COLLEGE ADMISSIONS CRACKED

COLLEGE ADMISSIONS CRACKED

SAVING YOUR KID (AND YOURSELF) FROM THE MADNESS

JILL MARGARET SHULMAN

Little, Brown Spark
New York Boston London

Little, Brown Spark
Hachette Book Group
1290 Avenue of the Americas, New York, NY 10104
littlebrownspark.com

First Edition: August 2019

Little, Brown Spark is an imprint of Little, Brown and Company, a division of Hachette Book Group, Inc. The Little, Brown Spark name and logo are trademarks of Hachette Book Group, Inc.

The publisher is not responsible for websites (or their content) that are not owned by the publisher.

The Hachette Speakers Bureau provides a wide range of authors for speaking events. To find out more, go to hachettespeakersbureau.com or call (866) 376-6591.

ISBN 978-0-316-42052-5
LCCN 2018967544

10 9 8 7 6 5 4 3 2 1

LSC-C

Printed in the United States of America

Contents

III: SPRING OF JUNIOR YEAR

Five Fantasy Responses to "Where's Your Kid Applying to College?"

IV: SUMMER VACATION

Five Ways to Sneak in College Visits Without Letting Them Consume Your Summer

COLLEGE
ADMISSIONS
CRACKED

In(tro)duction

WELCOME TO ANYONE NAVIGATING THE COLLEGE ADMISSIONS PROCESS (NOW OR EVER)

So, your child is a high school junior. You've known for a long time this day would come. You've heard other parents with kids older than yours whisper the word "college" like it was a terminal disease. You've seen the taut, maniacal grins of those parents trying to hold it together, and you've heard tell of the category five hurricane headed your way. Weathering and conquering the college admissions process with a teenager is a daunting affair. Maybe even the thought of it is daunting for you; maybe not. Regardless, very soon, advice will pour in through friends, your child's guidance counselor, and your mother's neighbor's cousin, if it hasn't begun trickling in already. The minute your child takes her first standardized test, glossy college catalogs will bombard your mailbox the way hundreds of Hogwarts invitations jetted through the Dursleys' fireplace at the beginning of *Harry Potter*. You'll feel the atmospheric pressure change when the seniors submit their college applications. Their parents' faces will soften and relax, and the flaming torch will be passed to you. That's where I come in.

Please put your hands where I can see them. Whether you're sporting a fresh manicure or your fingernails are bitten to the quick, it's okay. It's all okay here. Now slowly, put that torch down—yes, snuff it out right there in the water bucket. You have entered the safe space of our support group, and I am your facilitator. I have decades of experience as a college admissions evaluator, college essay coach, professional writer, college writing instructor, and parent. I have gone through the college admissions process with my daughter, and we both came out the other side. Now my son is a high school junior, like your child. Like you, I'm busy working, shopping for food, cooking it

3

(or begging someone else to cook it), making sure everyone's where they're supposed to be on time, managing who needs the car, paying bills, filling out school forms and tax forms and medical forms, taking out the trash, and feeding the dog. Life doesn't leave me much time to navigate one more thing, but here I am. Here we are. I'm your highly credentialed ally and resource who needs this support group as much as you do.

Look, you may have pictured yourself as a nucleus of calm with all those other crazy parents swirling around you like electrons when this time came. I did too, but I've learned that you cannot be that parent all the time. There will be moments when you find yourself with your toes dangling off the edge of Anxiety Cliff, where this process has driven even the sturdiest among us. My goal is to talk you down, arm you with information, and keep you laughing, even if it sounds like the laughter of an insane person. I've deployed backup in the form of an adolescent psychologist, college admissions counselors, and other parents and students who have survived college admissions just like I have (and you will). In the sanctuary of these pages, we are all here to help you maintain your strength and sense of self-worth, so easily lost somewhere between your teenager screaming, "I hate you! You're ruining my life!" and typing your credit card number into the College Board's website for the twentieth time.

You've got this, and now this support group has got your back.

THE KEY TO THIS BOOK

- Mom = Dad = Great–Aunt Agnes = You
- Daughter = Son = Gender Fluid Grandchild = Any Minor You Majorly Love
- College = University = Institution of Higher Education
- Wine = Double Espresso = Beverage of Choice (This is a judgment-free zone.)

PART I

FALL OF JUNIOR YEAR

FIVE THINGS YOU REALLY NEED
TO HEAR RIGHT NOW

1. That perfect baby you held in your arms sixteen years ago was only temporarily abducted and replaced with the moody, aloof, or melodramatic teenager who inhabits your house right now.

2. Just because you heard yourself say "SAT II, ED, EA," and "demonstrated interest" in a sentence does not mean you are *that* parent you vowed you'd never become when it was your kid's turn to apply to college.

3. You are not behind everyone else just because you have no idea what "SAT II, ED, EA," or "demonstrated interest" means.

4. You are not alone in this craziness. You have us (and your beverage of choice).

5. This too shall pass.

Chapter 1

The College Search Prequel

SURVIVAL (WHETHER OR NOT YOU'RE FEELING THE FITTEST)

You meet for coffee (or wine) with a mom friend, whose son is a high school junior, just like yours. She ticks off all of the colleges her son has visited, or is planning to visit, or are of interest to him. Your friend, who previously spoke English, is now dropping word bombs like "superscore" and "Coalition App" and "FAFSA" (?!) and using familiar words like "ranked" and "yield" in unfamiliar ways (see Glossary of College Admissions–Related Terms You Can Never Un-Know). You have taken your son to visit exactly zero colleges. You hide behind your coffee mug (or wine goblet), sipping (or chugging) with abandon, trying to hide your expression of concern (or terror).

Your friend's perfectly lipsticked lips are still moving, but her voice fades away, and your internal monologue takes over with something along the lines of... *Should my kid have already begun visiting colleges, or taking tests, or doing SOMETHING for college admission, and if so, what should I have been doing to help him all along, and what should I be doing right now instead of sitting here with this person who has her life totally together, lifting this cup of coffee (or wine) to lips I haven't bothered to lipstick, but maybe if I were a mom who bothered with lipstick, I'd be on top of this college thing. Am I behind? Is it too late?*

News flash: You are not behind.

You are right where you should be. You are so far from alone that I created this support group for you — for us. That other mom was just as nervous as you were. As a defense mechanism, she shored up as much information as possible to make herself feel more in control. That's just how she rolls. By expelling that information into the air between you, she didn't mean to make you feel like a teeny-tiny cowering bug of a parent. She was merely building herself up to boost her own confidence that she's been a good mother for sixteen years, good enough to handle this situation, which is less about college admissions and more about the gradual, painful, deeply emotional process that lurks beneath the entire act of parenting: letting go. Your friend applied that lipstick because when you proceed into the world perfectly coiffed with a red lip, you know for sure that despite any obstacle that may get the better of you, at least you started out the day doing something to arm yourself against it. Maintaining composure begins with a little self-care and a big dose of demystification of the college admissions process, which this book will provide.

The Cardinal Rule of Our Support Group: Forgiveness

No matter how weird it gets, *forgive other parents their trespasses, as you would want them to do unto you, and always forgive yourself.*

You will employ your own defense mechanisms during this time of upheaval, and they may not be pretty. You will make egregious parenting mistakes, as you have all along, and your child will survive them, as he always has. You're gearing up for a series of decisions you and your child will make culminating in the quarter-million-dollar question (literally, that's what four years of tuition can cost nowadays): Where will my baby land in the next stage of his life?

Let's start at the end of this whole process before we circle back to the beginning because, hopefully, it will make you feel better. At the end of all this college admissions brouhaha, your baby will be okay. He will get into college, leave home for real, and you both will wean yourselves from your daily collective worries and joys.

I recognize that right now you might only see a mourning period on the horizon. However, on the bright side, the time you spend carting your child to the doctor's office, or perpetually shopping for snacks to accommodate his teenaged friends' voracious appetites, will be freed up so you can finally try your hand at watercolor painting, or hang gliding, or learning to prepare tortellini from scratch. And your child will finally be liberated from the confines of the curfew you set when he was in middle school that—let's face it—he's grown out of (not that his curfew was ever unreasonable).

The scariest part is that at this moment, you can't picture this place where your child will land. Neither can he. The mystery of it is enough to freak anyone out. Some days, you might picture him tossing a Frisbee on a New England quad beneath autumn leaves exploding with color. Other days, you might picture him clicking on a keyboard in a sleek, chrome, state-of-the-art computer lab reflecting a row of palm trees. In both of these scenarios, the faces of those around him are redacted, their voices camouflaged, as if they are anonymous sources on a TV talk show. You can't picture the new friends he's yet to meet any more than you can envision his new habitat with any sense of accuracy. The one thing you know for sure about this picture of your child's near future is that you're not in it. I know how scary that is to contemplate when stress, longing, and worry are amplified by the unfathomable depth of love you feel for your child who will soon be spirited away from your home into a mysterious, dangerous alternative world. *I know.*

All these churning feelings can temporarily transform you into someone you'd rather not be, but even at your craziest, we'll forgive you. And we'll continuously remind you to forgive yourself. That's what we're all about.

APPROPRIATE VS. INAPPROPRIATE PARENT INVOLVEMENT: REALITY CHECKS

I grant you permission to trust your instincts on this.

Some of your peers, both professional and amateur, will insist that *all* parent involvement is inappropriate. They will encourage you to unleash your sixteen-year-old to make every decision all by herself about this next (expensive) stage of her life. Yes, it is *her* life, but in my estimation, the operative part of that sentence is *sixteen-year-old.*

Would you permit your sixteen-year-old to decide and pull the trigger on buying any other big-ticket item, like a house or a family car? No matter how brilliant she is, her sixteen-year-old cerebral cortex, the part of the brain in charge of decision-making, is not yet fully developed. Yours is. This is scientific fact.

It's entirely appropriate for parents to become involved in certain aspects of the college admissions process. After all, you have a lot at stake in this decision, starting with your bank account. I'm not advocating for you to micromanage. I'm encouraging you to help your child get started in a realistic way by applying your grown-up perspective to this upcoming transition barreling toward *your whole family* with the force of the Indiana Hoosiers' offensive line.

How far away is it realistic for my child to go?

Some kids love the idea of traipsing across the country for a big college adventure—in theory. The reality of actually living twenty-four/seven in that mythical place called college is harder for the only partially developed sixteen-year-old brain to process. You know your child. Go ahead and perform some reality checks on behalf of both of you:

- Is she someone who might be lost if she left the area?
- Honestly, would you be lost if she left the area?
- Is either of you willing to see each other only a couple of times a year?
- Have you factored the cost of plane flights into your budget for college expenses?
- What's the longest car ride that seems reasonable before motion sickness sets in?

Do I want my child to apply to my alma mater? Seriously, do I?

Over coffee (or wine) with your friend, you might have said, "I don't care where my son ends up in college, as long as he's happy." Chances are that comment was disingenuous if you've decorated your entire home in your college's colors and emblazoned the school's logo on your dining room chairs. I am *not* shaming you. The Latin "alma mater" translates to "nurturing mother," after all.

I loved college and dragged my children to my college reunions every five years as if they were religious pilgrimages. I mortified them more than once by accosting strangers in the airport security line just because I saw my college's name silkscreened onto their T-shirts. Somehow, though, I truly believed I was not pushing my school on my kids. I brought them on tours of similar colleges and patted myself on the back for my evolved parenting. Later, I realized I had subtly (and not so subtly) pushed my beloved college on anyone who would listen, including my children, since the day I graduated. If you went to college and you're having a light bulb moment, you're in good company. Rest assured, you have not permanently damaged your kid.

You may have heard that if your child's a "legacy" of a particular college, she'll have a better chance of getting in. If her aunt and uncle met there, or your second cousin's daughter attends, that does not count as legacy. If a parent or grandparent attended, your child's application may receive a closer look by admissions staff. That does not mean she'll definitely be admitted, nor does it mean it's as great a place for her as it was for you. So back to the reality check: Do you hope your kid will apply to your alma mater? If so (here comes the tough love), it is not acceptable for you to push it on her just because she might have an edge in admissions. It's her turn to own her college choice—you already had yours.

On the flip side, if you did not have a good college experience, have you been intentionally or unintentionally steering your child away from your alma mater? I aim to awaken your feelings about your child applying to your beloved (or reviled) college, not to control or judge them. Your feelings are always legitimate, and I validate your contemplating them in your own way. I will save you a bundle in therapy with the following message: If your child isn't as gung-ho about your alma mater as you are, or if she is excited to apply, this is about her, not a statement in favor of or against you or your parenting. I swear this to be true.

What can we afford?

I know you have big dreams for your child. We all do. I'm sure you've heard that big dreams can come true at myriad colleges. *Yes, so true,* you may be thinking, *but people only say this sort of thing to the disappointed soul rejected from her top-choice school.*

Not necessarily.

Sometimes a student is admitted into her top-choice school, but she receives devastating news from the financial aid department that makes enrolling there impossible. Then her parents end up in the nightmare role of dream-shatterers. You can escape this fate by assessing affordability now. Please have a seat in front of a computer, and let's get started.

- First you need to know that by law, every college that receives federal aid (most colleges) offers a Net Price Calculator on its website. If you plug in the numbers from your latest tax return, the calculator will spit out an Expected Family Contribution (EFC). That's an approximate assessment of your true sticker price for each college your child considers.
- If she's not considering any colleges yet, I repeat, *you are not behind.* Pull up the websites of one large state university and one small private college. Any will do. Then type in the numbers they request from your tax return, and use their cost calculators to find a ballpark figure of what college might cost you.
- Of course, variables abound. If you're an independent contractor whose income varies from year to year (or week to week), the numbers from your last tax return will still give you a sense. Improvising and estimating are all I'm suggesting here.
- Look for the phrase "covers full demonstrated need" on those websites. An often overlooked fact: A name-brand college with a hefty endowment can turn out to be cheaper for you than the

state school if you can prove "need" on the financial aid forms you will fill out fall of your child's senior year.

- Even if the college makes no financial promises, if your child applies to a college where his academic credentials are tops in the college's applicant pool, the college may offer a generous scholarship to lure your kid into attending. Many college websites will describe the scholarship awards they offer and what it takes to qualify for them.

- "Regional reciprocity" means that your kid might be eligible for an in-state tuition rate at an out-of-state university in the same region. For example, if a student from Arkansas wants to study nursing at the University of Kentucky, she only needs to pay in-state tuition due to the Southern Regional Education Board's tuition savings program for students interested in health professions.

- If you're divorced and there's an income discrepancy between you and your ex, some schools require financial information only from the custodial parent. If you can file for financial aid using only the tax forms of the parent earning the lower income, it could save you thousands (and thousands) of dollars.

- Don't forget that the savings incurred when you have one less family member at home will somewhat defray the cost of tuition. You'll save on expenses like gas to and from hockey practice forty-five minutes away, plus all that equipment and ten boxes of Honey Nut Cheerios per week.

If you thought your kid's tsunami of emotions was bad once she hit puberty, try telling a hardworking student that you can't afford her dream college, where she's just been admitted. It can hurl a family over the threshold from bickering to full-scale mortal combat. Do as much preemptive damage control as possible now, so you won't be forced to sell your home and live in your car while your kid's off enjoying college.

Is my child a contender for the most selective colleges?

We parents see unique and wonderful qualities in our children, including strengths that they often cannot see in themselves. They have so much *potential,* and we have spent their entire lives cheerleading for them to reach it. That potential reveals itself in various ways to the outside world. The student with the high school transcript so stellar you kind of want to frame it may be abysmal (and miserable) on the baseball field. The student who earns average grades may be a superstar on stage dancing in *The Nutcracker.*

There's a saying: *Everybody is a genius, but if you judge a fish by his ability to climb a tree, that fish will live his whole life believing he's stupid.* Let's call the tree Harvard College. If your child ended up at Harvard, would he embrace his new habitat like a monkey swinging happily from branch to branch, or would he become a beached fish there, putting on a game face as he stares up at those leaves but secretly dying inside?

There are more than 4,600 four-year college and university habitats in the United States alone. The Ivy League includes exactly eight of them. Maybe thirty-eight more are labeled "most selective" by one of those college ranking systems. (You can jump ahead to p. 188, The Toxic Impact of College Rankings, if you're ready to descend down that rabbit hole.) Statistically, it doesn't make sense only to consider 0.17% of colleges and universities in the nation and leave almost 100% of them out of the running.

To provide some perspective on just how selective these schools are, when Harvard advertises that their admission rate was 4.7% in 2017–18, that does not include 4.7% of all college-bound students in the nation. That means 4.7% of the students who *applied.* That kid who barely passed chemistry at your child's high school last year did not apply to Harvard. The class valedictorian might have applied, and it's the valedictorian who had a 95.3% chance of denial.

I do not mean to bring you down. Your kid will find her habitat. You will help her find it! We parents must bolster ourselves to answer some difficult questions so that we can determine whether or not an uber-competitive college has the potential to become the healthiest, happiest environment for our children.

- Think about all those nights of homework in your child's past. Did you nag, wheedle, and monitor that homework every single night? Or did your child nag and wheedle you into letting her please stay up just a little later to study for her social studies test?
- Did your child do her thing and earn a variety of respectable letter grades on her report card? Or is she a straight-A student obsessed with perfect test scores?
- Was your child content hanging out with friends at the local pond last summer by day and binge-watching *Game of Thrones* by night, or did she set her sights on an academic summer program and read fifteen classic novels?
- Now muster one more ounce of courage and answer this question: Is applying to a name-brand, highly competitive college your child's dream, or is it possibly your dream?

This is the part where I reassure you that whatever you answer is okay. Within the asylum of these pages, you are supported *no matter what*. Based on your answers to the questions above, I think you know in your heart whether or not packing your suitcase and embarking with your child on an expedition to tour all eight Ivy League colleges over spring break would be a useful exercise for your family. If not, then visiting the Harvard campus on a beautiful autumn day, trailing after a charming tour guide, will ultimately not do you or your child a whit of good. For you, maybe permission *not* to aim for a stiffly competitive college like Harvard for your kid was what you needed today. Permission granted.

If your heart suspects the Ivy League and the like would be just your kid's thing, I wish you safe travels. Hey, 4.7% of applicants *are* admitted to Harvard, after all, and your child could become one of them. Only promise me that upon return, you won't unpack your bags just yet. Dream schools are easy to identify. The important work of the college search is to locate "foundation" or "safety" schools where the odds are in your child's favor to—first of all—get in, and then feel intelligent, encouraged, and inspired as she transitions from a teenager into a full-scale adult.

BROACHING THE "COLLEGE SHOPPING" TOPIC WITH YOUR TEEN

Posing the Icebreaker Question: Big or Small, Urban or Rural?

Ultimately, your child will take her own sweet time to start talking to you about exploring college options. However, the "Big or small, urban or rural?" question can help launch the conversation. Let's troubleshoot. If at the dinner table one night, you scoop up some mashed potatoes and say casually, "So, about college, are you thinking of a big or small, urban or rural campus?" you will likely encounter one of two reactions.

The Active Volcano Response

If your child is a high-achieving, type-A student and hangs out with similarly academically ambitious kids, her reaction to the "Big or small, urban or rural?" question might resemble the eruption of Mount Vesuvius. If brilliant red creeps up her neck or epic shouting begins, this means that all your child hears all day long is college, college, and more college while she's just trying to get through AP Biology and, at this moment, dinner. (If steam begins spouting from her ears, seek immediate medical attention.)

The Oblivious Child's Response

If your child is completely oblivious to the fact that this behemoth of a thing called "his future" is about to transpire, when you ask, "Big or small, urban or rural?" he might look at you blankly. If he uses words at all to respond, the sentence might begin and end with the word "Huh?"

This bewildered reaction means your child has not spent one second thinking about college. Either he does not hang out with others thinking about college, he's very talented at ignoring anything that doesn't happen within his abbreviated event horizon, or he has assumed all along that his future would just automatically happen for him, the way his clean, folded laundry has always magically appeared on his closet shelves. (I'm not suggesting you're a bad parent if you still provide laundry service for your teenager. No law says we have to turn every household chore into a "teachable moment." See p. 93 for my take on this.)

The One-Size-Fits-All Solution: Schedule a College Visit

Make an appointment to take your child on one zero-stakes college visit as a remedy for both the volatile and catatonic responses. The point of the outing is to *show* (instead of *tell*) your child that getting started on her college quest will not hurt. It's not like you're taking her to the doctor's office to have her blood drawn. Here's how to plan it:

1. Log on to a college or university website. Big or small, urban or rural does not matter. It can be a local college your child has no intention of attending or a college convenient to an establishment that serves your beverage of choice.

2. Click on "Admission" on the menu, and then "Plan Your Visit" (or some such directive).

3. Sign up your child for an "Information Session" (commonly referred to as an "info" session), during which an admissions representative will treat you to an hourlong presentation, mostly consisting of talk, but usually with some audio-visual enhancement.

4. Sign up for a "Campus Tour," during which a current student at that college will lead you around campus for about an hour. If given the option, register for the info session for the first hour and do the tour second.

5. When you fill out the contact information form online, you can use your child's information but *your own email address* to register. Admitting you're the parent will not negatively affect your child. However, pretending she's really the one doing all of this planning merely ensures the email confirmation with directions to the Office of Admission, along with the parking pass, will languish neglected in the graveyard of her inbox, where emails sent to teenagers go to die.

6. If your child's disposition is volcanic, do your best to mitigate her reaction by telling her this first college visit requires no preparation on her part. It will only take two hours of her life plus transportation. If your child's default mode is oblivious, tell him that you hope this visit will rouse him from his current sleepwalking state to embark on his own college search. It's time.

Luring the Future College Student into College Shopping with You

Theoretically, the student himself should take charge of researching colleges and making all the plans for visits, but who are we kidding? Realistically, his classes have become more rigorous, he feels pressure to keep up his grades, he's slammed with homework, plays a sport or the cello, and wants some semblance of a social life. You have plenty of distractions too, but unlike many adolescents, you can see further into the future than your next Snapchat. If you're more on top of scheduling the college search than your child during most or all of his junior year, don't beat yourself up about it. *Your child is perfectly normal, and so are you.* Take one of the following approaches if you're hoping to persuade your teen to enter the vehicle with you for that first college visit you just planned.

The Positive Reinforcement Approach

Reinforcement: *the action of encouraging something.*
Bribe: *something that serves to induce or influence.*

Do you see the difference? I don't see much of a difference either. We could debate the nuances, or you can just call the reward you offer whatever you like, as long as it entices your child into the car for a college visit. You can offer a cupcake, a hike, or a Jaguar convertible after that first college visit, and there will be no judgments here.

The Optimistic Approach

If the positive reinforcement route doesn't sit right with you, optimism provides another effective gateway to teen involvement. I am not saying it's wrong if you're having ambivalent feelings about your kid going to college. Your feelings are your feelings. I'm saying, own your feelings, and if they're positive, demonstrate your eagerness. If not, fake enthusiasm as best you can.

"We're shopping for colleges!" I said to my daughter in the fall of her junior year. Notice the exclamation point, the cheerful tone, enthusiastic though hopefully not too cloying. (I was going for contagious.) Who could help but want to join in? My daughter went for it, but my husband did not. He says he hates shopping, but this man enjoyed house hunting so much that three years after we purchased our house, he still scanned real estate agents' ads. So I tweaked my verb and told him, "We're hunting for colleges!" That did it for him, and my husband hopped into the car.

My son was not so easily persuaded when his turn to explore colleges came around. He had professed a post-graduation goal of living in a van with minimal earthly possessions (#vanlife), so I knew the "college shopping" tactic would not fly with him. Yet I also knew that my so-called Spartan son could easily spend an hour "checking out" camping gear and such van-life necessities as rock climbing paraphernalia (and vans) online. "We're checking out colleges!" I announced when I scheduled my son's first college visit. He didn't exactly leap into the Subaru, but at least he didn't refuse.

Applying Dictator Tactics

When someone demands I "smile" when I'm in a crappy mood, I sort of want to punch that person in the face (though as a nonviolent person, my natural reflex is to smile obediently, then feel bad about smiling on command for a second or two). You should never have to endure anyone trying to force you to smile. If exclamation points and extreme optimism are not for you, there are other methods, such as introducing the first college visit as a fact of life, not a choice. I told my son, who fit solidly into the "oblivious child" category, "We're going to Burlington to visit the University of Vermont and Champlain College on October sixth and seventh. Please mark your calendar."

Planning ahead is the key to this approach. I chose two colleges, one big, one small, with access to both urban and rural environments. I chose Vermont in early October, when the fall foliage splendor would peak, admittedly, more for my enjoyment than his. Most important, I chose to inform my son a full month before that trip would happen. I've learned that teenagers rarely make plans earlier than the day before, and on October fifth, sure enough, my son received the inevitable tempting text from his friend inviting him to join a group hike the next day. By then, the trip to Burlington had been seared into the calendar for so long, he had no grounds to negotiate.

The Cardinal Rule for the First College Visit: Let Your Child Take the Lead

You can go ahead and log on to the college website. You can click on the "Admission" page and register your child for the information session and tour. You can transport your child to the college, usher him into the admissions office ten minutes before the planned activities will commence, and nudge him toward the front desk to announce his arrival. Thereafter, try to only speak when spoken to. Letting your child take the lead means erring on the side of silence.

Even if you're eminently curious, once on campus, do not be that parent who takes over the question-and-answer portion of the information session. You know the one. That person shows up at every presentation of any kind and asks a question, then a follow-up question, and then another, as if he and the presenter are the only two people in the room. Try not to judge this parent, whose sole motivation is—like yours—love for and devotion to his child. He just missed the memo about letting his child take the lead. Refrain from rolling your eyes when he asks that fourth follow-up question because as a parent of a teenager, you know exactly how it feels to sit there on the receiving end of an eye roll with no idea what you did wrong.

Instead of judging or *being* that parent, sit tight and write down your questions. You can ask them later, if this college ends up a contender for your kid. Bite your tongue until it bleeds, if you must, during the walk from the dining hall to the library. Then in the car afterward, you can morph into full "fun parent" mode, cracking jokes and offering to stop for donuts, to show your child how not scary this college search can be. "See? This is like shopping for a college!" you can say cheerfully, which will, at best, empower your child to feel in control of her destiny. At worst, it will elicit the eye roll you previously dodged when you didn't take over the Q&A, but you will laugh it off because you are a "fun parent" and wearing a full suit of positive attitude armor. Not even an eye roll can touch you now.

BECOMING AN EDUCATED CONSUMER

With that first college visit behind you, you may be asking, "How do I know where to take my child on her next college visit?"

Where to shop for a college is a serious, big-ticket shopping question, and for those kinds of questions, I always turn to my mother, who loves shopping more than anyone else I know. I'm just going to say it: My mother is "penny foolish." She'll splurge on a $199 T-shirt that looks and feels exactly the same as the $9.99 T-shirt I would buy. (Mom, if you're reading this, I hope I didn't offend, but can you see my point?) However, my penny foolish mom is "dollar wise." When it comes to shopping for big-ticket items, my mother is an ace consumer researcher. If you are buying a car or a house, or want to find the best doctor for an elective surgery, my mother's the one you call. One of the biggest-ticket items of any parent's lifetime is college, so when my daughter entered her junior year in high school, I called upon the master, and my mother was on it.

Choosing and Using Those Huge, Encyclopedic College Guidebooks

My mom is old school, so we beelined to a bookstore, where she bought three college guidebooks, which I will list in order of helpfulness to us:

1. The *Fiske Guide to Colleges,* recognizable from my college search in the 1980s, is still my favorite. I like the box that suggests "Overlaps" between the college I'm reading about and other similar colleges.
2. *The Insider's Guide to the Colleges,* created by the *Yale Daily News,* aspires to provide the inside scoop about each college's true personality to complement the facts. We liked having another perspective, although knowing which colleges had the "Ugliest School Colors" didn't feel essential to us (but it might be important to you because not everyone can pull off a brown and gold college sweatshirt).
3. Princeton Review's *Best 379 Colleges* goes a step beyond lists and provides rankings of schools in categories such as "Best Campus Food" and "Best College Radio Station." I preferred the books with less emphasis on "the best"—that's different for everyone.

In all, these books totaled more than 2,400 pages and cost my mother $72.97 (which I would not have spent). Of course, she turned right to the page in each describing her own alma mater and announced, "I would never get in there now," which is probably true for many of us.

My mother and I had a field day among the pages of the books she bought, window-shopping for colleges that might fit my daughter. We giddily discussed specific schools in hushed tones, since my daughter fell into the "volcanic child" category, but a parent can't tiptoe around a topic forever. My mother's visit ended, and then the challenge of raising the topic of college with my daughter for the first time since I'd orchestrated that introductory college visit was left to me.

I began by planting those books my mother had purchased around the house, like land mines. I placed the massive *Fiske Guide to Colleges* on the dining table that my daughter had commandeered for homework, so she couldn't miss it. My daughter piled her homework on top. I left the Yale *Insider's Guide* on the floor of her room, but I don't think she even noticed it was there among the wadded-up socks and sweaters that covered every other inch of carpet. My mother, known to my children as Cece, continued her shopping spree online and sprung for the hulking Peterson's *Four-Year Colleges* guide, a daunting 1,952 pages (and almost thirty bucks), which arrived by mail. I planted that one on the coffee table in the living room between the couch and the TV. Of course, busy high school juniors rarely have time to watch TV, and when they do, they watch on their computers, so that plant was a bust. For the record, Peterson's condensed each college entry into such brief sound bites that—though not unhelpful—it placed at number four out of four on my personal helpfulness list.

Eventually, I gave up and stashed all the books in my home office. At least my students would reap their benefits, even if my daughter would not. It was at that point that my daughter said, "I saw in that book Cece bought me…" and we were off. In this age of electronics, an old-fashioned book that takes up a significant amount of surface area is hard for your child to avoid, and, in my opinion, a worthwhile purchase for that reason alone.

Enjoy then ignore the college brochures stuffing your mailbox.

Colleges and universities invest liberally in direct advertising (a.k.a. junk mail). They'll send you glossy postcards and book-length brochures called "viewbooks" that will catch your eye with their museum-quality photographs, inspirational headlines, and heartfelt mission statements. One college even sent my daughter a poster in a tube.

I don't blame you if your heart beats a little faster when you open your mailbox to find a pile of postcards addressed to your child including one from Utopia University. Perhaps your child is a great candidate for Utopia (and Heavenly College, and Shangri-La Polytech, which in my fantasy universe is located on a beach in Hawaii), but it's my unpleasant task to tell you that Utopia sent that postcard to your home to use your love for and pride in your child to their advantage. In *their* fantasy universe, your family will hope that your kid's exactly whom Utopia is looking for. Then you'll pay them an eighty-dollar application fee to maintain that hope.

I don't know your child, so I don't know why Utopia targeted him. Perhaps your kid showed interest by signing up for a campus visit, and the Office of Admission is only doing due diligence and following up. Perhaps his name appeared on the list of students with high PSAT scores that Utopia buys from the testing company every year. (This happens in real life.) Perhaps Utopia expanded their mailing list to infiltrate every single mailbox in your family's school district to attract a greater number of applicants.

Colleges and universities play these games, and the charitable part of me doesn't blame them. Institutions of higher learning are businesses, after all. We should expect them to deploy marketing and other strategies to stay solvent. For the same reason, I also don't completely blame the periodicals that instigate these games with the college ranking lists they publish. And I certainly don't blame you. You've spent the past sixteen years believing in your child. It's almost impossible not to hope others have recognized his potential.

It's hard to disregard those beautiful viewbooks that make every campus look like a fairy-tale hamlet. In the end, though, all that college literature is direct advertising, like the other colorful catalogs and credit card offers also jammed into your mailbox. You can read them or not and then recycle them as such.

Online College Shopping

While our IRL mailboxes overflow, our children deal with a deluge of college solicitations in their virtual mailboxes. My daughter told me emails from colleges multiplied like bunnies. If she clicked one, two more would appear from the sender. Between emails and the college talk escalating at school, information and misinformation about colleges will assault our children no matter how much they try to avoid it.

If they don't realize it themselves early on, at some point we can remind our kids that they don't have to play victim to the information blitzkrieg. They can take charge, since they hold all of the world's knowledge in their pocket. I'm referring to their smartphones. For a generation that's grown up on Google searches instead of the *Encyclopedia Britannica,* the Internet's an excellent, age-appropriate alternative to paper books.

I suggest that for a list of the best college search websites, you consult the true expert on all things tech: your resident teenager. To start you off, the *National Center for Education Statistics* (NCES) site, though dull as dishwater, sticks with the facts about each college listed without providing opinions or rankings based on criteria that might not be yours. Plus, the NCES site doesn't require you to input personal information to break through a firewall, so you won't receive spam from them for the rest of your life.

You'll also find a research tool on the online platform your kid's high school uses for college planning, usually Naviance or College Kickstart. What? Your child did not tell you that the college counselor already introduced every single junior in the high school to this platform? If this is the first you've heard of such a platform, ask your kid, who will either drop his head sheepishly, vehemently deny ever knowing this platform existed, or scream "Stop interrogating me!" when you confront him about it. As another option, you can bypass your kid (who will never share his password with you anyway) and call the high school guidance office for access instructions.

CONSIDERING OUTSIDE INTERVENTION: OPTIONS FROM FLYWEIGHT TO HEAVYWEIGHT

Your ability to communicate with your teenager will change many times in the next few months, even in the next hour. Today, you may feel like teammates planning this grand college adventure. By the end of next summer, you may feel like your teenager's emotional punching bag. For our purposes, *outside intervention means help that is not you,* and at some point in time, you may want to seek it. Generally, rescue services offered for college admissions fall into four categories:

1. Preparing for standardized tests
2. Building a college list
3. Writing the application
4. Untangling financial aid applications

I'm going to say this here, and I'll repeat it later in case you are not able to hear me right now: Securing others to help with this process can be expensive, but it can also be free of charge, and either way, it can be an enormous relief for parents and students alike.

If you feel like your relationship with your teenager could have used a buffer *yesterday,* you might want to enlist the college admissions version of special ops Green Berets immediately. If you doubt you'll need help, or you're not sure, this is a preview of what's out there, just in case. Your child may need the adrenaline rush of an imminent deadline to leap into gear, but I don't know many parents who enjoy that feeling.

Option A: Code-Red Intervention — The Full-Throttle College Consultant

For those who can afford one, a full-service college consultant can organize the college admissions process for you so you'll never feel behind again. Big or small, IRL or virtual, these full consulting services have their benefits and drawbacks.

The Big College Consulting Company

You'll land on a website or hear about a local business offering multiple services provided by multiple players to guide you through college admissions. Some questions to keep in mind:

- Will they assign one person to your case to lead your family through every aspect of the process? Or will they connect your family with different specialized consultants to help with different parts (for example, a writer to help with essays or an expert cryptographer to help you through financial aid applications)?
- Will they meet you face-to-face at an office or conduct all of their business through phone, Skype, and email?
- Will they use an identical formula for every family, including worksheets to determine college match, or webinars for group financial aid instruction? Or does their consulting process vary significantly from family to family?
- While "en masse" treatment of their services might feel impersonal, will it fulfill your family's needs and make the big company the most economical choice?

The All-in-One-Person Consultant

Even if the pronoun "we" is used liberally on the website, the "About Us" page will reveal that "us" is really just one person who can provide a personal touch to the admissions process. Questions for her:

- This person will become your guru and amateur therapist. She may also become your temporary BFF, so assess right off the bat: Who is this person, will her experience satisfy your family's needs, and does her style jibe with yours?

- Does she meet with clients face-to-face at her home office, at your home, in a coffee shop, or in a public library? Or does she conduct all communication remotely?
- If you are a person who likes to bounce ideas off someone as they come up, who needs burning questions demystified, with compassion, before you lose sleep over them, will this consultant be that person for you? Will she take your calls or answer your emails whenever you need help (within reason), or does she keep restricted office hours?

Is a consultant really necessary?

Ask yourself the following questions to determine whether or not committing to a college consultant is an excellent plan or unwarranted at this juncture:

- Do you feel a deep sense of calm wash over you when you imagine someone else organizing all of this for you and your child? Or does the thought of relinquishing control stress you out even more?
- Will paying for this stretch your budget to the breaking point? Or relative to the cost of college does paying for a consultant feel more like grabbing a tin of mints at the grocery checkout counter than purchasing Kobe beef?
- Do you need help figuring out what colleges are out there? Or do you think the Internet and that fat college book you just bought will offer enough of a starting point?
- Will the support your child will receive at school make hiring a college consultant redundant or a godsend?
- Is it worth it to you to find someone who will do the dirty work, such as "prod" your child to hit deadlines, so you don't have to do the prodding. Or does the prospect of this type of interaction with your kid not concern you in the least? (And if it doesn't concern you, can we please trade kids during the college admissions process?)

- Does your child have learning differences that a trained professional could best help him address? Or have you filled out so many IEPs over the years that you can handle his accommodations blindfolded?

Based on your responses to the questions above, if your gut tells you that your family might implode trying to figure all of this out yourself, or that your child will probably respond much better to someone who is not you from the get-go, ask around. Search online. Ignore anyone who offers dodgy services because: integrity and jail time. If you decide it makes sense for you, secure a college consultant soon, deem it a worthwhile investment in your family's well-being, and *plug your ears when others question your decision*. Prioritizing how you spend your hard-earned money is up to you, not the people out there who will not hesitate to tell you how ridiculous it is to spend money on this as they pay the barista $5.25 for their daily latte. If you'd prefer to prioritize the expensive coffee, that's okay too, but don't give your friend a hard time if she prioritizes differently. It's all good. Remember, gentleness with yourself and other parents is our guiding principle.

Option B: Selective Outside Intervention

If you think you'll need outside intervention, but only for some parts of the college admissions process, I'll pipe up when time is of the essence. For now, here's a rough timeline to help you feel ahead for a change.

1. *This week, help your child look for academic outside intervention* if he is struggling in any classes. It's an important year for him to build an academic foundation, feel successful in the face of increased rigor, and acquire valuable study skills for his future. Your child should always approach his teacher first for extra help. Remind him that his teachers entered this line of work in

the first place because they want him to succeed. Private tutors are a luxury available as an added buttress.

2. *By the end of December, look for an SAT or ACT prep class or tutor* if a) you're concerned about your child's standardized test taking ability, b) you're not convinced he's self-motivated enough to use free online test prep, or c) paying someone else to nag him to study seems greatly preferable to your doing the nagging yourself.

3. *By April 1, find a college essay coach* if you think you'll want someone to guide your child through writing his college essays or the entire application because a) writing is not your child's strength, b) writing is not your strength, or c) writing *is* your strength, but you know your kid won't suffer your guidance well. This is not a hard and fast date, but if you wait until the week before an application deadline fall of senior year, it will cost you.

4. *Over the summer, line up someone to help you with financial aid forms* if a) you're not great with numbers, b) you don't feel up to learning a whole new language of financial aid jargon, or c) long, tricky forms make you feel faint. Check with the guidance office at your child's school to learn if they provide help for parents applying for financial aid. If not, the fun will begin next October, so summer (plus wine) is sufficient to secure the help you'll need.

If you are staring at this list with horror, thinking, *I have no concept of whether or not I'll need help, or who I might need, or if it's worth the added cost, or when I'll know if I might need them…* I am virtually holding your hand right now. The time is not necessarily now (or ever) to line up all (or any) of these people. I'll offer or introduce you to free help whenever I can, so your child will still have money left for her college textbooks, which can cost $250 each. (I kid you not!) Think about budgeting for potential helpers now, and remember that there's always backup out there if you start to feel overwhelmed. There will come a time when you will know whether or not you need outside intervention, and at that time, *it will not be too late.*

Option C: Mental-Health Intervention (For You, or Make It a Family Affair)

A complaint session with a friend over cappuccinos or a stiff martini might solve your problems temporarily, but it's not uncommon for parents and teenagers going through the college admissions process to seek outside help in the form of professional therapy. Come to think of it, it's not uncommon for people going through any process, including everyday life, to seek professional therapy. Any stigma that once existed is gone.

If you think your kid could use someone objective with whom to talk this through, consult her pediatrician or your friends for names of therapists with experience in adolescent and family therapy. Yes, we are here to support you, but if divulging your own fears and anxieties in the privacy of a therapist's office will help you remain calm around your child, find a therapist for yourself too. Cross-reference recommendations with your insurance company's list of local therapists and line someone up now. I'm a big fan of doing whatever it takes to emotionally support yourself and your child when all roads lead to enormous changes ahead.

TRANSLATING YOUR KID'S HIGH SCHOOL LIFE SO FAR INTO COLLEGE ADMISSIONS DATA

Freshman- and Sophomore-Year Grades

It's hard to get started when all the information isn't in yet, but let's make do with what we've got. Your child has accomplished half of her high school coursework. You've seen the ninth- and tenth-grade transcript. Don't fall into the trap of infusing the letters and numbers on that transcript with value judgments. Grades are not evaluations of your child's personality or life potential, and they are most definitely not evaluations of your parenting.

To college admission evaluators, your child's grades are data points that only convey meaning when placed in a context. Your child's high school will provide that context in the form of a "school profile" that accompanies every transcript sent to a college. The school profile includes a description of the high school's location, the student body's demographics, the honors and AP classes offered, the students' median grade point average, typical standardized test scores, and other particulars. You can ask the high school guidance office for a paper copy, or it may be posted online, if you want to see it. I hope it reassures you to know that college admission evaluators will know what grades mean within your child's world when they read through her college application.

What's already happened on your child's report card could serve as a motivator or a source of despair at this fragile time. High-achieving students may view a B– singed onto their otherwise pristine, straight-A transcript like the zit that's all you can see when you look in the mirror. For other students, that B– might be one of the higher grades on their transcript, with a D the grade that spawns despondency about getting into any college at all.

Your child might think that the lowest grade on her report card means "It's over" for her. She'll never get into a "good" college or into college period. One thing does not lead to the other, and it's our job as parents of these developing people who still need us (even if they don't always show it) to strengthen their spirit. This information may help: *Admission evaluators view an upward trajectory in grades favorably.* If grades improve as classes become harder in high school, evaluators feel confident that your child can succeed as classes become even more challenging in college. In fact, your child's lowest grade from the past is not the end of her college prospects, as some students may conclude. It's only the beginning.

Grades Happening Now

Junior-year classes are usually the toughest so far, and they offer a chance for your child to prove her mettle. Though it's impossible to predict the future behavior of a person whose hormones are in flux, if your child has always been the ambitious sort—signing up for all honors classes and studying late into the night to achieve As in them—

you can assume this behavior pattern will continue junior and senior year. The more As she accumulates as she tackles progressively more difficult coursework, the more that B– from freshman year fades into the background on her transcript.

If your child has done the minimum, and her grades show it, chances are that dramatic changes will not occur within the next eighteen months, but you never know. One of the most common refrains I hear from students is "I wish I had worked harder earlier in high school." Some students turn it on when the pressure rises. A chipper reminder from you that "junior year is a fresh start!" might motivate an upward shift. It's worth a try. As another incentive, that first visit to a beautiful college campus, where your kid hears about all the appealing opportunities offered there, can light a fire beneath a previously sedentary student's derriere.

The October PSAT

The PSAT/NMSQT (Practice SAT/National Merit Scholarship Qualifying Test) is a standardized test offered to high school juniors in mid-October. Usually people just refer to it as the PSAT without all those other letters. It's widely reported that standardized tests best evaluate family income and how well students take standardized tests, not intelligence or college readiness. Still, your child should take the PSAT fall of his junior year, and try his best, for these reasons:

- Most students need to submit some sort of standardized test scores to colleges, so any opportunity for test-taking practice will help familiarize your child with the format and environment for all similar tests.
- When he receives the scores (by December), he'll have another data point to help him begin researching realistic college options. Don't get too attached to this number, which will change, often significantly, in his near future.
- If he's riddled with anxiety on the days leading up to the test, and/or his scores are very low, he can visit the National Organization for Fair and Open Testing (FairTest) website and

browse a list of more than 1,000 "test-optional" (no need to submit any test scores at all when applying) and "test-flexible" (students can select which tests they want to submit) colleges and universities. Then you can talk about whether he'd like to have extra help studying for future tests or whether he'd prefer never to take another standardized test again.

- If he scores very high, he may become eligible for a National Merit Scholarship, a onetime, nonrenewable award of $2,500. I'm afraid this will only cover about one-thirteenth of one year's tuition on average at a private college, but if he wins, your kid's photo might appear in the local newspaper, so that's fun!

- Our state university also invites students to apply for other scholarships based on high PSAT/NMSQT scores. Maybe yours does too, so it's worth it for your kid to fill in a few ovals on a Scantron sheet and give the PSAT a shot.

Public service announcement: Before he takes the PSAT, your child should *create a new email address designated exclusively for the college admissions process.*

He should use this email address when he fills out the registration forms for standardized tests, campus visits, and everything else college-related. Once those testing companies and colleges get ahold of your child's contact information, there's no stopping them. Your kid does not want to miss his high school French teacher's email about rescheduling the exam for two days earlier because it was buried under college solicitations.

Extracurricular Life (Other Than Video Games)

While in my role as a college admission evaluator, I opened one student's file to reveal a personal essay that began, "My father ripped dance from my life." The applicant went on to say that her father had made her quit dance, which she had loved since she was a little girl, to free up time for her to join the debate team. Her dad had insisted debate would look better than dance on her college applications, but this kid hated debate. The student included a grainy photograph of herself posing in an arabesque in what looked like her bedroom, where, behind closed doors, she still danced, despite her father's dictum. After all that heartbreak, debate made no difference for this candidate at the college where I worked at the time. She was not admitted.

I implore you not to rip dance…or archery, or self-taught guitar, or babysitting, skateboarding, or anything else your kid views as vital to her very being…from your child's life. In the world of college applications, incessantly staring at a screen watching TV or playing video games is the sole activity I can imagine might raise eyebrows. Otherwise, everything your child does counts as a viable activity (as long as it's legal), whether organized by the school or not. If your child feels passionately enough about an activity to pursue it on her own, all the better.

A mom once asked me if she should sign up her daughter for crew. She wanted to know if crew would look good on college applications, since all of her daughter's other activities involved art. I asked this mom if her daughter wanted to row crew. The mom had never thought about that. *She was so determined to do what was best for her child, she'd lost sight of what was best for her child.*

We all let our anxiety get the better of us sometimes. We worry about disasters that have yet to happen, and probably never will. This mom needn't have worried. Her daughter's work in art earned her a Scholastic Gold Key award for a painting her teacher submitted to the contest, and school recognition from the art department. She developed an enthusiasm for art history, which informed her college search, and the all-out bliss she experienced spending hours in the art room after school every day naturally evolved into helping and encouraging younger students. For the record, that afterschool mentoring was bona fide, heartfelt "leadership." Crew might have made her daughter stronger on the outside, but this mom's good sense not to rip art from her daughter's life ultimately produced a happier child, as well as a stronger candidate for college.

TO-DO LIST

☐ Tune out others' mounting anxiety as best you can.

☐ Appreciate the teen POV (excitement, dread, denial about college looming, as well as other emotions you may be feeling, only magnified ten times because: hormones).

☐ Check your own reality, which is totally legitimate, regardless of what your teenager or anyone else tells you.

☐ Suggest to your child she set up a designated email address for all things college-related before typing a word into any college website or registering for her first standardized college entrance test.

☐ Take your child on a preliminary college visit if you intuit that it will do more good than harm.

☐ Buy or borrow a thick college almanac. Go with the *Fiske Guide* if you're undecided.

☐ Conduct an initial assessment of outside help you might need now or later to sustain family unity.

☐ Reinforce to your child that she should focus on her present classwork instead of wasting her valuable time and energy worrying about past grades.

☐ Make sure your child signs up for the PSAT. (Feel free to sign her up yourself and don't feel guilty about it, if it's easier for you at this moment in time.)

☐ Encourage your child to enjoy her favorite activities and try new ones that interest her, regardless of how she thinks they will look to colleges. College admission evaluators will admire your kid for being her authentic self.

PART II

WINTER OF JUNIOR YEAR

FIVE HELPFUL MANTRAS FOR THE WINTER
OF OUR DISCONTENT

1. Inhale. Exhale. Repeat.
2. You are the sky. Everything else is just weather.
3. Patience means counting down without blasting off.
4. Okay, that happened (or didn't happen). What's next?
5. Speed doesn't matter. Forward is forward.

Chapter 2

January

Me: "How was the SAT this morning?"

My son: "Long. Tiring. Painful like a sharp knife repeatedly stabbing my aorta."

EVERYTHING MY CLIENTS EVER WANTED TO KNOW (THOUGH PERHAPS MORE THAN YOU EVER WANTED TO KNOW) ABOUT STANDARDIZED TESTING

The Majority Report

When the trees in my New England neighborhood flaunt their fall colors, the world appears golden and possibilities seem endless. When those leaves begin to drop, the world looks a little bleaker, and by the time naked branches claw at the gray January sky, my neighborhood looks the way standardized tests make me feel. From what I've gathered, testing malaise plagues the general populace, so I'm making the sweeping assumption that standardized testing will be one of the lower points, if not *the* low point of the college admissions process for most people leaning on this support group.

If you're thinking, *How do I know what tests my kid should take?* or *When should he take them?* or *Does he need a tutor?* or *Am I late signing him up?* or *Oh God, I have no idea how this all works!*...

Stop. Repeat after me: *No need to bother God with this. We've got testing covered.*

It might feel like something out of Homer's *Odyssey* to get your kid through all of this testing, but let's slay the six-headed monster together.

The Minority Report

My friend Dan thinks standardized tests are fun. He makes a game out of them. He has traditionally performed well on them. Even among those who test well, Dan is special. You might know someone like him, or you might *be* one of these "Oh, goody, a test!" people. The last thing I want to do is offend.

There's also Carolina, who works at a standardized testing company. She is like the Mother Teresa of my Facebook feed. When Hurricane Sandy flooded New Jersey, my other Facebook friends argued about the politics of cleanup while Carolina went house to house with a bucket and a mop. That's how wonderful she is, and that's how I know smart, compassionate people work at these testing companies, which makes me feel a little bit mean about making them the villain of my story.

But only a little bit.

SAT vs. ACT

Don't let all the different names for these tests make you feel less than.

The "College Board" is the first confusing name you'll come across, if you haven't already when your kid took the PSAT/NMSQT/ZKRL-CYYY. (I'm just messing with you on that last bit, except for the *why, why, WHY* the need for such an unwieldy abbreviation?) Even though the word "board" usually means "exam" — as in, doctors take the medical board exam and become board certified — the College Board is not a test. It's the name of the company that tortures our children with the SAT, among other things. This is important to know because you'll eventually visit the College Board's website more times than you'd imagine, for much more than SAT registration. (You'll see.)

The ACT, the name of both a test and the company that develops it, is the College Board's only competitor. Most colleges require your kid to submit scores from one of these two standardized tests. Think: SAT or ACT. Do not let all the other names for these tests throw you off-kilter.

A brief history of the name-calling:

- The SAT began as the Scholastic Aptitude Test in 1926.
- It was renamed the Scholastic Assessment Test in 1990…
- and renamed the SAT 1: Reasoning Test in 1993.
- The letters ACT originally stood for American College Testing in 1956.
- By 1997, both testing companies agreed that the acronyms SAT and ACT really stood for… nothing.
- The names SAT and ACT are both just brand names now.

Think: Lots of names, still just two tests, SAT or ACT.

The SAT is split up into four sections: Reading, Writing and Language, Math, and the optional Essay. However, your child will see only three scores on his score report: one score for Evidence-Based Reading and Writing (combining two sections together), one score for Math, and a third score for the Essay (if your kid opted in). I've given up trying to understand the logic of separating the test into four sections but only sharing three discrete scores with our children. I'd keep trying if I thought it was important.

Now it gets trickier because sections within the SAT have also been called various names over time.

- The SAT's Reading section was initially called the Verbal section.
- Then it was changed to Critical Reading (CR).
- Then it was changed again to Evidence-Based Reading and Writing (ERW).
- Now the combined Reading plus Writing and Language sections are called Reading, Writing, and Language (RWL).
- By the time your child takes the test, it will probably be called something else (WTF).

Think: I've got this. These are just different names for a section within the SAT test.

The ACT consists of five sections total: English, Math, Reading, Science, and an optional Writing section. The science section of the ACT began as Natural Sciences, and now it's called Science Reasoning, but otherwise, the section names are pretty straightforward (and your kid will receive a score for each).

Are you still with me? Think: Still just two tests, the SAT or ACT.

You will hear these tests and the sections within them called all these different names, but the upshot is the same. Despite all of society's steep advances in technology, your child will arrive in a fluorescently lit room early on a Saturday morning with his sharpened number-two pencils and fill in ovals on an answer sheet for three or four consecutive hours, exactly the way students did in the 1930s, when electronic scanners were first invented, and exactly the way you did, if you took either of these tests.

If another parent lets "the SAT's RWL section" tumble trippingly off her tongue, she is not better informed than you are, a showoff, or inherently evil. She knows memorizing abbreviations will not help her child take this test, but like many of us, she probably feels helpless while she watches her son exchange Snaps instead of studying for it, and she feels like she has to do *something* to regain a modicum of control. If you look more closely, you'll notice the dark rings under this parent's eyes that she's tried to conceal with makeup. Behind those eyes, she's looping, *My child is going to tank the SAT's RWL section, and never get into college, or get a job, or find a mate, and he will live in our basement playing video games until we die, and then what will happen to him?*

Instead of feeling less than or judging this other parent, take her hands with their ragged, chewed-off fingernails in yours, and whisper, "I will not let you take that leap off Anxiety Cliff." She may…

A. whisk her hands away as if from an open flame and through her clenched teeth say, "I am not anxious."

B. squeeze your hands tighter, cry off that thin layer of under-eye concealer, and say, "I have already leaped."

C. share a much-needed laugh with you (best-case scenario), or

D. all of the above.

What exactly do these tests test?

This is such a great question. Upon inception, allegedly the ACT tested "achievement," while the SAT tested "reasoning." Neither of these tests has been proven to accurately assess either. In 2012, the ACT surpassed the SAT as the more popular of the two tests, and then in 2016, the SAT replaced their old "reasoning test" with the "New SAT," which is supposed to test "achievement" too. Your child will take the "New SAT." Honestly, if you can parse out the College Board's language on their website describing the reasons they redesigned the SAT, I will symbolically award you 800 points (a perfect score) on the reading comprehension section.

What's the difference between the SAT and ACT?

Science is the main content difference between the two tests. Only it's not really science. It's more about reading graphs and charts, analyzing data, and applying scientific reasoning. If your child is good at that stuff, the ACT might be the better test for him…

…unless he's a slow test-taker. *The biggest difference between the two tests is the speed required to take them.* Both tests are fast, but the ACT is speed-of-light fast. The ACT allots students only approximately 49 seconds per question, while the SAT allots 70 seconds per question on average. For some students, this will not be a problem. For others, it's a deal breaker. Your child can learn to speed up through practice, but if she's always needed extra time on tests, consider that a sign.

Is the SAT or ACT the better test for my child to take?

Most colleges will accept the SAT or the ACT interchangeably. Therefore, the choice comes down to a few factors.

- *Convenience:* My children's school serves as a test site for the SAT, but we must travel at least 45 minutes to take the ACT. The SAT wins by proximity and an extra hour of sleep.
- *Superscoring:* Some colleges will "superscore" (which I will cover momentarily on p. 47) whatever test is tossed their way, but

some will only superscore the SAT. (Superscoring is good for your kid.)

- *It's a state requirement:* Some states offer either the SAT or ACT for free and require all students to take it. Check the Education Commission of States website to see if the decision will be made for you.
- *Coachability:* Is it really easier to coach students for the SAT than it is for the ACT? Some of my clients think so and choose the SAT for that reason.
- *One test feels less odious to your child:* I recommend students try each test once, either a timed practice test or the real deal, and then if they want to improve their scores, retake the one they like better or dislike less.

Is it worth it for my kid to spend the extra hour on the optional writing section?

I get it. After entering a school building early in the morning for the sixth day in a row, and slogging through three hours of testing, your kid's exhausted and burnt out. But later, he may choose to apply to a college that requires the writing section. Since he's already there, tacking on another hour is a lot better than going through the whole rigmarole again.

Should I seek outside intervention for test prep?

The Most Economical Approach: Self-Motivated Practice

Whether you're sixteen or sixty-one, there is no way to make standardized test prep sexy (except maybe for Dan). For that reason, unless your child is superhumanly motivated, procrastination will ensue, regardless of ability or intentions. Here are some pointers for those who want to try taking the free road.

Free test preparation materials are available online. Your child can sync PSAT scores to Khan Academy, or use Method Test Prep through Naviance, and those programs will advise your child what she needs to study. The ACT website offers free downloads of Stanley Kaplan test prep booklets. If any or all of those names I've dropped sound like gibberish to you, you can consult the Glossary, or your kid, who probably already knows all about them.

If you are determined to go the free route, sit down with your child and schedule when and where practice sessions will take place because there is always something more fun to do than prepare for a standardized test, like empty the dishwasher, clean toilets, or poke pins into your own eyeballs.

Relying on luck is also free. Some kids will talk you into letting them take the test without studying at all to see how they do. Note that every time your child retakes the test, it costs a baseline fee of $64.50 for the SAT with essay (plus $29 if you register late), or $67 for the ACT (plus $30 for late registration). I'm not saying that paying this fine is a bad thing. It might be the best way to teach your child the lesson that doing well on a test actually requires studying.

The Second Most Economical Approach: Buy a Book

The ACT offers free practice tests online, but you can also buy their pudgy test prep book. The College Board offers an entire bookstore on their website. From what I've seen, if a child isn't self-motivated enough to practice for free, he's not going to be self-motivated enough to crack open that book for which you spent $28.99. Your child might be different. And honestly, if you can afford it, and buying that book makes you feel like you are taking action on behalf of your kid, I am not one to talk. I spent about fifty dollars on SAT practice books that sit to this day on the desk in my daughter's bedroom — the bedroom she vacated for college — with their spines intact.

Bonus advice: If you've managed to convince your child to sit down with his SAT workbook but his face looks like he's being electrocuted, in my experience (with my son, within the past fifteen minutes), it's a waste of time to say, "The more oomph you put into these practice tests now, the fewer times you'll have to take the test later!" You're going to have to do better than the optimistic approach if you want your kid to study on his own for these tests.

The Not-Economical Approach: Classes and Tutors

Not-so-economical group classes: Companies such as Stanley Kaplan and Princeton Review offer live test prep classes, and a great local guy may teach group sessions in your area. Some students need the accountability of a real live adult (who isn't you) and peer pressure from classmates to prepare in any way for these tests.

Not-at-all-economical private tutors: You can also find a slew of in-person and remote private tutors for hire, if group classes are inconvenient or your child works better one on one. The variety and costs of these services depend on where you live and how dizzyingly the college admissions frenzy has spiraled there. Your child's more likely to study if he's the only student in the room with the tutor, which may make the extra cost on your end worth it.

Turning to experienced, ethical professionals can help your parent-child relationship, though if you can't or won't unearth the funds for such an endeavor, no one here will shame you when you do whatever you must do to make test prep happen. Threatening to confiscate a cell phone is a powerful tool many otherwise-nurturing parents have used throughout time immemorial to force their children to plant their butts in chairs and take those free practice tests.

What do the different scores mean?

How Scoring Works

Possible SAT scores:
- The highest possible score on the SAT is 800 Evidence-Based Reading and Writing + 800 Math = 1600 total.
- The lowest possible score for each SAT section is 200 points, which your kid's awarded just for showing up.
- The highest possible score on the SAT's optional writing section is 24 points. The Essay score is split into three parts, but do we really need to go there?

Possible ACT scores:

- The highest possible score on the ACT, in each section, is 36.
- All sections are averaged into a composite score ranging from 1 to 36.
- The highest possible score on the ACT's optional writing section is 12 points.

What exactly is superscoring?

Superscoring means colleges take into account only your child's very best scores on each section of a standardized test, and they recalculate for a higher total score. It's like the lower scores never happened. As a hypothetical example:

Johnny's March SAT scores: 610 Reading + 720 Math = 1330
Johnny's May SAT scores: 600 Reading + 680 Math = 1280
Johnny's June SAT scores: 680 Reading + 700 Math = 1380
Johnny's superscore: *680 Reading + 720 Math = 1400*

Johnny's May test magically disappears because through "score choice," he only has to submit the test scores he wants to submit to colleges. His superscored composite is higher than his composite score from any individual test date. Do you see how this works in your kid's favor? Calculating the student's superscore is as much in the college's interest as the student's because higher scores help boost colleges' rankings. Most colleges will superscore the SAT, but fewer superscore the ACT. You can learn which colleges superscore what tests on their websites or by anonymously calling the admissions office.

What is a "good" score?

When your child receives his score report, he'll see where his score fits into national percentiles. Then he'll compare his test scores to his friends'. These comparisons are irrelevant. The only comparisons that matter are the ones between your child's score and the scores earned by students at the colleges where he might apply down the road.

1. When you receive the first score report for any standardized test (look online; your child will already be in college before the paper version arrives in the mail), you'll have a baseline score for your child. That score is just a place to start.
2. Since we're at the very beginning of the college admissions process, turn to a random page in your college reference book or choose any college's website. Somewhere on that page (the Admission or Student Profile tab if you're online), you'll find average standardized test scores for current students.
3. If your child's score is at or above the top of their median score range, it's a "good" score for that college. If her score is below the 50th percentile, she's got some studying to do if she wants to apply to that college.

As an example:

- The median ACT score range for the University of Michigan's 2017 freshman class was 31–34.
- The median ACT score range for Miami University of Ohio's 2017 freshman class was 27–31.
- Maryellen's composite ACT score was 31. Her score fell in the lowest 25% of applicants to the University of Michigan in 2017 but in the top 75% of student test scores in Miami University's applicant pool.

What if my child's scores are way lower in one section than another?

It's okay. Students' test scores are more often than not uneven across the curriculum. We as a society don't need a computer programmer to write the great American novel, and I doubt anyone expects a professional novelist to write elegant computer code. Some can do it all, but if your kid is a budding theater major and the one blip in an otherwise outstanding application is a Math SAT score 160 points lower than his Reading score, that depressed Math score will not overwhelm the rest of his record. Conversely, if your kid is applying to an engineering program, a college admission evaluator might weight his higher math SAT score more heavily than his lower reading score. Polymaths are rare, these tests don't accurately predict if students will succeed in college, and admission evaluators recognize that. Your child's best is good enough. Test scores are only one part of the admission equation. If he's taken a test three times and his scores have flatlined, for the love of God, please urge him to stop.

How are my kid's test scores viewed if he is considered "privileged" or "underprivileged"?

More affluent students tend to have higher standardized test scores than poor and working-class students. This has nothing to do with who is smarter. It's because their environment commonly offers access to resources—such as the opportunity to take that $1,600 test prep class or to retake the SAT a couple more times for $64.50 a pop—that can help them appear more qualified. Plus, if a student attends a school where almost everyone else assumes college is in their future, she'll be surrounded by peers prepping for the test, making her more likely to study for it too, and her scores will improve.

As college admission evaluators review applications, they strive to gauge every student's potential for college-level work and include those who have been historically underrepresented in the student body. Evaluators appraise test scores, like grades, within the context of an applicant's environment. On that school profile the high school submits with your child's transcript (see p. 31, Freshman- and Sophomore-Year Grades), one significant statistic is the percentage of students at your child's high school who will attend four-year colleges.

If 98% of your child's peers are college-bound, chances are your child enjoyed a number of ambient advantages that will help her score higher on standardized tests. This does not mean that her high score is less impressive, or that it came easily. I know she's worked hard for everything she's earned, and you are not being penalized for doing well by her. It means that when you check the college's website, you should look at the upper end of the college's median score range to determine what's a "good" score for your kid. If your child studies within this privileged culture but does not enjoy the presumed privileges, don't worry. Other parts of her application will alert college admission evaluators to this discrepancy.

If fewer than 20% of the students at your child's school will go to college, evaluators will know that your child's environment is not necessarily supporting her to achieve all she can. Application readers will recognize that she doesn't have access to expensive test prep, or peers and mentors to push and guide her, and her test scores will not be compared apples to apples to those of kids who can afford private tutors. Any score within that median range listed on a college's website is a "good" score for your kid. Please hear me that if your child achieves a score that perches at the top of the charts within her school context, it will shine as brightly as a perfect 800 to the evaluator's trained eye.

I am well aware that your child is like no other, so, no doubt, she doesn't fit into my either/or description. The great news is that beyond test scores, your child has lots of control over how she presents herself in her college application. In Part IV: Summer Vacation, we'll go step by step through the ways she can make her application pop while you're lounging on the beach (because that's what I hope you will do). I promise.

Does my kid have to take all those other tests?

What exactly are SAT Subject Tests?

SAT IIs, SAT Achievement Tests, and SAT Subject Tests are all the same thing. More name-calling. Most people just call them Subject Tests. They are one-hour timed tests on twenty different subjects offered by the College Board.

The Subject Tests are not equally distributed across disciplines. If a student speaks twelve foreign languages, there are more tests for her to take than the student whose best subject is English or History. On most SAT testing dates, students may take up to three Subject Tests instead of taking the regular SAT test, but most will agree that two of these tests are exhausting enough for one day.

Beware: Not every subject test is available at every test site on every test date.

My daughter needed to submit two SAT Subject Tests to one of the colleges on her list. She insisted that she could decide which specific tests to take on the morning of her test date. That is true in most cases, but not all.

I told her, "Sign up for your SAT Subject Tests."

She did not sign up for the SAT Subject Tests.

I told her, "You'd better sign up for the SAT Subject Tests *today*, or all the seats will fill up."

She did not sign up for the SAT Subject Tests.

(Repeat above dialogue five or six times.)

Finally, on the last possible day to register, she decided she wanted to take the English Literature and Spanish with Listening tests.

Good news!

Both were offered at her high school, a two-minute drive or thirteen-minute walk from our house.

But wait!

Bold red letters on the College Board website announced that Spanish with Listening was no longer available. The language listening tests require a listening device, and there are a limited number of those devices available at each test site.

But wait! Good news!

My daughter found a school forty minutes away with space left for her to take Spanish with Listening.

So on the Saturday morning of her Subject Tests, I awoke at 5:15 a.m. to cook a hearty breakfast for her, and then drove her the forty minutes to arrive at 7:40 sharp for her SAT Subject Tests.

Just kidding.

The *real* good news was that she had a driver's license and could drive herself because there was no way on God's green earth that I was going to awaken before the sun on a Saturday morning and reward my sixteen-year-old's procrastination with scrambled eggs and a free ride.

Are there good reasons to take these extra tests?

Most colleges and universities do not require any SAT Subject Tests, but they're necessary in some cases:

- Some highly selective colleges and universities still require that students submit SAT Subject Tests (in addition to the SAT or ACT) with the application, though this list is shrinking.
- Some specialized colleges may have additional testing requirements. For example, in addition to either the SAT or the ACT, the California Institute of Technology requires students to submit two specific Subject Tests: Math Level Two, and the student's choice of Chemistry, Biology, or Physics.
- If your child's a great test-taker, more excellent test scores are especially desirable if other aspects of the application might raise questions. For example, a high score on the Biology SAT Subject Test could help mitigate colleges' concerns about a low grade in high school biology, especially if she's applying to a program requiring more biology classes.
- Some universities' internal college programs require Subject Tests, while others might not. For example, at this writing, Cornell University's College of Arts and Sciences requires two Subject Tests of the student's choice, the Engineering school requires one math and one science Subject Test, and Cornell's other six colleges require none.

Wait a minute. What's the difference between SAT Subject Tests and AP Subject Tests?

Little-known fact: The College Board—the same company famous for the SAT test and the SAT Subject Tests described above—creates, administers, and oversees the entire Advanced Placement program. Unlike the SAT and ACT, there is no market competition for either the SAT Subject Tests or the AP program that holds such cachet in our society. (Cue scary organ music.)

Monopoly: *exclusive possession or control.*

AP exams are additional tests offered in May to students who took an AP class during the school year. Some private schools offer these tests as part of their tuition, but most schools require families to pay for them. In exchange for $94 per AP test (the price hits triple digits if you live abroad or in a U.S. Territory like Puerto Rico), plus $15 to send a test score report to *each* college, your child...

- gets to take another laborious four-hour test
- has another test score he can choose to display (or not if it doesn't go well) on his college applications
- earns the honor of including "AP Scholar" on his college application *if* he receives a score of at least 3 (out of a possible 5 points) on three AP exams
- can earn college credit at 2,600 of the approximately 10,000 colleges worldwide (that's one out of four), in exchange for a high enough score
- might be able to use his score to test out of entry-level college courses

Another little-known fact: Not all high schools require AP tests for credit for an AP class. My daughter's school did not. She chose not to take any AP tests for the four AP classes she took senior year. They were offered in May, after we'd already put a deposit down for a college that did not offer credit for APs. She decided that taking a free Spanish placement test once she'd arrived at college would place her at a more accurate language level, bearing in mind all the Spanish she'd forget over the summer. Her decision saved me hundreds of dollars, and saved her sixteen hours (plus study time) of her life.

I'm getting ahead of myself. Your kid's only a junior and doesn't know where she'll apply to college, let alone if the college she'll ultimately choose will or will not accept AP credit. If she's taking an AP class now, she should take the test in May to hedge her bets. Then if the college your child ends up choosing accepts AP scores for credit, it could be worth taking those tests senior year too, even if they're not required. One friend's son graduated from a private college a semester earlier and saved $35,000 (minus the $376 AP test fees) because he'd earned scores of 4 or 5 on four AP tests to account for the needed credits.

When? How Much? And Other Things You'll Want to Know About Testing

When should all of this testing happen?

My friend said her son took the Chemistry Subject Test right after our kids took chemistry together last year, so why am I learning about this for the first time now? Should my kid have done that? Have we missed the boat?!

Deep, cleansing breaths. Now is a perfect time to plan a testing schedule.

A TYPICAL TESTING TIMELINE FOR JUNIOR AND SENIOR YEAR

JUNIOR YEAR

- November: Take the PSAT
- March: Take the SAT
- April: Take the ACT
- May: Take AP tests (if enrolled in AP classes)
- June Option 1: Retake the ACT or SAT (whichever went better the first time)
- June Option 2: Take SAT Subject Tests for subjects recently completed

SENIOR YEAR

- September/October: Last chance to retake tests before November deadlines

- November/December: Last chance to retake tests before January deadlines
- May: Take AP tests (if enrolled in AP classes and a college that accepts AP credits)

Troubleshooting:

- The ACT and SAT offer tests on alternating months most of the year. Both companies offer tests in June, October, and December, but on different weekends, so in those months, your child could experience the joy of sitting and filling in ovals for four hours straight two Saturdays in a row. Hooray?
- June is the best time to take the SAT Subject Tests for subjects your child has studied this year, when content is fresh in his mind. If that doesn't happen next spring, or didn't happen last spring, he can always study and take the test at any time.
- It takes a few weeks for test scores to reach colleges, so if your child takes a test the month before an application is due, she must send her scores directly to colleges, sight unseen. Some kids are wigged out by this idea. Plan accordingly.
- By May first of senior year, your child will know where he's going to college (only a year and a quarter away—you've got this), and you'll know whether taking senior AP tests will be worth his while.

How much will all this testing cost me?

We paid $921.21 for my daughter to take standardized tests (SAT, SAT Subject Tests, ACT, AP) and then submit her test scores to colleges. Two years later, we paid $926 for my son's testing, totaling $1,847.21 for both of them. Of that amount, $1,717.71 went to the College Board. These numbers do not include test prep books, tutoring, massages (that only happened twice), or the amount I spent at the salon to cover fresh sprouts of gray hair (which I attribute to my kids' standardized testing, whether that's fair or not).

While we're on the topic of cost, other expenses, such as college application fees and submitting financial aid forms to private colleges, also add up. I'll provide a breakdown of college admissions expenses you might encounter (before paying a cent of tuition) and point out hidden costs you can avoid on my website, and I will not charge you a single red penny for any of it. Extract what you will from my numbers to help you plan your own budget.

"Every Test Is Practice" and Other Advice from the Trenches

I've gathered pep talks from parents, in case you need to borrow one in a pinch to combat your kid's test anxiety:

- *Get to bed early enough. Eat a good breakfast. Relax. Show 'em what you've got.* (Scott, Ohio)
- *Just do the best you can, and remember, each question is worth the same amount. If you're stuck, skip it.* (Nadyli, New York)
- *No single test has the power or ability to define you, your worth, or your intelligence. No matter what happens, we love you, and you will be fine.* (Andrea, Massachusetts)
- *Pain is weakness leaving the body. Suck it up.* (While not exactly a pep talk, some kids need tough love. David, Connecticut)
- *You have conquered long portages with a fifty-pound pack on your back.* (Substitute your child's most impressive feat of strength.) *You can do this.* (Suzanne, Pennsylvania)
- *If you do well, that's amazing, but everyone gets into college, so don't get sick over it.* (Rona, Florida)
- *Every test is practice.* (Me, Massachusetts) With superscoring and score choice (see Glossary), it's true, with the exception of only a handful of schools.

Introducing Katherine Appy, Psy.D., a clinical psychologist, who has worked with families as well as her own three boys through the psychological aspects of the college admissions process. She more than gets it. We'll be calling upon Dr. Appy from time to time throughout this book to help us as difficult emotions surface. Here's her ammunition against test anxiety to add to your cache:

- *Remind your child that he is not alone. "We are going to figure out some ways for you to prepare and relax and come up with a plan prior to the test to set you up for success."*
- *Set up a study schedule that will make your child feel prepared. Preparation is a great inoculator against test anxiety or any performance anxiety.*
- *Encourage your kid to try a practice test before the big day so he knows what it looks like and feels like.*
- *Talk through the "worst-case scenario" and then come up with some responses. "I will fail the test" is the most common worry. Your response, "So let's imagine you fail. What happens then?" "I won't get into college," etc. Teens realize that of course their worst fear is most likely not going to happen.*
- *Teach your child a basic relaxation exercise, like deep breathing, or tightening and relaxing his feet, then ankles, then calves, all the way up his body.*
- *Embed a new script or narrative to replace his negative thinking about the test. This is where studying comes in handy. "You know this stuff. Just remind yourself of that!"*
- *Reassure your child, "This test does not define you as a student. If a college is only going to look at you based on this score, this may not be a college for you."*

If my child tanked the PSAT, does that mean he will tank the SAT when it counts?

Showing up and taking the test provides practice and valuable information that will help improve future scores. My daughter entered her PSAT cold. The breakneck speed shocked her, she didn't finish, and she knew she'd have to work faster on the SAT, which improved by more than 200 points. Her friend learned that math would be no trouble for her, yet she'd have to study for the reading section. Studying between tests helps more than simply showing up. The College Board reports that after twenty hours of practice, SAT scores increase 115 points on average.

What if I'm pretty sure my child will crash and burn on these tests?

Your kid's worked her tushy off for years, and her grades are outstanding, but her standardized test scores are not. Her guidance counselor will say something like, "Her testing does not accurately reflect her academic achievement or potential," as if you didn't already know that.

Here's what I want you to remember: *Your kid's achievements over the span of four years are more important than her achievements over a span of three or four hours on one test.*

Please allow me to take your hand and escort you back to the FairTest website for a pick-me-up. You will be thrilled when you see a list of more than a thousand institutions—some colleges you've heard of, as well as some you haven't—that are test-optional or test-flexible (see Glossary). A handful of these colleges and universities may be terrific for your child and exempt her from any more testing hell.

What if my academically average student crushed it on the SAT?

> **Late bloomer:** *someone who becomes successful, attractive, etc., at a later time in life than other people.*

Some mediocre students stun everyone with really great test scores. Admission evaluators can interpret this in two ways.

The charitable interpretation: He struggled with the transition to more rigorous classes in high school, but then he figured it out, his grades have improved over time, and high standardized test scores strengthen his application.

The skeptical interpretation: The dominant variable between four years of average grades and one morning of focused testing is probably effort.

Fantastic if your child's enthusiasm and motivation for academics has begun to surge! In the best of all possible worlds, his high test scores will instill him with newfound confidence and he will resolve to try harder throughout the rest of high school and on all those tasks he won't want to do (and yet he must) when he enters the adult world.

How important for college admission are test scores, anyway?

I think you know by now that to me, standardized tests are like gnats I want to swat away. Like it or not, they keep buzzing around as an important part of the college admissions process for the colleges that require them. Even I will admit that sometimes they're the best that college admission evaluators have to compare kids from nontraditional learning environments, such as homeschooled students, to the rest of the applicant pool.

If a student's grades and standardized test scores will not be competitive in a college's applicant pool, admission evaluators may not move on to review everything else your child has to offer, no matter how many essay revisions he labored through or how many clubs he presides over as president. This may not be number one on the list of things you wanted to hear today, but sometimes, as your ally, I need to deliver news point blank.

If avoiding testing altogether will give your child and your family peace, applying exclusively to test-optional schools is a legitimate thing to do. If she might apply to any colleges that require standardized test scores, testing matters, and she should skip the party the night before, eat her Wheaties the morning of, and do her best.

THE INS AND OUTS OF ATHLETIC RECRUITING

You read about that eighth-grade football player offered the athletic scholarship to the University of Alabama. Your kid plays football, but recruiting wasn't even on your radar. Ye olde internal monologue takes over with something like *Maybe MY kid wants to play her sport in college. I never thought to ask her because I am clearly, without a doubt, the worst parent ever. Is she even good enough? Is it too late? Have we totally missed the window?*

Here's what I have to say to you. Fauja Singh of London ran his first marathon when he was eighty-eight years old, and then he ran eight more. Certainly junior year in high school is not too late for your sixteen-year-old to pursue something she wants with her entire heart and soul. If your child is an exceptional athlete, athletic recruiting is a whole separate process that warrants a whole separate book (which I will not be writing), though I can get you started.

Sizing Up the Divisions

The National Collegiate Athletic Association (NCAA), the governing organization for college sports, divides colleges into three "divisions" by size of student body and the amount of resources dedicated to athletics.

Big universities usually field *Division 1* teams, which are serious business. The honor of playing a Division 1 varsity sport usually comes with a significant scholarship (though not within the Ivy League), which makes athletics like a job. If your child is good enough at her sport to be a Division 1 recruit, she's likely already entered the NCAA clearinghouse. If she hasn't, she can march up to her coach now and learn how to make that happen.

Medium-sized colleges and universities usually field *Division 2* teams, though "medium-sized" is hard to define. For example, the California Collegiate Athletic Association, a Division 2 sports league, includes schools with student bodies ranging from about 5,000 to 30,000. At a Division 2 school, expect a Division 1 level of commitment to the sport in terms of hours but less scholarship money to compensate for that commitment.

Small colleges usually participate in *Division 3* sports leagues, a different story. At a typical small liberal arts college with a student body of around 2,000, academics come before sports. Your child won't receive any financial aid for participating, nor will she be obliged to attend practice if it conflicts with a big sociology test, but she could enjoy extra attention in college admissions if the coach supports her.

Should my child approach coaches, or will they come to her?

The most relevant thing for you to know is that coaches are not allowed to approach your kid before a certain magic date, which is different for every sport. (See the NCAA's recruiting calendars.) Before that date, if your child wants to participate in college sports, she should contact coaches. She can go ahead and do that now. First, she'll fill out the brief athletic recruitment form on the college's website. Then she'll email the coach prior to visiting the campus and schedule to meet him, as well as the team, if possible, which could become her second family at a Division 1 or 2 school. Depending on the sport and the division, she might need to create an "athletic reel," for which outside intervention options abound. You can hire a Hollywood producer or DIY those videos. Your child's high school or club team coach will know how it's done.

How does my child know if she's a top athletic recruit or not?

One of my students was encouraged to attend intense soccer camps (and by "camp" I do not mean songs around a campfire) at six different colleges the summer before his junior year, yet he didn't end up as a top recruit anywhere. If a coach shows interest in your kid, it does not necessarily mean your kid's at the top of that coach's list. Coaches don't mean to be misleading. They want to keep their options open, as would anyone. Your child has to build up the courage to ask the coach where he stands, and most coaches will tell him the truth — not always easy for a kid (or any of us) to hear.

Even if he is a top recruit, encourage your child to do some soul searching:

- How much does he love his sport, and what percentage of his college life does he want to devote to it?
- Do the colleges recruiting him have the academic programs he wants and needs to prepare him for life after college? (Not to

squelch his dreams, but this might be a good time to break it to him that very few college athletes go pro.)

- Do these colleges offer an environment where he will thrive even if he's injured? (I am throwing salt over my shoulder right now on your child's behalf.)

A Timely Lesson on Letting Go

Approaching adults in person or in writing may sound easy to you but might be really hard for your kid. Athletic recruiting forms and other forms your kid will be asked to fill out during the college admissions process provide fertile training ground.

Teenagers see every adult—whether wearing a business suit or a sweatshirt and cleats—as an authority figure. I remember showing up at the middle school open house ready to meet Mr. Smith, the infamous math teacher, reputed to be old, out of touch, and gray bearded (I'd added that last detail in my head), to find that Mr. Smith was about twenty-seven years old and fresh out of grad school. No matter how young he looks to you, or how warmly a coach greets your family, to your child, that coach is an intimidating gatekeeper to something she wants with all her heart. It might seem like no big deal to fill out a brief, impersonal form or send a quick email to schedule with a coach, but for your child, it can take gumption. The same goes for requesting teacher recommendations, scheduling a college interview, etc.

Since those simple-looking forms can stress kids out, parents often complete them. I know that a few keystrokes can erase that pained expression on your kid's face. I know that filling out a silly little form or writing a two-sentence email—the same way you've always done for her—is much easier and quicker than expending the energy required to motivate your kid to do it. I know your life is busy, and you are strapped for time, because so am I. Let your child take the lead and fill out that form herself anyway.

There's a saying, *Give a man a fish and you feed him for a day. Teach him how to fish and you feed him for a lifetime.* One of the best things I ever did as a parent—beyond providing food, shelter, and *life* for my children—

was to force my daughter to stumble through the American healthcare system the summer before she went to college. She needed a doctor's appointment, nothing serious, so I handed her the doctor's phone number. From the shocked expression on her face, you would have thought I'd sent her off to navigate the Tokyo subway system. I transferred her insurance card from my wallet to hers (for the long term). I instructed her to make another call to check if the specialist was covered by our insurance, call the primary care doctor's office for a referral, be Zen about the Musak while she sat there on hold, ask for the referral, call again and check with the specialist that the referral had arrived, and call her primary care physician's office again when it hadn't. On the day of her appointment, I provided directions to the doctor's office, shooed her out of the house to make it to the appointment more or less on time, fielded her text questions about the medical history form, and bada boom, bada bing. A person capable of advocating for her own healthcare *all by herself* was born.

Was this a painless process? It was about as painless as natural childbirth. Am I sorry? No way. My daughter's personal healthcare manager has officially retired. Besides, once your child turns eighteen, you'll see that the American healthcare system becomes very serious about patient privacy, which provides a great excuse for you to retire from uncompensated healthcare management too.

If you've already filled out that recruitment form for your child, I don't mean to shame you. There will be many moments throughout the college admissions process, and after she goes to college, and forevermore, to either do some simple task for your child or compel her to do it herself.

TO-DO LIST

☐ Look at a few college websites to make an educated decision about which standardized tests your child will need to take.

☐ Make a testing schedule. No one will hold you to it if things change.

☐ Sign up your child now (or better yet, he can sign up himself) if he wants to get started earlier than most and try the ACT test in February. To avoid a late fee, register for all standardized tests a month before the test date.

☐ Forgive yourself if you've been enabling your fledgling adult's helplessness, as all of us have at some point or another. There's no time like the present to start teaching her to take on some of the tasks you've always done for her.

☐ If your child is an athlete interested in participating in a college sport, familiarize yourself with the NCAA recruitment calendar and show her how to let college coaches know she's interested. Then you can leave the room to show her you have faith in her abilities and to prep her for adulthood.

☐ Looking ahead, think about using February break for some zero-stakes college visits. See how to schedule a college visit in Part I: Fall of Junior Year, and I'll cover what to do (or not to do) once you arrive on campus in the next chapter.

☐ Looking even further ahead, I know this sounds a little neurotic, but if your kid is interested in any summer programs that require an application (such as an academic program, employment, an internship, travel involving a visa or plane tickets, or any activity with limited space), you might want to start looking into that now because some have February deadlines. Don't worry if you hadn't thought about this. You will see in Chapter 6: May that I recommend your child does not sacrifice one of the last two summers of his childhood trying to impress colleges.

Chapter 3

February

How are you doing so far?

I, for one, am ecstatic we've gotten that testing section out of the way. I think we all deserve a little breather after that, so I invite you here with me, poolside, to the house my parents have rented in Florida.

My family takes this February break trip almost every year, and in some ways, it is always the same. My mom is here, so you know there will be shopping. She stocks the fridge with our favorite fish salads from Morton's deli before we arrive. My parents' patterns are thoroughly predictable. Every so often, my mom yells, "Jeffrey!" and my dad shrugs his shoulders and says, "I'm innocent," before she accuses him of anything.

Earlier today, I took a walk on the beach. Come along for the walk because I want to show you something. Can you hear the surf? Can you smell the salt and sunscreen? Can you see among the striped umbrellas, where a young mom in a Lilly Pulitzer bikini squats beside her toddler, who bends over, swim diaper pointed at the blue sky, and reaches toward the sand? The toddler pinches her tiny fingers around a shell. It's one of millions of shells on that square of beach, but to her, it's *the* shell. Under the flap of her flamingo sunhat, this tiny little girl, one of millions of tiny girls on beaches today, is *the* little girl to this mom. In unison, as if planned, the two of them look at each other and say, "Wow."

Back at the table beside the pool at my parents' rental house, what I want to share with you is that although so much feels the same on this annual Florida trip, much has changed. I was once that young mom (minus the bikini), and my sometimes-ornery teenage boy, splashing around in the pool acting silly with his father, was once that little toddler. Right now, my kid is saying, "Look, I'm walking only on my big toes." His legs bent outward underwater, he looks ridiculous, like a crab, but I am looking. And I am so glad we chose to come here together, even though it's his junior year and I felt a little nervous before we booked the flight, as though maybe we should've used this break to tour colleges like some of his friends are doing.

Please promise me, and promise yourself, that you will not become so caught up in the college admission hoopla that you miss the moment when your child wants you to ogle her perfect shell, no matter how ordinary, or wants you to bear witness as he crab-walks in a swimming pool, no matter how silly, because this is what's important. This.

PLANNING WHEN AND WHERE TO VISIT

When to Visit: Pros and Cons of IRL College Shopping over February Break

If you've already booked a February break trip to visit colleges, I respect that. When my daughter was a junior, we were so itchy to get started that we skipped the Florida trip and college-shopped instead, and it worked out fine. I relished other "Wow" moments with her before she left for college.

Even if your kid's school doesn't allot a full week of vacation, February is flush with long weekends, random teacher workdays, and early dismissals when — in what seems like a million years ago, and also yesterday — we scrambled to find childcare for our second-graders. Now those free days and afternoons can come in handy for college shopping. Whether you've already leaped into that first college visit, you're planning to start now that the holidays are behind you, or it still feels premature, *you are right where you should be.* I wouldn't lie about this.

Pro and con: The weather in February doesn't lie.

If you live in the Northeast, you may recall the brutal winter of 2014. If not, you might have heard about the subzero temperatures and record snowfall. That winter, forty inches of snow accumulated on our roof in Massachusetts, and I learned that a "roof rake" is a tool with a telescoping handle that, had we discovered it before the hardware stores sold out, could've prevented water from pooling on our eaves into "ice dams" that leaked into our kitchen and caused thousands of dollars' worth of damage. Surprise! That was also the winter I decided to embark on a February break college tour in the snow belt of upstate New York and Vermont with my daughter.

Yes, I did this.

We started urban, in New York City, with such glacially cold wind lashing the campus that our tour guide wrapped her scarf over her face and we could hardly hear her speak. As we continued to rural colleges upstate, temperatures never topped negative ten degrees *without* factoring in wind chill. Believe me, it's hard to differentiate building façades on college campuses when you've seen them all through a blizzard. Touring six colleges—all great options for my daughter—in arctic conditions backfired, and none of them appeared on her final college list. Not a one.

I suppose it's a pro that my daughter saw (and felt) a realistic representation of what it would be like to live on these campuses during the academic year, but the bigger pro (especially for the parent) is that you can choose weather when traveling. As many students stay warm on campuses in Florida and Southern California as freeze in New England in February. They ski on the weekends in Colorado and wear tank tops to classes in Louisiana. There are lovely hotels on or near all of these campuses, and if you can tack on a beach or mountain vacation to your college visits, I'm all for it.

Pro: You can preempt the spring break and fall crowds.

Spring break is the most popular time for college visits, with fall senior year a close second. That makes college visits in February similar to traveling on the Monday instead of the Wednesday before Thanksgiving. We once packed into an overflowing auditorium that must have held three hundred people for a spring break information session.

Twelve tour guides barely managed the surge of humanity that descended upon campus that day. However, most info sessions in the dead of winter are small enough not to intimidate prospective students from asking questions, and tours, equally small, can cover more (admittedly frozen) ground. At one college, our tour included only my daughter and me with a tour guide so warm and personable, I wanted to either adopt her or enroll there myself and request her as a roommate.

Pro: The students are on campus, and classes are happening.

Some colleges' spring breaks will sync with your child's—good news for family unity if you have one kid in college and another in high school, but bad news if you arrive for a tour and find the campus deserted. However, in February, almost all college campuses are happening places, where your child can observe students and sit in on classes. We toured one college in wretched weather with a lackluster tour guide, but sitting in on an exhilarating class transformed my daughter's impression of the school (and perhaps reminded her that the point of college is to engage in learning). That couldn't have happened if classes hadn't been in session.

An overnight visit is another option available only when students inhabit the campus. While your kid eats dining hall food and sleeps on a dorm room floor, you can enjoy a night alone in a nearby hotel, with room service, zero responsibilities, and full control of the remote and the minibar. There's no rule that says college visits must be all about your offspring.

Pro: The concept of "college" is demystified for the nervous child.

My daughter's nerves surfaced well before February break. Back in the summer before her junior year began, I was caught off-guard when I picked her up from a weeklong teen wilderness trip. After ten days in the woods, before she'd even taken a shower, she said, "Izzi has already visited two colleges. Should I be looking at colleges now too?" Then she opened fire with a battery of questions like: *What happens on a college visit? Do I have to say anything? Am I supposed to know what I want to study?*

Does this sound familiar?

While I'd envisioned my child transfixed by mountain views and skipping stones across an alpine lake on her wilderness trip, she'd been preoccupied with *this*. The solution was as simple as visiting a college—any college—a little earlier than I'd anticipated (but after she took a shower) to demystify the experience.

If you haven't yet made a preliminary college visit, it might be a good idea to visit one now if your child's on edge about it. We toured an abandoned campus, but the giant, scary void my daughter saw when she'd tried to visualize her future began to fill in with familiar, more comfortable, tangible details, such as a row of cereal boxes in the dining hall, and a classroom with a math equation lingering on the whiteboard, as if the class had just been dismissed.

Con: It's still a little early.

A few more months of grades, test scores, and brain development may provide more clarity about which colleges are worth visiting. Even if the likelihood of admission is already starting to look pretty clear, winter break feels too soon for a week's worth of college shopping for some families. If that sounds like yours, consult Google Flights (or CheapOair.com if you're feeling brave) for last-minute deals, and come join me in Florida. Or stock enough hot chocolate, marshmallows, and firewood for a fabulous stay-cation in your hometown. Don't even think twice about it.

Con: Just because school's out doesn't mean everyone else's work stops.

Oh yeah, there's that thing called *your life outside of your child's world* that needs tending. You might have taken time off from work during that week between Christmas and New Year's. If your child has another vacation, it does not mean you do. If sacrificing your sick days for February break college visits would mean working through that next 101-degree fever, please prioritize your health.

Where to Visit: Big, Small, Urban, and Rural Campuses

Let's dig deeper into the icebreaker question introduced on p. 16 in Part I. Discussing the differences between big and small, urban and rural campuses with your child will help you choose colleges to visit, whenever you visit. This won't be the only criterion for your child's choice, by a longshot, but it's a great way to begin narrowing down her search. Each college is unique, but here's a general picture:

SMALL LIBERAL ARTS COLLEGES	BIG UNIVERSITIES
Lively discussion seminars on day one	Huge lectures first, seminars after your kid's major is declared
Accessible professors who live for undergrad "Aha" moments	Demigod professors at lecterns and TAs in discussion groups (at least, at first)
Academic exploration until a major is declared	Apply to a specific program and start career prep right away
36 majors offered at Haverford College	160 majors offered at Penn State University
Personal advisors hold students' hands	Many advisors are available for students who take initiative to find them
Your kid can play sports or land a theater role as a first-year	Your kid can appear on a Jumbotron and join the Concrete Canoe Club (or another of the six hundred clubs)
They recently built a new gym with a modest climbing wall	He can pedal a recumbent bike in an athletic center fit for Olympians
He'll see his crush at parties for three weekends straight (until he finally summons the nerve to introduce himself)	He can join a fraternity (or one of those six hundred clubs on campus) to make his big school feel smaller

RURAL SCHOOLS	URBAN SCHOOLS
Beautiful scenery surrounds a one-horse town	The library is one of the skyscrapers surrounding a public park
Tranquility is perfect for undistracted study	City energy is perfect for inspiring creativity
Your kid climbs a bucolic mountain for geology class	Your kid visits a famous natural history museum for anthropology class
Entertainment: an indie band at the fieldhouse	Entertainment: a concert at Madison Square Garden
Room and board payments cover just about everything	"Hey Mom, can you subsidize fifty bucks for a concert? It's cultural."
Home is a double in the sophomore quad	Home is five roommates in an apartment without a chore wheel
Your child's roommate harkens from a neighboring state	Your child's roommate grew up in Zimbabwe
Your kid needs a car or a 3-hour Uber ride to the airport	Public transportation should get him wherever he needs to go

A shout-out to suburbia:

Not to confuse matters, but down the hill from the verdant campus, your kid hops on a train that takes him four stops in one direction to his bank internship, and four stops in the other direction to the beach.

HOW TO VISIT: DOS AND DON'TS

Prep for College Visits

Try "the afterthought approach" if your child doesn't feel like looking at colleges when it's convenient for you.

In Part I, we covered the positive reinforcement approach, the optimistic approach, and applying dictator tactics to persuade your kid to get on board. But what if you happen to be in Florida (where I find myself this February break), which happens to be a potential college mecca? What then? In this fortuitous situation, here's a script for you to adjust as appropriate:

As long as we're in Florida, I have the most awesome idea! Let's road trip to the Devil's Millhopper Geological State Park, where there's a 120-foot-deep sinkhole in a rainforest! It also happens to be in Gainesville, where the University of Florida, home of the Gators (!), was spared from the sinkhole, thank goodness! Maybe we should stop there too!

If you can pull it off, dropping in words like "awesome" and "fun" maximizes effectiveness. Even if your teenager senses what you're up to, he may go along with it because he feels sorry for anyone who is *that* excited about a sinkhole.

The cardinal rule of college shopping: No falling in love with one college.

Multiple adults in your child's life have told her there's a college out there that's a "perfect fit" for her. This drives me crazy. Almost every teenager I have ever known (not an insignificant number, since I work with teenagers) has translated "perfect fit" into "love at first sight." Your child will sense pressure to find her divine paradise, and that pressure escalates when a campus tour guide says that the first time he saw the college he's hawking, he "fell in love" or "just knew" it was the "perfect" school for him.

What if your child never experiences that smitten, love-at-first-sight feeling at any school? Or what if your child feels giddy heart palpitations, and the college doesn't feel the same way about her when she applies?

> **Perfect:** *being entirely without fault or defect.*
> **Fit:** *to be suitable for or to harmonize with.*

I'm adding this cardinal rule to protect your child from unnecessary heartbreak. "Fit" is a reasonable thing to look for on a college visit. Lots of colleges out there are suitable to accommodate her needs and desires, and the college you're touring next week could be one of them. But it's 100% up to your kid to enter college with a good attitude and then tailor her experience into a "perfect fit" once she arrives there. Others may have hexed your kid with idealistic expectations, which leaves you in charge of breaking the spell. As you drive through the campus gates, reassure her that you're only here for a first date, and falling instantly in love is neither expected nor advisable.

Your child and her BFF visiting a college together: Good idea or big mistake?

It can go either way.

Big mistake: Peers' opinions can disproportionately influence every aspect of a teenager's life, including this one. In an extreme case of "big mistake," one mom told me her suggestible daughter had chosen a college based on her trusted friend's insistence that it was "the best." It was not the best for her kid, who applied to transfer to another college after one semester.

Good idea: On the flip side, another set of eyes can prove as positive as negative, and the presence of a friend can provide a buffer between your child's annoyance with you and your dwindling patience with her. (This too shall pass.) As an added benefit, if the friend can't visit the school any other way than in your car, it's a good deed to shuttle her along with you. The way I see it, good deeds lead to good karma, and you're going to need all the positive karma you can get to survive the remaining year of college admissions challenges.

Don't worry if the college is too far away or too expensive to visit.

If you live within a two-hour drive and you can carve out the time between work, school, your child's flu shot, and your dog's rabies shot, colleges will expect you to make the effort to get your kid there for a visit. With a driver's license, she can make her way there herself. But this expectation is null and void if a visit requires a two-hour plane ride.

Wear the right clothes.

I'm not talking about a jeans-versus-business-attire conundrum. I'm talking about dressing for the weather. When I brought my daughter on the arctic college expedition of February 2014, trust me when I tell you not one soul who saw me or my daughter could've cared less if we were wearing cute shoes. Pity that Southern family on our tour who had packed only fleece jackets. College tours require lots of walking, and no one is spared the outdoor sections of a tour just because she wears high heels instead of sneakers, sneakers instead of snow boots, or can't feel her fingers because she forgot to bring mittens.

Brace your child for the info-session introductory questions she'll have to answer.

Before our first college visit, I promised my daughter she didn't have to say a word. Then, not ten minutes later, a process of going around the room announcing home state and potential major began, and my daughter shot me her best glare. When it was her turn, she declared that she was interested in "English and study abroad," which I interpreted as a passive-aggressive way of saying, *I'm interested in clear communication about what really happens at an info session, and in moving as far away from my parents as possible.*

"Why didn't you prepare me?" my daughter hissed afterward, as if it were my fault.

Now you can be the prepared parent I was not. During the info session, the presenter generally goes for audience participation right off the bat by asking students where they're from ("Is anyone from Nebraska? We could use a student from Nebraska, haha!") and what their academic or extracurricular interests might be. Your child will have to answer those questions in front of everyone present. If not at the info session, surely it will happen during the tour, and teenagers do not like to be caught off-guard.

Once You've Arrived

"Demonstrate interest" upon arrival.

Have you heard about "demonstrated interest"? If you have, you might have heard it's all a ridiculous game, but it looks a little different from a college's vantage point, so hear me out.

Next year, your child will fill out one universal application, aptly called the Common Application. (I cover every corner of this application in Part IV: Summer Vacation.) She can fire off this application to twenty schools without much extra effort, a vast improvement over the tools available to my generation (typewriters, carbon paper…do they still sell Wite-Out?). Some students use this convenience to play the odds, figuring the more applications they submit, the greater chance they have of getting in somewhere "good."

From an admission evaluator's perspective, I can tell you that the odds for these blitz attackers are no better than they are for the students who thoughtfully target seven viable colleges. I understand the fear that seduces kids into throwing in a couple more applications, and so do other admission evaluators, but they have hundreds of applications to read in about six weeks. Do you see how taking the time to thoroughly review an application submitted as an afterthought, from a student who isn't really interested in the school, is not at the top of their priority list?

If a student shows up on a campus that's within a reasonable distance from her home, it's one way a college can gauge if she's genuinely interested. There are other ways, too, so there's no need to get all hung up about it. It's hard to tell which colleges track applicants' demonstrated interest and which don't bother. Either way, if your child checks in at the front desk of the Office of Admission upon arrival, voila! She's counted as present and included on the college's mailing list (sometimes forever). If you didn't pre-register (see p. 17 for instructions), rest assured, a college won't turn away potential students (a.k.a. customers) who show up.

Whatever you do or don't do, you'll embarrass your child, so just try to blend.

Also at the first college I visited with my daughter, I made the mistake of raising my hand during the question and answer period at the end of the information session. I only asked one question, but by the horrified look on my daughter's face, you'd have thought I'd committed a felony. Then, during the tour, our guide asked, "Does anyone have any questions?" I think you know where I'm going with this.

I couldn't help myself. I asked another. My daughter slouched to make herself as small as possible, maybe figuring that if her head completely disappeared into her shoulders, no one would see her standing there associated with the crazy lady beside her asking questions right and left.

I know how thrilling it can be to land in the lobby of an Office of Admission and interact with other parents who've boarded the same rickety boat. Keep in mind that if you chat with other parents or ask a question during an info session (even if it's burning inside you like a mouthful of cayenne pepper), it might feel to your child like you've worn a clown nose to her piano recital. Since the goal here is to blend, when in doubt, err on the side of keeping your mouth shut so you don't detract from the main event.

If your child announces a different major at each college visit, roll with it.

That very afternoon—after the drama of the info-session introduction debacle and my rowdy question-asking unfolded—my daughter and I attended our second college visit. Sure enough, the presenter at the info session there asked the students the exact same questions. This time, my daughter was ready. She announced where she was from, and that she was interested in "art history and women's and gender studies." On future college visits, she would declare majors in American Studies, political science, and psychology to the roomful of potential applicants. She would tell them she was interested in the cross-country team, or studio art, or sometimes she'd choose various social justice clubs. All of these were honest answers, and that led us to a mutual understanding that a liberal arts college would be right for her.

Staking Out the Info Session Like a Spy from the NSA

Not that I'm paranoid that the National Security Agency (or Facebook, or my smartphone) is listening in on everything I say, but approach the info session during your college visit like an NSA secret operative (who might be reading everything I'm typing right now — not that I have anything to hide).

Probe beneath the propaganda.

If you're on time for the information session (which of course you *would* be if you didn't have to wrangle a teen out the door), you'll sit there waiting for the latecomers while slides of happy people dwelling on the campus you're about to tour flash on a screen. This is a perfect time for you and your child to sift through the papers they handed you upon arrival or that you picked up in the waiting room of the admissions office, which probably list programs and majors. For the rare kid who knows exactly what she wants to study in college, she can home in on specifics. Does this school offer a pre-law program? Does it offer a study abroad opportunity in New Zealand? For the regular kid who has no idea what she wants to study in college, those lists of majors and programs will give her ideas.

After the happy-people-on-slides, you might see a marketing movie featuring the same happy people perambulating the campus. If not for this movie (and the parents who embarrass their kids during the Q&A), that hourlong info session could easily be condensed into half an hour, tops. If you were a real NSA spy (please Facebook-message me if you are because I have some questions), you'd excuse yourself to the restroom, but you'd sneak past the restroom into an office and rummage around in the desk drawers. (I have learned about this exclusively from television.) Second best and less risky, while the movie rolls, you and your child can finish reading those papers. You should do so silently because you might be sitting beside someone like my husband. He resented my daughter and me shuffling papers, whispering, and distracting him during a perfectly good film.

Determine how they do academics.

When the movie ends and the presenter starts talking, begin your investigation of the school's academic requirements. Some kids do best when they are never told what to do, while others prefer more structured environments (though they don't want their parents to be the ones structuring them). Here's what to listen for:

- Some colleges offer an *open curriculum,* meaning students can take whatever classes they want.
- Some obligate students to fulfill *distribution requirements,* meaning students must take classes within a few categories (for example: humanities, STEM, foreign language) to graduate, but they can choose their specific classes within those categories.
- Some require a *core curriculum* of assigned classes all students must take, regardless of major.

Additionally, listen for unique academic opportunities. One school we visited offered a cool semester-at-sea program. Another offered dozens of foreign languages, and still another boasted a state-of-the-art science lab with student access to a working nuclear reactor (!), which I'm sure some parents found more appealing than alarming.

How do extracurricular activities work?

You'll get a sense of what the student body values when you hear about what they choose to do with their time outside of class. Start listening for clues about student life during the info session, and continue looking for them during your tour.

- What are the most popular clubs on campus?
- Are most activities as selective and time-consuming as a job, or are they all pretty casual and inclusive?
- Are athletics a big part of the school's culture? If so, are varsity football games and tailgating the big events, or does the Ultimate Frisbee club team draw the largest crowd?
- One college we visited offered students music lessons with members of the city's symphony orchestra, and another loaned students original paintings from the college's museum to hang

in their dorm rooms for a semester. Does this school offer any-thing special in the arts?

- Is Greek life huge or nonexistent at this school?
- Are there opportunities for service in the surrounding community?

Will this college help your kid get a job?

We all want our children to have a delightful and fulfilling college experience, but afterward, we hope this investment yields returns.

- What's the story with career counseling, internships, and the school's alumni network?
- What career fields are popular among graduates?
- What percentage of students continues on to graduate school (requiring how many more years of tuition payments)?
- Do most students land jobs that will cover their rent, or can you expect yours to return to her childhood room, searching the want ads indefinitely?

Try to interpret the nitty-gritty of admission and financial aid.

The official literature will reveal admission rates, but listen for more nuanced intel about admissions and financial aid beyond the published statistics. Take notes, and if this school rises to the top of your child's list, you may have some questions to ask come fall.

- What percentage of students do they accept early decision versus regular decision? (See Glossary or Part V: Fall of Senior Year to decode application terminology.)
- If your child will need to apply to a specific college within a larger university, which are most or least competitive for admission or for transferring among departments?
- Is financial need a factor in the school's admission decisions? Listen for the terms "need blind," meaning it's not a factor, or "need aware," meaning it is.

- Does this college award financial aid on the basis of "merit" (your child's academic record) as well as financial need? If so, do merit scholarships require an additional application?

Encourage your child to record tidbits that make the school stand out to him.

It's easy to find elements colleges have in common. They're all institutions of higher learning, after all. But if you can entice your kid to use that free pen he snagged when he checked in, it would behoove him to write notes about the colleges' differences. As incentive, give your kid the following reasons:

- If he's shy, he can jot down questions so he'll remember to ask them later in front of five people on the tour instead of the fifty people at the info session.
- He'll have information specific to that college and informed questions ready for an interview if he has one.
- He will thank himself while writing supplemental essays next summer or fall (covered in The Writing Supplement FAQs, p. 175), trying to recall what distinguished this college from every other college on his list and why he wants to apply there.
- A bribe, such as paying him a penny per word, provides a good incentive for your teen to take notes, but it might make you feel grimy inside.

Don't worry about interviews. They are not happening yet if your kid doesn't want them to.

Most colleges do not offer admissions interviews until spring break, but some will offer the option now. Especially if you're traveling a significant distance to visit the school, check ahead to learn if interviews are required or recommended. If so, let your kid make the call about interviewing on campus while he's there. If he's not ready, keep the college shopping low pressure by reassuring him that he can arrange an interview with a regional representative or alumnus later if he decides to apply. If he does choose to interview now, you can read my interview tips on p. 120, and your child can refer to the notes he took during the info session.

The Campus Tour: Observing the Natives in Their Habitat

Think about splitting up and going on separate tours.

At one college, where separate parent and student tours were compulsory, I cannot begin to describe the relief I felt releasing a question into the air instead of struggling to hold it in like a cough in the middle of a philharmonic concert. When you split up, you'll rest easy about asking questions as they arise, and see and hear different information from different tour guides. And when you reconvene, it's fun to compare notes.

Don't let your child (or yourself) fall in love with the tour guide.

Colleges choose tour guides for their charm. They walk backward and provide good, interactive fun when they ask you to let them know if they're about to bump into anything. They linger in the lobby of the library and tell an engaging story about how the school's mascot originated, or about that time when their professor invited them over for dinner. By the end of the tour, you'll feel maternal toward your young tour guide who has given this show his all.

This tour guide will become the representative your child will most remember from the college. If you happen upon a good tour guide, your child will either have a crush on him or want to be his best friend. The dud tour guide can become detrimental to your child's impression of the school. Remind your child that the tour guide is only one student among many at said college, and chances are, the tour guide will graduate before your child enrolls. Then cross your fingers and hope your kid can summon the strength not to rule that college in or out based on the tour guide's personality.

Will your child live in a castle or a concrete bunker?

One mom told me that on a college visit, her son wandered through the dorms unfazed, as if this were happening to someone else, when it hit her, while standing in some other kid's dorm room, that her baby would live somewhere other than home. She knew then she'd probably cry a little each time she saw his ten-speed bike gathering cobwebs in the garage. If a similar reality sinks in for you, try not to let it steal your focus away from assessing the housing situation at the school.

- Are the rooms organized into singles off a hallway, doubles with a shared living room, or the occasional "forced triple" (three roommates stuffed into a double-sized room, for which you'll pay the exact same amount as the parents of the two kids sharing the identical room next door)?
- Do all the first-year students live together in a dorm near the library, or are they spread out among three campuses that necessitate taking a bus to class?
- Does the college guarantee housing for all students, or do most upperclassmen move off-campus?
- Are there themed options that might appeal to your child, like language houses, sororities, or a health-and-wellness dormitory?
- Are students enrolled in the Honors College or School of Engineering housed separately from the rest of the student body, or is everyone integrated?
- How does the arrangement of living groups correlate with campus social life?

Look beyond the yellow brick road.

Your tour guide has been trained to show you the Wonderful Land of Oz, including the shiniest new buildings, and to tell you the college's most flattering stories. But pay attention to "the man behind the curtain" while you're touring the campus.

- Does your tour guide say five times, "Students work really, really hard here," implying that's all they do?
- Is the library standing room only, while the student union's a veritable ghost town? Or is the student union the hopping place where students seem to congregate?
- Have you seen an even or uneven ratio of lip piercings to students carrying hockey sticks and gym bags?
- Do the school traditions your tour guide mentions off the cuff sound fun (Winter Carnival) or potentially dangerous (hazings)?
- Have you noticed any ethnic diversity or foreign languages spoken among the students? Is it a priority for your kid to meet students with different backgrounds from hers? Are you worried she'll feel marginalized at this school because of her own race, religion, or background?
- Does the art building consist of three small rooms, while the rest of campus orbits around the football stadium? Or is the flashy new art museum this school's equivalent of the castle in the Emerald City?

Try to meet people other than those paid to sell you the college.

If your child is too shy or embarrassed to strike up a conversation with a random student at the snack bar and you know it will mortify him if you try to do it, let's troubleshoot options:

- Emphasize that a real live student has nothing to lose by telling the unabridged truth about his experience on campus.
- Perhaps your child would be willing to pre-arrange a rendezvous with someone he knows from his high school who now attends this college.
- Might he allow you to arrange a lunch in the dining hall or coffee with your friend's kid, who happens to be a current student?

- If you've made it this far and a meeting is planned, take cues from your child to determine if he wants you to accompany him when this meeting goes down.
- If he resists this type of college-visit bushwhacking, respect his wishes, and get as much as you can out of the info session and tour instead.

Meeting with college faculty or staff can also be helpful. If your child is an athlete, she can set up a meeting with the coach, who might suggest joining the team for a practice or meal. If your child's a potential math major, she can email ahead and arrange to sit in on a math class and meet the professor. She can learn more about irrational numbers and derivatives while you dine on a cinnamon bun at the snack bar and text your friends about how old you feel as the future parent of a college student.

After the college visit, be Alexa.

During the ride home, you are the shining halo of light.

My mother gave my techy husband an Amazon Echo as a gift. Most of the time, I forget the cylindrical device is sitting there on top of the wine rack (usually I'm more focused on the wine). But sometimes, when I'm cooking dinner, I like to hear the news, and so I say her name, "Alexa," and a blue halo of light swirls around the rim as she comes to life. "Play news," I tell her.

She responds in that eerily calm robot-woman's voice, "Playing news highlights."

Then she gives the bare minimum of news—not opinions about the news—just ten minutes of headlines. Before she circles back to the beginning and repeats the news summary for a second time, I say, "Alexa. Stop." She obediently stops talking and sits there on the wine rack, alert for the next time she can be of service.

After a college visit, you are Alexa, waiting for your child to summon your blue halo of light. You will have opinions, thoughts, and feelings about this college you've seen, but so will your child, who needs time to process them *without your influence.* You may be the driver of the car on the way home, but you must wait patiently for your kid to drive the conversation. If she asks what you thought of the college, you can respond with the news headlines. Then follow her cues to determine when it's time to stop.

Don't judge your teenager for judging colleges like a teenager.

I am going to warn you right now that regardless of how thoughtful and smart your teenager may be, many of the details that distinguish a college for her might seem mind-numbingly shallow to you. She might pronounce the students walking to class — with whom she has never spoken or interacted in any way — "snobby" or "nice" solely based on hearsay by her friends who toured last summer when there were like five students on campus. Here you are, excited about the incredible variety of computer science classes they offer, and your kid has silently ruled out this college based on the dining hall smell because you happened to visit on taco day.

Here's the chronology of events for one college I visited with my very intelligent daughter:

1. My daughter saw a student walk past wearing the same sweater she was wearing.
2. My daughter commented, "That girl's wearing the exact same sweater I am wearing."
3. Three beats after she spotted the girl wearing her sweater, I swear on my life my daughter said, "I could really see myself here."
4. I realized my daughter's entire impression of this college would come from a chance encounter with a student wearing a familiar sweater.

After the visit, ask yourself, *Did my child hate this college because I woke her up early on a rainy, cold Saturday, or because she hated this college? Did she love this college based completely on the sunshine and free Vitaminwater in the admissions office?*

The vibe your child felt on that college visit could have more to do with the weather and the funny or boring tour guide than the school's curriculum, but at least you can now start a conversation. For instance, you can ask, "Did you like that quaint little college town, or would you like to look at colleges in the city?" "Did you like the idea of studying every subject, or would you rather look for programs that focus more on music or engineering?" Listen to her answer with the under- standing that her feelings about this college and all the others you visit will change ten times (and I'm lowballing it) before this whole process ends. As the prospective applicant, that is her prerogative. You are, in essence, just another tour guide—much like Alexa, escorting us through the cyber-world (and she never judges).

Don't beat yourself up if your kid doesn't act her sparkly best on college visits (or you don't).

Both my husband and I can look very sparkly in certain situations, even stressful ones, but dull and tarnished in others. Case in point: When my daughter was learning to drive a car, she wanted her gadget- savvy father, not her anxiety-prone mother, in the passenger's seat. However, she wanted me there during college tours *not* taking videos on my iPhone.

If you don't meet your own expectations during college visits and you say something you immediately regret, or your usually kind, con- siderate child disappoints you and says something mean, and your mind begins droning, *I should never have pointed out "fashion don'ts" on the subway because now she's a judgmental mean girl and it's all my fault*…don't go there. Go back to the cardinal rule of this support group and *forgive yourself.* Forgive your kid, too. I do not think Alexa would linger on this. Do you?

SIGNING UP FOR SENIOR CLASSES:
RIGOR VS. GRADES

Around this time of year, schools ask juniors to sign up for senior classes. I know because this exercise triggers an onslaught of emails, phone calls, and parents stopping me at the grocery to ask "one quick question." The question, phrased in a variety of ways, is almost always the same:

Which is more important, rigor or grades?

You will hear this question asked by some parent at almost every info session you attend.

You will hear college admissions representatives respond, "It's best to earn top grades in the most rigorous classes."

The audience will give a courtesy laugh, or at least a half smile, in response to this totally unhelpful answer.

Wearing my hat as an admission evaluator, I can tell you that the rare student who achieves straight A-pluses in six AP classes each year is in great shape for the transcript portion of his application. Ditto for the kid who maxes out of math classes at his high school and ends up in a college multivariable calculus class by junior year. In other ways, his shape is not always so good. If he's achieved that kind of transcript, his extracurricular résumé might be filled with one-week service trips or a sport he played freshman year but dropped because *all he had time to do was study*. Recommenders might write that he's quiet in class because perfectionists can be afraid to talk and say something wrong. And his health…forget about it. The Additional Information part of his application might explain that he received an A instead of an A+ in AP European History sophomore year because he missed a month of school due to a mysterious hospitalization, where he probably luxuriated in the most sleep he's had in years. Sure, some of these students with perfect transcripts are superstars in three sports, virtuoso cellists, and happy, but they are the exception, not the rule.

The rule is that your child should challenge himself with top rigor in the academic subjects he most enjoys learning. The potential astronomy major should go for it with AP Physics, but he is under no obligation to sign up for AP English. Also, why does the future art major who has always struggled in math think he has to take calculus? He will hate it, he will earn his first C ever, and he will get more out of taking a statistics class, which will actually come in handy for calculating his odds of making a living as an artist.

I'm not going to lie and say that it doesn't look good at first glance when a student is signed up for a bunch of AP classes and a college course senior year, but to what end? If your kid is truly that brilliant kid who would be bored otherwise, let him sign up for a superhuman program of study. If he's doing it because everyone else is doing it and he's scared not to (which I'm guessing describes 98% of our children), or you're scared for him not to (because you've caught college admissions fever, which is highly contagious), think about balance for your whole child. A whole child does need intellectual challenge. He also needs some semblance of a life outside of school, and he needs more than two hours of sleep per night. If he uses common sense instead of following the herd when signing up for classes, he can still experience a rigorous academic program, but his grades will be better, and he'll be much happier and more fulfilled. You can help him recognize that.

"But is it better for my child to take a higher-level class and get a B or drop down a level and get an A?" the parent who has listened to my entire schpiel will ask.

It's the same question worded in a different way, but if it's on your mind, I'm happy to address it more specifically. If he drops down a level in his least favorite subject, in which he's fared worst in the past, what makes you think that he'll definitely earn an A? Similarly, if he signs up for the more advanced class, why do you feel so sure he'll earn a B and not struggle just to pass with a C or lower? Signing up for any class your kid might not be able to handle sets him up for late nights, tears, possibly the flu, and extra time and money spent on tutoring or therapy. One class can cause all that, and when it does, the level of rigor in your child's schedule becomes a family affair.

TO-DO LIST

- ☐ Spend some quality time with your kid, who won't live with you forever.
- ☐ Sign up for March testing. (for the majority of students)
- ☐ Around this time, your kid's school will instruct him how and when to register for May AP tests if he's taking AP classes, but you might want to remind him.
- ☐ As a place to start, contemplate some big-picture questions: Big or small? Urban or rural?
- ☐ Let the college visits commence! (for some)
- ☐ Start planning spring college visits. (for others)
- ☐ If your child's spring break takes place in March instead of April, skip ahead to the Spring Break College Tour Extravaganza section on p. 116 so you'll know what you're in for.
- ☐ When your child signs up for senior classes, inform him that all classes are not universally appropriate for all students and help him prioritize the level of rigor to keep his (and your) life sane.
- ☐ Check when applications are due for summer programs, but if you missed a deadline, don't sweat it. You'll find plenty of other ways to spend your money this summer.

PART III

SPRING OF JUNIOR YEAR

FIVE FANTASY RESPONSES TO "WHERE'S YOUR KID APPLYING TO COLLEGE?"

1. "Doom on you."
2. "Stop talking! I have duct tape in my bag and I'm not afraid to use it."
3. "As far away as possible."
4. "UNH, UMASS, UCONN, USUK, SOS."
5. Silently strike a power pose until the inquisition ends. (Watch Amy Cuddy's TED Talk or read her book, *Presence,* for instructions.)

Chapter 4

March

MARCH WINDS BLOW

Helping Your Kid Survive the Squall

Before we venture forward, let's take a moment to acknowledge the truth in the saying *The hardest year of college is junior year in high school.* By spring, your junior's classes are hard, getting harder, and come with reams of homework. He also has extra tests (SAT, ACT, AP), chorus rehearsals, Latin club, baseball practice, driving lessons, babysitting (for gas money), and he's juggling Instagram, Snapchat, and Facebook (for Grandma). Even if your kid's main extracurricular activity is playing Xbox, I'm sure he *feels* as busy as the student body president. Plus college notifications are rolling in for seniors, which means college talk hums in the background of juniors' busy lives like the soundtrack from a horror movie. A simple acknowledgment of the stress your kid is under will go a long way toward goodwill in your household. Then, if your child's riled up, and if you truly love him more than yourself, and if you're willing to give up hours of your life in the service of his, you can offer to help.

I reached a moment of reckoning during the spring of my daughter's junior year when I found her hunched over her homework at midnight. It was a heartbreaking sight. She wore a sweatshirt with the name of a college on her fledgling list. She'd gathered her hair into a messy bun. Her bloodshot eyes were barely propped open. It had been fifteen and a half hours since her day had begun. I heard "What can I do to help you?" burst from my mouth.

"It would give me ten extra minutes of sleep if you could please make my lunch," she said.

Flash back to the day my daughter began middle school and I'd announced she was perfectly capable of making her own school lunches.

When I resumed spreading the mayo and stacking turkey slices onto her sandwiches spring of her junior year, it was as if my big empowering lesson about self-sufficiency had never happened. It didn't feel right to prepare only my daughter's lunches, so I started making lunches for my (also perfectly capable) son, who preferred ham to turkey and his bread crusts cut off. I felt so ashamed of reverting back to my indulgent parenting days that I hid my lunch-making relapse from my friends.

But you don't need to hide anything from us. We in this support group know that your child is insanely busy. It's *your choice* how much help you're willing to dole out. Please don't waste time feeling guilty about it, like I did. In retrospect, sacrificing ten minutes of sleep for a few months was a small price to pay to help my kid through a difficult stretch, and I'd do it again. If you feel unsettled about the help you're providing, you can always either stop providing it or compensate in some other way. I replaced the fizzled lunch-making empowerment lesson with one involving my children doing their own laundry, which made me feel much better as I slapped those sandwiches together.

What if my kid can't seem to squeeze anything college-related into her busy schedule?

My friend Karen's oldest daughter, Min, was a typical busy teenager and a reluctant college shopper. The summer before Min's junior year, Karen started to detour and drive through college campuses during family trips.

Min wouldn't get out of the car.

Karen suggested touring campuses over winter break.

Min wouldn't entertain it.

In March of Min's junior year, Karen tried to have a family planning meeting of the variety I'm about to suggest to you.

Min sat at the table but didn't speak.

Spring of junior year, Min still would not talk about college, let alone visit one.

Min wasn't ready.

All summer long before Min's senior year, Karen tried to persuade Min to write her college essays.

Min wouldn't write them. No arguments. No tears. Just nothing.

In the fall of her senior year, Min was finally ready to deal.

She pulled her act together and applied to colleges (sight unseen) the day each application was due.

By then her mother's tongue hurt from biting it so hard. Min's college search had not gone at all the way Karen had thought it would go, based on her friends' experiences.

But it eventually went.

Min received college acceptances spring of her senior year, like everyone else.

On May 1, the last possible day for her to make a decision, Min chose among the colleges where she'd been admitted.

She enrolled, loved college, graduated magna cum laude, went to graduate school, and graduated early (for a change) with an MA after only a year and a half.

Now she has a job that pays the rent, and she is not living at home looking for work like some of the other children of Karen's friends, who had pulled their act together much earlier in high school than Min had.

Most important, Min is happy.

If your child is not ready to deal with college yet, it is nowhere near too late. Your kid may feel ready at the last minute, like Min, or she might plan to take a gap year, if she's still not ready in the fall. If you read through this March chapter or this whole book thinking, "My kid is not ready for any of this," hold the information in reserve. It will come in handy…when your kid is ready.

TYPE-A PARENTS, THIS IS YOUR MOMENT TO ORGANIZE!

The Art of the College Calendar

There comes a time in every parent's life when she must stop holding the accumulated family calendar in her head. Now is as good a time as any. If you love organizing your sweaters in accordance with the color spectrum more than almost any other activity, this is your lucky day. If not, we've got you covered.

The giant paper calendar: During my friend Sarah's college admissions adventure with her son, Sarah bought one of those enormous monthly calendars you'd find in front of a kindergarten classroom. She hung it in the kitchen of her open plan house, and it was the first thing you saw when you entered. This method worked well for her family. Deadlines were hit. Her son went to college.

The 8x11 paper calendar: Being a pen-and-paper person myself, I hung the free calendar we received in the mail from the World Wildlife Federation (with cute baby animal photos) in a place where it would be the *second* thing everyone saw upon entering our house. I figured if it was the *first* thing we saw, one or more of us might avoid the house altogether. This method could work for you, but it did not work for us. That calendar quickly became wallpaper to everyone but me. My daughter still went to college.

The Filofax: Even I don't carry one of those anymore. If you do, I'm sure you'll agree that it's impossible to share.

The online calendar: Apparently, my husband had created a shared Google family calendar that the more tech-oriented people in my family (everyone but me) had been contributing to for over a year, which explained all those times I'd felt like they were conspiring against me. If forced to embrace technology, I decided I'd make it enjoyable for myself through color-coding. As of this writing, my son's shared Google college calendar appears in fuchsia.

The downloadable college calendar: I've heard about parents printing these out and then filling them in by hand, giving a digital-age solution a retro vibe.

Whether paper, digital, or a combo of both, I'd advise you to set up a shared college calendar now because the entries will begin this month. By fall, it will include enough deadlines to make your head spin, but you'll already have your calendar ready, so no problem.

The College Search Spreadsheet, Worksheet, or Whatever Works for You

This is different from your calendar, as you can include more detail on it. The extent of the detail is up to you. If you are an analog person like me, you might prefer a simpler worksheet. I can help you with that. On p. 98 I've included a template I created. If you go to jillshulman.com, you'll find a blank version with ample space to fill in particulars that you can download for your very own.

If you're a digital person, I'm sure the worksheet I concocted won't do. For you, I inquired after my friend Debbie's more elaborate spreadsheet for her daughter's college search, which is a thing of beauty. Debbie was happy to share her masterpiece on my website, too. When you access Debbie's Dazzling Spreadsheet, you'll see that it goes into much more detail than mine, including tabs and links and what-have-you. According to Debbie, sharing it on Google Docs was the key to family harmony during the college admissions process, since she and her teenager could communicate about colleges through the spreadsheet without having to talk. If you want to change the column headings and use Debbie's spreadsheet as a model to create your own, Debbie says she's 100% cool with that, but before accessing it online, I need you to swear to me you will not freak out when you see all the columns of information to fill in. Most of them are not relevant until next fall. We will go through everything before any deadlines sneak up on you. You have my word.

Keeping it in perspective: You're still just shopping — only with a list.

When my friend Katie and her husband were newlyweds looking for their first house, it was a huge purchase, a big transition, and a big deal to them. Each time they toured a property, they asked themselves practical questions like "How's the neighborhood and the school district?" and "Can we really afford this?" And they asked more emotional questions like "Could this house feel like home?" Your child is asking herself similar questions about colleges.

COLLEGE SHOPPING WORKSHEET

College	Size (# of students)	State	Setting	Admitted %	Foundation, Target, or Reach	Academics	Extracurriculars	Will my kid apply?	Notes

Katie and her husband chose a house, had a baby while living there, and threw a great New Year's Eve party there (with cheese, meat, and chocolate fondue: a perfect food trifecta). That house created a strong foundation for their family. Then they moved on to other houses, two more children, and the rest of their lives.

Right now, you're starting a college shopping list, and *that is all.* Including details about a college on your spreadsheet or recording the date of a college visit on your calendar is the equivalent of Katie and her husband circling real estate ads with a pencil when shopping for their "starter" home. Later, you'll cross out some colleges on your child's list and add others. The college your child ends up choosing will create an important foundation for his big transition into adulthood. Then he will move on to the rest of his life, as Katie and her family moved on to their next house and made it a home. It can be fun to shop for a house, or a college, if you keep it in perspective and don't let it overwhelm you.

GUESSTIMATING YOUR KID'S CHANCES

How do I know which colleges are realistic for my child?

We've addressed this topic once, and we'll address it again because this question is a doozy. If I had access to a crystal ball, I'd dress up in clanking gold jewelry, rub my crystal ball, and show you images of your child in class, in the library, and in his dorm room, happy at his new college. I wish with all my heart I could end the interminable not-knowing for you, but guesstimating is as close as we can come until college notifications roll in next year.

Guesstimation Categories: Reach, Target, and Foundation Schools

For our purposes, *reach* (a.k.a. dream or stretch) schools are shoot-for-the-moon colleges, where it is unlikely your child will be admitted if he applies. He should be prepared, at least in theory, for that outcome. In this category, we're including all colleges and universities with acceptance rates under 20%, as well as any college where your child's GPA and standardized test scores fall short of the college's admitted students' average.

I'm defining *target* (a.k.a. match, 50%/50%, or core) schools as those for which your child's credentials fall within the range of the advertised criteria. Since this category tends to make up the majority of colleges on most students' lists, some people further separate colleges into "more likely target" (or target +) and "less likely target" (or target –) schools.

Foundation (a.k.a. backup, safety, or probable) schools are colleges your child found appealing, and where his academic credentials are well above the average cited for admitted students. He's more than qualified, and you (and everyone else) would be surprised if he didn't get in.

The trick to making this entire college search a success is to find one or more foundation schools where your child would be excited to enroll.

The Tools of the Guesstimating Trade

PSAT scores and first semester grades: Use the method introduced on p. 47 to determine if your child's test scores are "good" for a specific college. While you're on the college's website, compare your kid's GPA so far (including recently reported first semester grades) with the median GPA of current students.

Online tracking tools: These can be helpful, but they can also lead to a black hole of worry, doubt, or inflated expectations. Consider yourself warned. Naviance (a software interface commonly used in high schools for college planning) includes a tracking tool called Scattergrams that shows the GPA and test scores of students from your child's high school who were accepted, denied, and waitlisted at specific colleges. If your school does not use Naviance, I'm sure the guidance office can direct you to an equally perilous Internet tracking tool. I introduce you to these tools with trepidation. While useful as a starting point, the tools only track grades and test scores, leaving many other factors in admission decisions to the imagination. Wildly misleading conclusions can result from such omissions. They're a gateway drug that's both addictive and destructive for some parents. I am keeping my promise to share every tool in my arsenal with you, but proceed with caution if you use this one.

Above all, constantly remind yourself and your kid that likeliness for admission can change by the time she applies.

Personal limitations can make any college a reach for your family.

Take a gulp of wine or do a few push-ups or whatever you need to do before you have to tell your kid if geography or finances will limit her college options. Let her talk about her feelings about these constraints, at least to vent, if not to change your mind.

Discussing the "Likeliness for Admission" Factor with Your Kid

Option one: You know your kid, and if she's not ready to deal with likeliness of admission to specific colleges (or anything else college-related), prioritize her mental health (and your relationship) over pushing a college agenda, and don't bring it up.

Option two: If communication lines are open and not too crackly, address the topic of likeliness at the family meeting you're about to have.

Option three: If you are at all in doubt about how your kid will handle the likeliness for admission factor coming from you, wait until the school meeting and let your child's guidance counselor be the messenger. It's part of the counselor's job (God bless).

SPRING MEETINGS: WHEN COLLEGE TALK IS RELEASED INTO THE OPEN AIR

The Spring Family College-Planning Meeting

Schedule a meeting and stand your ground.

This meeting is not required, but I recommend you designate time for a discussion with your kid instead of bringing up college every night at dinner. When you cement a definitive date for a family meeting, not one soul can say you didn't tell her it was happening because: shared college calendar.

Record this meeting on the calendar in indelible ink or its online equivalent.

Email and text reminders to your kid and any guardian whose presence is expected.

Direct-message your kid on Facebook.

Send her a Snap on the hour every hour for twenty-four hours before the meeting.

When the scheduled time arrives, your kid will present whatever conflict has come up in the interim as extremely urgent, and it will *feel* genuinely urgent to her. She'll need to study for a test the next day. She forgot about her friend's track meet, and if she doesn't go, her friend will *never* forgive her.

You have to stay strong.

When the scheduled time for our family meeting arrived, my daughter informed us she only had fifteen minutes to discuss her future because she had promised Lydia she would meet her at the frozen yogurt shop in town. My husband and I insisted that our daughter text Lydia to reschedule this urgent engagement, and then *put her phone in airplane mode and place it beyond arm's reach*. Best move ever. If you do the same, you will not be sorry. Then follow through with the family meeting you've scheduled ahead of time, as grownups do.

Stock up on your beverage of choice prior to the meeting.

You'll need sharp focus and agility during this meeting. If your kid's really upset about that extremely urgent thing she's missing, you'll need to parry her advances, lunge to restart the conversation, and then quickly retreat when your volcanic child begins to freak out, or your oblivious child shuts down. It can be exhausting. It helps to know that wine is chilling in the fridge for afterward.

Sometimes, your teenager will surprise you. The traditionally volcanic child might calmly tick off her colleges of interest, or the child you thought was oblivious will take over and lead the meeting. Some kids feel relieved when all of the swirling, vague, overwhelming details start to take shape as they're discussed out loud. If this happens, uncork that wine and celebrate.

To summarize, the wine comes in handy either way.

AGENDA FOR A SPRING FAMILY COLLEGE-PLANNING MEETING

Questions for the future college student:

THE BIG PICTURE

- Size: When you say you prefer big (or small), how many students does that mean?
- Geography: When you say you prefer urban (or rural), what are you picturing in your head?
- Distance: How do you feel about a plane ride versus a drive to college?
- Climate: Do you want eternal summer, great skiing conditions, or other?
- Characteristics of other students: Liberal? Conservative? Fraternities? Techies? Outdoorsy? Artsy? Sporty? Academically motivated? International? Diversity? Do you care?

ACADEMIC PROGRAMS OF INTEREST

- Do you want to explore everything for as long as you can or concentrate on studying one subject early on?
- What college majors have you heard about, and do any interest you?
- How can we translate favorite activities or future goals into academic disciplines you might explore in college?
- Do you want to see any specialized schools (like those geared toward art, music, or technology)?

STARTING A LIST OF COLLEGES

- Have you thought about specific colleges? If so, which ones?
- On the list of schools on our spreadsheet (the unveiling!), do any sound good?
- (Or if starting from scratch) Let's begin with one feature you want in a college and look up colleges that have that feature together.
- Optional: Do you want to discuss likeliness for admission? We can talk about what's likely for you now, and what factors could change that in the future.

QUESTIONS AND GOALS FOR THE COUNSELOR MEETING

- What are your burning questions so we can be sure to ask the counselor?
- Heads up: Here's a list of questions that I plan to ask.

It helps to promise this conversation has a time limit.

Your kid's more likely to agree to it if you tell her this discussion will not go over thirty minutes or however long before her mind wanders back to that silenced phone on the kitchen counter.

It might not be fun.

Remember that hormones will be present in the room (incoming for your teen, and perhaps some outgoing challenges for you?). I want you to know that however prepared you might feel behind the armor of your printed agenda and stocked bar, this meeting could end with the slamming of a door within six minutes. If so, *you haven't done anything wrong.* (If you're the one slamming the door, we will forgive you even before you forgive yourself.)

When you ask a volcanic child if she has any thoughts about specific colleges, it may take fifteen minutes of the allotted half-hour to calm her down. Dr. Appy, our consulting therapist, suggests that you ask your child what the anxiety is all about and then forget about your agenda for now and use the time designated for the meeting to listen. Or the oblivious child may throw up her hands and say, "I have no idea where to start." For her, Dr. Appy suggests following up with, "That's okay. We can start together now."

Add your thoughts about the college list only after your child has had a chance to voice hers.

If your child comes prepared with a preliminary college list on the "notes" app on her phone (which is reason enough to give her back that phone), or on paper, seriously entertain her thoughts about the colleges she's included (even if most of them come from the hearsay of her peers) before you comment or add to it. If she arrives with no ideas and tells you she is totally lost, you can whip out your geeky spreadsheet or your college reference book to start educating her.

As the discussion unfolds, record the list or addendums to her list in writing. It doesn't matter at this early stage if the list includes three or thirty-three schools. Everything starts to feel clearer and less overwhelming when you have a working list you can hold in your hands or access on your computer. With lists come plans, and with plans come relief for everyone involved. Plus, if you listen closely and record everything in writing, when your kid complains that you woke her up on a Saturday morning to tour a college, you can remind her, "*You* were the one who added this college to the list," and show her your notes as evidence.

Your kid may not understand that no college will have every single detail she desires.

She wants to attend a large university but wants no big lecture classes. She has a preference for a rural setting, by which she means oceanfront, like she saw on the Pacific Coast Highway during the family trip to California. A three-hour drive from home would be ideal, she tells you. After you explain the situation with class size at larger schools, you — the one in the room with the fully developed cerebral cortex — will have to tell your kid that after driving three hours in any direction from your home, she will not be anywhere near the ocean because you live in Kansas.

Talking about future academic majors could overwhelm her.

The same people who told your kid she needs to find her "perfect fit" college have asked her, "What are you going to major in?"

To teenagers, this question translates into *What exactly are you going to be when you grow up? You really need to decide this right now, so you can find the right college to get the right job to live in the right place to make enough money and love your career for the rest of your life and find happiness.*

If your kid, like most sixteen-year-olds, has no idea about what she wants to study in college, a less stressful way to think about this is to focus on her passions now. For example, if she loves camping, what are her favorite parts of camping? Admiring the vegetation on the hike to the campsite? Journaling in the tent by lantern light? Then think about how that can translate into academic disciplines she might love.

Botany? English? I guarantee, she'll talk about her passions with much more enthusiasm than she'll muster for abstract potential majors.

Your kid's ideas about what she wants to study in college may sound unrealistic or incompatible with the child you know.

If your kid is a hard worker and high achiever who has a plan for her future career path and how college will get her there, support her ideas about her future major while simultaneously letting her know it's okay to change course. If your kid is clueless and overwhelmed by all the possibilities, reassure her. You can point out that the adults surrounding her, no matter how successful they look (yourself included), are all winging it through life. We try things. When they don't work out, we change direction. We do this forever. She might feel comforted to know she has that freedom too.

The Spring College Counselor Meeting

If your child has unlimited access to her college counselor, lucky her! Since most students don't, I'm providing tips for you to harvest as much as possible from one family college counselor meeting in the spring of junior year, and then one in the fall of senior year.

Tips for a productive meeting with the counselor:

- *Don't hijack the meeting.* Think of it this way: Your child is forging a relationship with another adult, and you are privileged to listen in before you chime in. This meeting is a practice session for letting go. Baby steps.
- *Listen to your child* talk about his vision of himself and his college prospects. He might express them differently to his counselor than he does to you.
- *Let the counselor give your child the pep talk he deserves.* The counselor can deliver compliments that your kid won't believe coming from you because you've been positively reinforcing him since birth.

- *Use the counselor as the harbinger of doom.* Even if your child earns the top grades in the school, he needs to hear that some colleges are "safe for no one," not even him.
- *Learn where your kid stands academically.* What's his calculated GPA? He can use it to assess likeliness of acceptance at specific colleges (when he's ready), and you can plug it in to those Internet tracking tools that I know you'll use despite my warning. (Already forgiven.)
- *Discuss standardized testing.* The counselor can give your kid the lowdown about the scores he'll need to reach his goals for admission and scholarships.
- *Get advice for senior-year classes.* At most schools, there's still time to retool a student's senior schedule to set him up for success.
- *Ask the counselor for specific colleges to research.* She'll often know about colleges you and your kid will not.
- *Mine the counselor's high-school-specific expertise.* She'll know how students from your kid's high school have fared in the past at colleges of interest.
- *Learn about foundation schools.* Guard her office door until she's provided names of at least two potential foundation schools that fit your child's criteria so far.
- *Pick her brain about available resources.* For example, your kid's school might offer a free college-essay-writing workshop, or ACT prep at a discount.
- *Make sure the counselor knows your kid's strengths.* This will embarrass your kid, but if they weren't revealed naturally in conversation, sharing them judiciously will help the counselor point your kid in the right direction.
- *Bring up questions that came up at the family meeting* that have not yet been addressed at this one. Your kid may sit there beside you turning fire-engine red, but don't let that stop you from asking remaining questions as the meeting winds down.

Handling Disappointment if Ambitions Were a Little Loftier Than Your Kid's Credentials

The college counselor does not enjoy this part of her job, but *taking on the role of "bearer of bad news" is possibly the greatest gift she can give your family.* If your child has a 2.8 GPA and wants to go to Dartmouth, his college counselor will set him straight. There may be tears while the counselor paints a more realistic picture of the colleges your child should explore. You may feel anger or despair bubble up inside you, as you watch this counselor hurt your child.

Any feelings you feel — in the counselor's office or ever — are okay.

Listen and take thorough notes because you'll be too emotional to remember anything about this meeting other than the image of your child grabbing another tissue from the box on the counselor's desk. After you've had time to thaw from the initial shock, feed your child his favorite dinner, process this new perspective, and look up the counselor's new suggestions in your fat college bible. You can decide if her professional guidance makes sense to you or if you disagree. You're allowed. Your child's counselor might function as an especially knowledgeable resource, but hers remains only one opinion.

Planning Next Steps Based on Info from the Counselor

You've finally achieved open communication with your teenager, and then the topic of standardized testing appears out of nowhere, like a bush of stinging nettles on an otherwise lovely hike.

- We already know every test is practice, but your child might not. Tell her.
- Discuss the counselor's advice about which tests to take or retake, your child's objectives for testing (if any), and when those tests will happen.
- Add test dates to your calendar, as well as the registration deadlines about a month before test dates.

- If you're planning to hire a tutor or register your kid for a test prep class, go for it now.
- Making your kid part of the conversation enables you to say stuff like "Don't sweat this. You have four possible times you can take and retake the test." The prospect of having to sit for that test four times may inspire her to study for the one coming up.

While we're on the topic of testing, early March is the registration deadline for May AP exams if your kid's taking any AP classes. Chances are the counselor won't mention this because usually taking care of registration is on your kid, but you'll hear about it when it's time to cut a check for the $94 test fee, which at most schools is on you.

On a more cheerful topic, go ahead and register for visits to colleges the counselor recommended before something else comes along to steal your kid's focus.

TO-DO LIST

☐ Take stock of your busy teenager's time management skills and help when you can or want to (no guilt) or don't help (also no guilt).

☐ Maintain a positive attitude (still shopping!) in the midst of all the info funneling your way. Someone in the family has to hold it together.

☐ Start your kid's family-accessible college calendar. As an update, I'm doing well with my online calendar so far, and if I can figure out the technology, anyone can. Seriously. *Anyone.*

☐ Prepare a system to compile a college list. For analog types, my College Shopping Worksheet appears on p. 98. For techies, Debbie's Dazzling Spreadsheet will start you out. Both are available at jillshulman.com.

- ☐ Schedule a family college-planning meeting. If that sounds too formal for your family, you can call it a "chat." Either way, you'll want to stock up on your beverage of choice.
- ☐ If possible, schedule a meeting with the high school college counselor and add it to your new calendar.
- ☐ Schedule college visits, and add them to your calendar too.
- ☐ I would not keep bringing up testing if I didn't have to, but you'd better revisit testing plans. Register for April tests (for some) and double-check on your child's May AP exam registration (if applicable). Then I promise I won't bring up testing again (until next month).

Chapter 5

April

SURVIVING APRIL SHOWERS OF CONSTANT INTERROGATIONS

March roared in like a lion... and keeps getting louder.

They corner you in the grocery produce aisle, slide into the seat beside you in the eye doctor's waiting room, and stalk you at intermission of the high school musical. They all ask, "Where is your child applying to college?" (Henceforth: the Question.)

If you say, "We don't know yet," they will not let it rest.

They push: "Where is she *looking?*"

They stand there expectantly, and your mind reels with *What if I don't answer? What if I do? Will I betray my kid's confidence? If I list brand-name schools, will they gossip about how she'll never get in? If I mention colleges they've never heard of, will they think my kid's not very bright, or unmotivated, and judge her, and think I'm a crap parent, which might be true whether I answer them or not?*

You promised yourself you would be different from all those parents of juniors last year, planted in the grocery aisles like ticking stress bombs. Yet now this person (who has spoken literally ten words to you in the ten years you've lived in this town) is torturing you with unsolicited advice and then says, "Relax. It will be okay. Your child will end up in college somewhere."

I give you license to feel what you feel.

You can relax when you damn well please — a bit by the time you reach the frozen foods, and a little bit more by bedtime tonight. For now, let's go over some strategies for dealing with these inquisitors.

Defense Strategies for Dealing with Interrogators' Shenanigans

The Rule of Five Defense

In the moment, you may hem and haw and not know what to say, and then rattle off a list of colleges, when pressed. Then you may spend the rest of your shopping trip ruminating about what you should have said, or if you shouldn't have said anything at all. Look, you know full well that guy you barely know wasn't going to let you progress beyond the condiments aisle to do the rest of your shopping until you said *something.*

The Rule of Five states: If it won't matter in five years, it's not worth more than five minutes of stressing about it now.

That thing you said was not right or wrong. It just was. Banish the remnants of that conversation no more than five minutes after it happened, and push your shopping cart directly to the aisle with the ice cream.

The Zen (a.k.a. Don't Be a Hater) Approach to Fending off Your Assailant

You may not feel a Buddhist compassion for all sentient beings while someone pummels you with a string of endless questions you can't or don't want to answer, but you can resist his advances *with your mind.* Turn hatred into love and avoid making an enemy by remembering: *Whatever your assailant is saying has nothing to do with you, your child, or your parenting.*

There are so many reasons this person might need an audience for his protracted monologue about all colleges everywhere more than you need to escape the aisle with the Tide Pods. Examples:

- He may not have any clue he's causing you to suffer (and if he knew, he would feel much worse than he's making you feel).
- He may feel deeply insecure about his own child's college choice, or about his own lack of a college education.

- Perhaps the word "college" triggered a hypnotic trance under which this overworked, exhausted grownup felt young and hopeful again, and that's why he's telling you your kid should, without a doubt, go to Tulane University and pledge Beta Theta Pi.

If you can stomach it, sacrifice a few minutes of your time to listen to him, and think of it as a community service. If not, Dr. Appy suggests, "Don't be afraid to set gentle limits on anxious question-askers." Remaining patient and kind as you put a halt to this conversation means you can move on to the checkout counter without even a hint of regret.

The In Cahoots with Your Kid Strategy

You can choose to make your grocery run at a time when you're unlikely to bump into anyone you know, but school is compulsory for your kid. She's stuck there fielding the Question all day long. College talk runs rampant in high schools this time of year as seniors frantically deliberate the choice they need to make by May 1 (a.k.a. National College Decision Day). Your child is watching them, even if she's not talking to you about it. The best wall of defense against the impulse to cement your ear canals shut during every inquisition is to consult with your child and build a strong, united response. For example, my child chose the Politician's Defense strategy (which I will share with you next) for the whole family to employ spring of junior year, and we all stuck with that.

The Politician's Defense Strategy (a.k.a. Saying Something Without Really Saying Anything)

When I asked my daughter what I should say when confronted with the Question, she told me, "Just say I'm interested in small liberal arts colleges."

"But what do I say when they ask which ones you're considering?" I countered.

"Say I don't know yet."

"But what about when they ask which ones you think you *might* consider?"

"No one would really ask that."

"They would. They *have* asked," I said.

"Tell them all I know is that I want to stay in New England," she said.

"Is that true? Do you know that?"

"No, but you can just say it to end the conversation."

So I took her lead, and the conversation did not end. They asked, "Which small New England liberal arts colleges look most interesting right *now?*"

I could honestly say, "That's all I know right now."

If they still persist, Dr. Appy suggests saying, "That's really my child's information to share," which might sound more abrupt than some of us can handle. Pretend you're a politician on the campaign trail, and feel free to use whatever vague response pops into your head when someone poses a question you don't want to answer.

The Magician's Maneuver

Sometimes you might need to resort to trickery to tame an especially persistent interrogator. Magicians use sleight of hand, a type of skilled manipulation, to plant a card on top of a deck without your realizing it. Then they use misdirection to draw your attention to the deck of cards while they're stealing your watch.

If a conversation's going south, you can skillfully manipulate and redirect it due north. Instead of responding to an aggressor's question, you can go on the offensive and ask *him* a question before he knows what hit him. Ask anything. "How's work treating you?" "How about that Red Sox game?" "Do you think Trader Joe's Wheat Crisps are really Wheat Thins in different packaging?" You'll find immediate relief from the hot seat because the only thing people love to talk about more than college admissions is themselves. It's magical.

The Truth Without Apology Strategy

My friend Elaina's son was not the most motivated high school student, but he wasn't the least motivated either. When the first person asked her the Question, Elaina apologetically began with the disclaimer that her kid was not shooting for anywhere overly ambitious, and followed with his college list.

The interrogator responded, "Oh, that's okay," as if he were trying to console her.

Upon remembering this moment, Elaina gripped the handle of her coffee mug so tightly I thought she might break it right off. *Console her!* Elaina's wonderful son, though not *the best* student, was certainly a *good* student and a good person, destined for a good college and a good life. Elaina was proud of her kid! Why had she felt the need to apologize for him as if she wasn't? "What should I say next time?" said Elaina, her tone a cocktail of despair mixed with anger.

"If they ask you where he's applying to college, say, 'Ah yes, the proverbial Question'" (the Politician's Defense strategy of saying something without really saying anything).

Elaina cocked her head. "Really? Is that all you've got?"

"Have you discussed this with your son?" (The In Cahoots with Your Kid strategy.)

"He's not super communicative about college," said Elaina.

I knew better than to suggest she go Zen when she was this upset. "What about the truth, but without the apology?" I said.

Elaina nodded. A plan fell into place. The next time someone asked the Question, Elaina proudly rattled off a list of colleges the inquisitor had never heard of, with no caveats or apologies.

Predictably, the person's face went blank. He said, "Huh. I've never heard of any of them."

"Isn't it great how much easier the Internet makes researching everything, including colleges?" Elaina said. Then Elaina threw in the Magician's Maneuver and calmly redirected the line of questioning.

The Zipped Shut Lips Strategy

Though widely used, this strategy usually proves less effective than the others. A friend of my daughter's was a top-notch student who kept her college plans to herself, except for that one time she told that one person she planned to apply early to Harvard…and the floodgates opened. That one person told one more person, who told another, and soon it seemed like everyone in the community, whether they knew her or not, whispered and speculated about the college admissions destiny of this very private kid who wanted to keep her decision to herself, *which was her God-given right.*

When Harvard denied her along with the other 95.3% of Harvard applicants that year, it was a very lonely time for the girl and her parents (who had exercised the In Cahoots with Your Kid strategy by keeping their lips zipped too). They suffered alone while the gossip mill jabbered on, "She wasn't even deferred!"

I am not suggesting your family should blab your child's preliminary college list all over town. I'm only arming you with the fact that the Zipped Shut Lips strategy, though tempting for many (and justified for all), rarely works well against insensitive interrogators. As with my daughter's friend, it's usually like a futile attempt at piling sandbags beside a river that's going to overflow no matter what.

THE SPRING BREAK COLLEGE TOUR EXTRAVAGANZA

Pros and Cons of College Tourism During the High Season

Pro: It feels like a festival in the admissions office, and there are cookies.

Spring break is the most popular time for juniors to visit colleges. Admissions offices are in full swing, creating a festive atmosphere to entice kids to apply. You can feel the anticipation, and you may get a cookie! Remember that your child will likely never set foot in this office again once he's on campus (unless it's for his work-study job), so enjoy, but don't judge the school by the scent of fresh baked goods wafting through the swanky new Office of Admission building.

Con: More stressed-out people generate more stress vibes.

Beneath the thin veneer of excitement lurks the stress of every person in that info session going through exactly the same process you are. Some kids are so juiced up with the desire to please that they practically jump out of their seats to announce their state of origin and future major. Others are so nervous that they shrink into their seat cushions to the point that they might disappear into the fibers. And the parents...some glisten with sweat trying to entertain a bored five-year-old sibling, while others strain their necks, birdlike, every ten seconds or so, as if trying to peck away at their teenagers' private thoughts about the college. Anxiety does not even begin to describe it. I suggest saying "We're just shopping!" over and over again until both you and your child believe it.

Pro or con: You could run into the same people at every school.

Especially if colleges are relatively close in proximity, families tend to follow the same tour loop. In addition to running into the same strangers from campus to campus, your child may run into kids she knows from school over and over again because, of course, they are also on spring break. These encounters can ease tensions for some kids, while for others, exacerbate them.

It might help you and your kid to know that the rumor you've probably heard, that colleges have a secret quota and will only admit a limited number of students from each high school, is a myth. That friendly girl from your kid's English class poses no more of a threat to your child for admission to this college than anyone else sitting in the lobby waiting for the info session to begin. Besides, after the college admissions process is over, you'll still be neighbors with some of these people, and your kids might be classmates. It's in no one's best interest to alienate each other now. You'll feel better about the college admissions process, and about yourself, when you rise above the cutthroat competition and think of the families you run into at college visits as fellow travelers instead of rivals.

Pro but also surprise con: The weather, though milder, can be "iffy."

I know I brought up weather in February, and it may sound like a secondary concern to you, but it can disproportionately temper your kid's perception of a college. If the weather works in your favor, spring break is an especially pleasant time to tour campuses. Students may throw Frisbees in the quad like you've seen in the movies, and did I mention the cookies?

However, you also run the risk of getting caught in torrents of April showers. A campus on a chilly, rainy gray day before one green bud has emerged on a tree can be a damp, dreary affair. If the college's spring break coincides with your kid's, the empty campus can look downright spooky. I doubt it will surprise you to know that the college we visited over spring break, where chilling wind whipped the rain sideways beneath our umbrellas until, eventually, they blew inside out, did not end up on my kid's list.

Pro: You know that college too far away to casually visit, but in a really appealing place for a spring break trip?

Yeah, that.

Pro or con: Your child could knock out an interview during the visit.

Many colleges begin interviewing juniors in March and April. On the pro side, interviewing while on campus means your kid will check one more item off his to-do list, learn more about the college, and demonstrate interest to boot. An awkward interview will rarely count against him.

On the con side, some kids feel so apprehensive about interviewing that it ruins a college-shopping trip. If yours is not in the right mind-set to interview yet, that's a definite con, and he should skip it. This will not be his only chance. Besides, interviews are low on the list of importance in most admission decisions. They're not worth ruminating over, no matter how those thirty minutes play out.

HOW MANY SPRING BREAK COLLEGE VISITS ARE TOO MANY?

The math according to parents surveyed:

If campuses are ≥ a 1.5-hour drive from each other
    then pay 1 visit/day

If ≤ a 1.5-hour drive between them
    then possible 2 visits/day (but no lunch)

If ≤ 1-hour drive between them
    then possible 2 visits/day (quick lunch)

If 1 week spring break = 2 travel days + 7 full days
    then 14 college tours possible

If 14 college visits happen over a 1-week break
    then overload (= gap year)

If 2 college visits in 1 day
    then it's easier to compare them (for some)

If 2 college visits in 1 day
    then you're too exhausted to like the second one (for others)

If your kid's enthusiastic and energetic
    then 2 visits/day every day = possible

If your kid's easily overwhelmed
    then 1 visit/day = maximum *ever*

If you eat in dining halls and meet students and staff
    then fuller picture possible

If you spend time exploring the area beyond college gates
    then better experience

If you take a full day off with no college visits
    then superior vacation

INTERVIEW TIPS FOR INTROVERTS, EXTROVERTS, AND EVERYONE IN BETWEEN

The Key to Admissions-Speak Regarding Interviews

Most colleges don't require interviews, which is important information if your child breaks out in hives at the thought of one. Check each college's website and look for these code words:

- *Required:* If your child wants a chance of admission to this college, he ought to interview, whether on campus or remotely.
- *Highly recommended* or *recommended:* If your kid doesn't make the effort to interview, he'll still have a chance of admission, but if he demonstrates interest with an interview, he'll have a better one.
- *Evaluative:* Notes from the interview will appear in your child's file and become one component of his application.
- *Informational:* Your child is welcome to schedule an interview, but it's for his own information and will not contribute to the admission decision.
- *Not offered:* Your child will not have a leg up if you somehow finagle an interview for him. If the college does not include an interview on their list of priorities, nor should you.

When will interviews happen?

Colleges are all over the place with their interview timing and venues. Note that many small liberal arts colleges start offering interviews on campus now if they offer them at all. They require students to set up their own interviews before applying. Other schools, like Yale University, for example, will contact students senior year, after they apply, to set up interviews with regional alumni or via Skype. Auditions for performing arts programs also don't usually happen until senior year.

Dress for Success

Erika Blauth, senior assistant director of admission at Colorado College (and formerly of admissions at Bates College, Wellesley College, and Harvard College—she's interviewed a lot of undergraduates), describes appropriate interview attire as "on the spectrum from nice casual to business casual." Your child is not expected to wear a three-piece suit for college interviews. If the student sitting next to your kid in the admissions office waiting area is wearing khakis and a tucked-in collared shirt (the teen-boy uniform for everything from bar mitzvahs to Grandma's birthday party), he probably has an interview scheduled. Boys should appear neat and clean, which means showered and wearing a presentable shirt without holes or the college's archrival's logo, and skip the flip-flops. Girls should remember that short skirts become shorter when they sit down. It's not a high bar.

The Types of Interviewers Your Kid May Encounter

- *Seasoned admissions officers* are usually closer to your age than your kid's and experienced at putting the student at ease and making sure the conversation flows.
- *"Green deans"* are recent graduates who have remained at the college, working in the Office of Admission full-time, as an interim job between college graduation and real life. The interviewer may look about the same age as your kid, though dressed better. He's newer at this, but he'll still carry on an adept conversation. (Extroverts tend to work in admissions.)
- *Student interns* work in admissions offices and interview candidates. Do not assume this interview is a throwaway. Current students provide valuable information for prospective ones, and interviewers of any age will record thoughts about your child and slip them into his file.
- Colleges train *alumni interviewers* across the country to interview prospective students who live far away from the campus.

Best-case scenario, your child and the interviewer hit it off, your kid learns tons about the college, and the alumnus writes a positive review of the meeting. Worst-case scenario, it's an awkward half-hour at a coffee shop. On the bright side, the worst-case scenario is not nearly as bad as a morning of standardized testing. So there's that.

- *An online interviewer* could be any of these people. It's hard for some students to feel like they're in the room having a conversation when they're not. As long as your kid doesn't Skype or Facetime from his rumpled bed wearing his pajamas, he'll do fine.

Advice for extroverts: Don't forget to listen as well as speak.

When extroverts get nervous, they tend to babble to fill lulls in the conversation as a defense mechanism. Since it's impossible to speak and listen at the same time, suggest to your child she plan on listening first. Then tell her not to fear pausing for a moment after the interviewer poses a question to formulate a more thoughtful answer than the one she might automatically expel if she lets nerves get the better of her.

Advice for introverts: Don't worry about clamming up.

The interviewer won't let the interview go by in silence. She knows your kid is anxious, like everybody else. She has seen kids like yours, whose nerves render him silent, many times before, and she has strategies to draw him out. Your kid should try to hold up his end of the conversation by responding to questions with enthusiasm and multi-word answers. However, reassure him that he's not expected to drive the conversation, if that's not his way.

My Personal Interview Trick Worth the Price of This Book

When I returned to the full-time workforce after spending some years working primarily as a freelancer and stay-at-home mom, well-intentioned friends offered a litany of advice. I was told:

"Don't include the date you graduated from college on your résumé."

"Wear pearls. You'll look professional."

"Whatever you do, don't wear pearls. You'll look too old-fashioned" or "too conservative" or "like you're trying too hard."

I left my college graduation date on my résumé and dressed up, though not in pearls (only because they didn't work with the outfit). Then right before I walked into the office for my interview, I made a mental switch.

I changed this: "They're going to interview me now and see if I'm a good fit for them."

To this: "*I'm* going to interview *them* now and see if *they're* a good fit for *me.*"

Throughout the interview, I assessed things like *Would I like working here? Would my work style fit in? Would I both serve this workplace well and feel challenged?* Instead of worrying, *Am I saying what they want to hear? Should I smile more? Should I have worn pearls?* I executed that interview as my most confident self because I was focused on determining if that job was right for me. Merely substituting a few pronouns psyched me up for a conversation much more likely destined for glory, and I was offered the job. This little trick can turn a frightening experience into an empowering one for your kid, or for you, if you happen to have an upcoming interview.

INTERVIEW CHECKLIST FOR STUDENTS

- If you're nervous, you can lower the stakes by interviewing at a college lower on your priority list first, or role-playing an interview with a parent, with your high school counselor, or on a Skype call with kind Uncle Mel to make your first interview feel like your second.

- Check out the college's website the night before your interview and attend the info session and tour first so you won't enter the interview clueless.

- Prepare a few questions to which you genuinely want to know the answers. Jot them down while browsing the website, and take notes during the info session like the outstanding student I know you are.

(Hint: If you can find the answer on the college's website, it's not a good question.)

- Think about the story you want to tell about yourself, and how you'd fit with the college you're visiting. The interviewer will surely ask you why you want to attend the college. Beyond that, he'll want to learn about your academics, activities, personality, and values.

- Wear clean, decent clothes like you'd wear to church or your personal equivalent, not to a backyard barbecue.

- Arrive for your interview ten minutes early.

- If you feel anxious, turn it around in your mind so you're the one doing the interviewing (but in a curious, not arrogant way; see "My Personal Interview Trick," p. 122).

- Don't forget to listen as well as speak, if you're an extrovert.

- Don't forget to respond in full sentences instead of grunts, if you're an introvert.

- Write a thank-you note afterward like your parents taught you to do after receiving birthday presents. When someone devotes half an hour to you, it's a gift.

THANK-YOU NOTE CHECKLIST FOR STUDENTS

- Just do it within twenty-four hours, while it's fresh in the interviewer's mind (and yours). Use email to expedite the process.

- Spell the interviewer's name right, the exact way it's spelled on the business card she handed you at the end of your conversation.

- Thank the interviewer for her time. Yes, it's part of her job, but an interview also requires the interviewer's undivided attention on you.

- Refer to a specific moment in the interview to remind the interviewer, who may have interviewed twenty students that day, that you were the dancer (or martial artist, or chess player, or...).

- Be positive about the college. Authentic enthusiasm is an appealing character trait and makes people feel good about sacrificing their time on your behalf.

- Keep it short and to the point. This is not a college essay. People are busy and appreciate a brief, gracious note.

- Proofread carefully. Everything sent to the Office of Admission is a "point of contact" (see Glossary) included in your file.

- Write the thank-you note no matter what. Even if you're not sure you want to apply to that college, you'll have a template handy for thank-you emails after future interviews. Plus, it's good manners.

THE SKINNY ON RECOMMENDATIONS

It requires a leap of faith to trust other adults—whom you met only once at the school's open house back in the fall—to do right by your kid. They will. Teachers enter their profession because they want to make a positive impact on students' lives. If a teacher doesn't feel he has the time or the knowledge about your child to write a meaningful recommendation, he will turn your kid down. Therefore, your child's recommendations will be positive, though *how* positive is out of your hands completely. The lessons on letting go will come fast and furious from here on out.

The people who will write recommendations in support of your child:

- The guidance counselor
- One or two teachers of the major academic subjects (English, math, science, social studies, and foreign language)
- An additional person of influence in your child's life as an optional recommender

The Counselor Recommendation

You would not be the first if you're thinking, *What if my kid attends a huge high school, and her counselor doesn't know her at all?* or *What if the counselor is new and inexperienced?* or *What if she's overloaded and writes short, generic recommendations or doesn't write recommendations at all?!*

Inhale.

Exhale.

Now please listen, *really listen,* to what I'm about to tell you: *No big deal.*

Many, many parents have these worries, but you can save the brain space for something that is both in your control and actually matters. I will tell you why I felt it was worth slowing down and taking a deep breath. Some parents consumed by college admissions mania cannot contain their anxiety about recommendations and take action on their concerns. They try to control the content of recommendation letters, and it backfires. As an admission evaluator, I've read recommendations in which counselors embed code phrases, such as "Renata's parents have been extremely involved in her college admissions process." (Translation: They micromanaged it.) Every parent aches for her child to receive as much support at school as she receives at home, but this is your reminder not to lose sight of the negative effect a well-intentioned parent's assertive behavior can have on other people involved. (Translation: Relinquishing control has its rewards.)

The Long and Short of It

You might hear that the neighbor's kid, who attends a private school, has a guidance counselor who writes novella-length recommendations. You might suspect your kid's community school with its overburdened guidance office includes only a few sentences. This is not your child's fault, and it won't count against her. While evaluating applications, at one extreme, I've read three-page single-spaced recommendations from school counselors. At the other extreme, one esteemed high school in California annually includes the disclaimer that due to heavy caseloads, counselors cannot include recommendations at all. Every year, students with recommendations representing both extremes are admitted to the same colleges.

Filling Out the Counselor's Questionnaires

You do have some agency here. If the high school guidance office disseminates questionnaires to parents, that's an appropriate place for you to include all the information you hope the counselor will address in your child's recommendation letter. Often counselors quote directly from student and parent questionnaires in their recommendations. If the counselor is new to the school or doesn't know your child well, he will be grateful you've provided him with something more specific to say. If no questionnaire graces your email inbox, you can share whatever you feel colleges should know about your kid in a gracious email or at the counselor meeting next fall, right before most counselors will write their letters.

The Academic Teacher Recommendations

Asking can be tough.

The counselor automatically writes a letter, or at least submits school materials, but your child will need to ask for teacher recommendations. As previously discussed, asking adults in authority positions for anything can be hard for a kid (see "A Timely Lesson on Letting Go," p. 62). To add to the stress, at some high schools, jockeying for a recommendation from a popular teacher can seem almost as crazy as the college admissions process itself. I dropped my daughter off at school early on the first day students could ask teachers for college recommendations. The line of students waiting to enter the school building was already so long, you'd have thought they were giving away Taylor Swift tickets. By the time my son was a junior, the school had wised up and changed the policy. Warn your kid to learn the protocol in advance to eliminate surprises. Convey to him that if a teacher says no, it's a reflection of the teacher's time constraints, not your child's worth.

Whom should my kid ask to recommend her?

Many colleges will require two recommendations from teachers of the five major academic subjects (a.k.a. "majors" or "solids," if you hear those words batted around). Some colleges only require one, or don't require any recommendations but will accept them. Your kid's junior or senior year teachers are better equipped to recommend her as a future college student than teachers who knew her as a wide-eyed underclassman.

Guidance counselors will advise students to ask for one recommendation from the science/math cluster and one from the English/humanities/languages cluster. If your child is a well-rounded student and applying to a liberal arts college, this is good advice, but if the math teacher barely knows your kid, how can he possibly write compellingly about her? *A student should choose the teachers who know her best in classes where the student glitters most brightly.* If that means two teachers from the same cluster, so be it.

The recommendations don't have to come from teachers who awarded your kid an A+, but the biggest mistake I see is the recommendation from the teacher of that class where the student received her lowest grade. The student hopes the teacher's description of her work ethic in the face of adversity will somehow mitigate the grade in the reader's eyes. It won't. Your child should only choose that teacher if all those hours of extra help led to a rapport unmatched by any with her other teachers.

The Optional Additional Recommendation

The thicker the file, the thicker the student.

A file overstuffed with recommendations can raise a red flag. Evaluators wonder if perhaps the student has some academic deficit he hopes to bury beneath recommendations from three teachers, a coach, an employer, a private violin teacher, and an alumnus family friend.

Even if your child has five people who would give him great recommendations, I'd advise him to choose only one additional recommender. Remember, application evaluators already have teacher and counselor recommendations to read. One more recommendation that might reveal a new perspective on your kid might help. If the chosen academic teachers and counselor pretty much have it covered, *it will not count against your kid if he stops at three recommendations.* Either way, beyond four, enough is enough. Multiple recommendations, no matter how effusive, will not obscure a student's shortfalls or endear the student to the time-crunched reader.

Good ideas for an added recommendation:

- A private or school teacher of the visual or performing arts—especially if your kid wants to continue to pursue her art in college
- The coach who can speak about her conduct on the field and with the team
- An employer or volunteer coordinator who can share how your child interacts in the grown-up world
- A clergyperson who can describe your child's participation or leadership in the religious community
- Teachers of electives (school classes that are not academic majors), such as computer programming, theater, or yearbook (especially if that elective relates to your child's potential future studies)
- A third teacher of a major academic subject if that teacher can provide a fresh perspective (example: the teacher advises your kid's favorite club).

Bad ideas for an added recommendation:

- Peers (even if they attend that college)
- Family friends (even if they are luminaries)
- Family members (even if they are alumni)
- Boyfriends or girlfriends (evaluators are not looking for character references or telenovelas)
- Anyone who only met your kid once (even if it was under impressive circumstances)
- You (even though you know her better than any of these other people, and you could write a dissertation on your kid). Caveat: If you homeschool your child, of course you need to write her counselor recommendation, but focus on details of the rigorous curriculum and let outside, objective recommenders sing your kid's praises.

Trust in Thy Educators

Should my kid waive his right to read his recommendation letters?

Here's another fun abbreviation to add to our Glossary: FERPA, which stands for the Family Educational Rights and Privacy Act of 1974 (a.k.a. the Buckley Amendment). If your kid's under eighteen, FERPA gives you the right to see her recommendations and records before they're sent. Once your kid turns eighteen, this right transfers to her. Checking the box on the application that waives the FERPA right is a nod of trust, so your child should check it. Colleges will take the recommendations seriously when they know recommenders did not write those letters under the duress of overzealous parents or with an anxious student looking over their shoulder. Under this agreement, once enrolled in a college, the student can usually visit the admissions office and read those letters, but by then most students have forgotten all about them.

Your Kid's Turn to Nag

Your child must trust her recommenders to write on her behalf, but it is up to your kid to stay on top of her application materials and nudge teachers to nail deadlines, if necessary. It may be the first time in your child's life she has a little empathy for the less glamorous side of being a parent.

TO-DO LIST

☐ Survive inquisitions by everyone you know, in whatever way you must, without shame or resorting to violence. No easy task, but I know you have it in you.

☐ Let the Spring Break College Tour Extravaganza begin! (Or for some, carry on with the college shopping.)

☐ Hand your child the interview and thank-you note checklists I've included. You can emphasize they came from me, not you, so your kid won't accuse you of burdening him with yet another thing to add to his busy schedule.

☐ Register and pay for May and June standardized testing (if applicable).

☐ Let your child make her own decisions about whom to ask for recommendations, though share my advice with her, if she'll listen.

☐ If a summer program requires a deposit by May first, you know what to do.

☐ If not having summer plans is stressing you out, skip to p. 139, Summer Activities That Look Impressive vs. Just Doing Life, and you will feel better. Then flip to Resources for a few ideas.

Chapter 6

May

YOUR JUNIOR'S SPRING FEVER AND STRESSORS

May Day: *May 1, celebrated as a springtime festival.*

Here in New England, May means we are definitively done with all the nor'easters, power outages, and nights when the electric blanket is our only salvation. The garden sprouts awaken us from hibernation. We escape the confines of our homes with thrilled, stir-crazy dogs, and we reconnect with friendly neighbors, who are sometimes a little bit nosy, but now we have strategies for that! By May Day, also National College Decision Day, seniors must send a deposit to secure their place at a college or university. On the upside, their admissions slog is over. On the downside: senioritis.

Senioritis is contagious. Combined with the kinder, gentler weather, spring fever is a tough ailment to cure. If you had the option of frolicking outside or staring at a sunny spring day through a classroom window, which would you choose? While seniors can frolic, juniors must continue the heads-down charge through final papers, exams, and continued assaults from the College Board in the form of May AP exams *and* more SATs. Some juniors also feel pressure to visit colleges during the last couple of weeks students remain on campus. I'm sorry for your kid, who just wants to be a kid sometimes. I'm afraid she will have to wait a little longer to tiptoe through the tulips.

Mayday: *used as a distress call.*

Another chance for tests!

May presents all manner of testing opportunities: AP tests in early May, and there's an SAT offered too! Students can register now for SAT Subject Tests in June, an especially good time for them because, hello! With finals and AP exams, students have already studied! I keep hoping that if I use lots of exclamation points, as if all these opportunities delight me, my attitude toward testing will improve! It's not working!

WHO WILL HELP MY KID WITH THE INFAMOUS COLLEGE ESSAY AND EVERYTHING ELSE?

It's check-in time.

How is your family doing? Take this short quiz to find out.

When the topic of college comes up, your heart rate is about the same as when you're...

   A. lounging on a beach chair cradling a mai tai.
   B. waiting in a line of traffic at a highway toll booth.
   C. out of shape in the middle of a spin class.

If you bring up the topic of college at the dinner table, your child...

   A. answers your questions with an update on what she's been thinking.
   B. quickly shoves asparagus into her mouth, even though she hates asparagus so she won't have to talk about it.
   C. screams, "Why can't you just leave me alone!" and throws down her fork hard enough to crack your wedding china.

When you run into curious acquaintances in awkward places—say, the waiting room for your first colonoscopy—and they ask you about college, you...

A. feel perfectly fine. You've got your answers down.

B. want to crawl under a rock until the answers sort themselves out.

C. start shaking. You relive the horror as your kid slams and locks the door to her room and blasts music with angry lyrics to drown out your attempts to talk about college.

Answer key: If you answered mostly…

A. You are on top of this. No need to add outside intervention to the mix.

B. You're okay for now. Compile a list of contacts for outside intervention as a protective measure.

C. You need help. No joke. Seek help now before your evil twin takes over your body and turns you into someone who will not make you proud.

Should I call in the cavalry?

Summer is coming, and it can be tough to keep the momentum of your child's college admissions journey humming along without the structure of school. I'll introduce you to everything you need to know about writing applications, but it's up to you to communicate the information to your kid. If your relationship is suffering and you need a buffer, hiring someone to help your kid write college applications or study for standardized tests over the summer is an investment decision. Period. It is not an acknowledgment of failure, or something to feel guilty about. This decision does not hinge on whether or not writing or test-taking is your child's strong point or yours. It hinges only upon whether you answered mostly a's or mostly c's on that quiz you just took.

You might have told someone you were thinking about hiring an essay coach or maybe an ACT tutor. And that person replied with something to the tune of "We've chosen to spend our money on Charlie's college education instead of giving him an unfair advantage in the admissions process because we can." I want to reassure you that these are the very same parents who will call me, desperate for help, the week before Charlie's applications are due, and by then I'm completely booked.

I told you earlier that I'd repeat this again later, and I believe now is the appropriate time: Securing others to help with this process can be expensive, but it can also be free of charge, and either way, it can be an enormous relief for parents and students alike.

Pros and Cons of Teachers Serving as Essay Coaches

God love the compassionate English teacher willing to take time out of his busy day, for no extra pay, to help his students write college essays. Let's recognize those benevolent teachers right here and now. They provide community service every single day. They are warriors for our children. I hope some of them are reading this book and feel appreciated. I'm sorry I cannot give every one of them an eighty-million-dollar raise.

- Pro: Some teachers have a creative writing background and understand the craft of personal essay writing. If your child is lucky enough to score the willing help of a skillful teacher, this is a massive pro.
- Pro: Other than the mega thank-you gift and the twelve-page thank-you letter you will feel compelled to write, this teacher's services are *gratis*.
- Pro: Working together on an additional project might develop the student-mentor relationship in ancillary positive ways.
- Con: That wonderful teacher may be willing and skillful, but she may have limited time to critique the multiple drafts your child's essay will require.
- Con: Teachers deserve a summer break too, so your kid might have to wait until fall to tackle his essay.
- Con: Many teachers are amazing at analyzing literature and teaching students the five-paragraph essay, but they may not be knowledgeable in the creative writing and college admissions arenas.

- Con: Teachers will evaluate your child with grades. It's part of their job, like a year-end review from your boss might be part of your boss's job. Personal essays require students to reveal vulnerabilities of the sort you probably wouldn't want to reveal to the boss who will decide your year-end bonus or promotion. Do you see the problem here?

Myths About Hiring Professional College Essay Coaches

- *No one else is doing it.* Lots of people are doing it but not talking about it.
- *Everyone else is doing it; it will place my child at a disadvantage if I don't.* Many families are toughing it out or finding free resources for help.
- *Hiring an essay coach is cheating.* A good college essay coach would never write any part of your child's application for him. In addition to adhering to a code of ethics, she'd know that she could not possibly duplicate your kid's voice, nor could she tell your kid's story with the potency of the person who lived it.
- *My kid is too shy to open up to a stranger.* It's amazing how quickly kids warm up and spill their guts to people who are not grading them or adoring them with every bone in their body.
- *A private essay coach or consultant will get my child into her top-choice school.* An outstanding essay can tip the scales in your child's favor, but it is not a guarantee of admission. You should know that before you open your wallet.
- *A face-to-face or online coach is better.* It's not a one-size-fits-all decision. For kids with horrendous time management skills, meeting with someone in person might better keep them accountable. For some kids, revealing personal details is easier when there's no chance they'll run into their coach at Target.

Whom Not to Hire

Do not hire the guy who advertises: *I have a new secret weapon that will get your kid into Columbia, Berkeley…any college of your choice!* He is selling tap water and calling it holy water.

Also, do not hire this woman: *I am expert in academic admission essay writing and I will provide the best essay for you in any admission level let me know what you want and you will have your essay in few hours.* It would be like hiring someone to rob your own house for the insurance money. I've seen ads like this, and unethical is just the beginning of its problems. The grammar almost offends me more.

Avoid these charlatans like you'd avoid that stranger with the wet cough even if he was sitting beside the only empty seat left on the bus.

Let's Talk Truth About Parents as Essay Coaches

You are the person who held up your kid's head when he was three weeks old and couldn't hold it up himself. You potty-trained him and then tirelessly advocated for him throughout that playground-bullying incident. Now he can do these things for himself, and your job is to let him.

The role of a parent, when it comes to writing the college application, is "cheerleader."

You may feel incensed that someone who doesn't know anything about you or your kid is advising you to take a back-seat role in this important part of your kid's college admissions process. You may be thinking, *This doesn't apply to me.* I apologize in advance. This is the part where I slap you across the face—not a mean slap, but a friendly slap by someone who cares enough to wake you up and give it to you straight because I am your *ally.* This might not apply to you, but it probably does, and here are the reasons.

This essay is deeply personal.

Did you feel comfortable revealing every thought to your parents when you were sixteen? It's a teenager's job to begin separating from his parents and defining himself on his own terms. This essay can empower him to do so. If he has to run every draft by you, his essay will end up reflecting the way you see him, or the way he wants you to see him, and not the way he has grown to see himself. Regardless of how well you're doing relinquishing control over this process to him (and you are!), a child always has that niggling desire to please his parents. Your teenager will read "constructive feedback" differently from his parents than from anyone else, quite often as "I've disappointed them."

This essay is different from the kind of writing most parents do at work.

The most common parent misconception is that this essay is meant to sell their kid to colleges.

The personal essay is an exercise in creative nonfiction, not the kind of persuasive professional writing required for cover letters, legal briefs, marketing, grant writing, academic writing, etc. Many parents instruct their children to write 650 words boasting about their greatest achievements, and then they revise and polish the language to impress the judge. I've seen so many parents sterilize a student's lively, impassioned, memorable prose into stiff, formal, and unoriginal (though grammatically correct) language that it breaks my heart to think about it. When they take over the essay altogether and add two spaces instead of one after periods as well as the word "awesome," which teenagers don't use anymore, it's a dead giveaway. These parents think they're helping, as they sabotage the work of the creature they love most in the world.

We parents are (way) too invested.

You still might think that you would *never* interfere and ruin your child's college essays, and I know you wouldn't—consciously. Sometimes, when it comes to our kids, we have a blind spot. In all but the rarest cases, it's best for everyone involved for you to step back and let your child take the lead on this. You know your kid better than anyone else, but he knows himself better. Although his brain is not fully developed, he's still the foremost expert on his inner life and the best person to document it in writing.

SUMMER ACTIVITIES THAT LOOK IMPRESSIVE
VS. JUST DOING LIFE

You may have heard that those who work in college admissions groan when they see "service trips" pop up on a student's application. It's true that a two- or three-week trip to Guatemala to "build a school" or "teach kids English" is not nearly as helpful to anyone as a commitment to weekly service at a soup kitchen for all four years of high school. It's also true that most people don't need to travel beyond their own community to find kids who need English tutors.

That doesn't mean traveling away from home on a service trip this summer is not worthwhile. If your child is super excited about a three-week service trip to Ecuador with other teens, and you can afford the $10,000 to send her on such a journey, what a wonderful gift! If it's her first time visiting another continent, traveling without you, or participating in any service project, then an experience like this can blow the mind and alter the path of a developing person. That's why so many kids write about these trips in their personal essays, and why, despite what you've heard, a powerful essay about a service trip experience can make an applicant stand out. These trips can be of great service to the student travelers, not so much the countries' residents or the students' college résumés.

The same goes for summer study at Johns Hopkins, Brown, or other such popular programs for "gifted and talented" high school students. For the kid who is eager to learn whether architecture is the right path for her, or wants to commune with peers as enchanted by quantum mechanics as she is, it may be worth it to spend the $6,000 to treat her to a three-week academic summer program. If she's just participating in an academic program or an internship because she thinks it will look good on her college applications—or because she thinks you want her to do it—your child will lose precious weeks of one of her last childhood summers to something that feels like a chore. She will spend gorgeous summer days in a windowless basement science lab, and you will be out thousands of dollars, all for something that doesn't look any better on a college application or inspire a more original essay than life-guarding at the neighborhood pool, or a week visiting your quirky family in Wisconsin, or working at the local donut shop, or hiking part of the Appalachian Trail, or dancing, or volunteering at a farm, or teaching tennis...

TO-DO LIST

- ☐ Turn to friends (and your beverage of choice) if your teenager catches senioritis. They will give you the strength to help your child fight off his "illness" before final exams and his next SAT.
- ☐ Register for the last round of standardized testing before summer break.
- ☐ Support your child (financially and emotionally) through AP exams, if she's taking them.
- ☐ Visit colleges still in session during school days off and begin planning summer visits.
- ☐ Line up outside help for summer college application writing or test tutoring, *if you choose.*
- ☐ Schedule summer activities to benefit your child, not her college application.

PART IV

SUMMER VACATION

FIVE WAYS TO SNEAK IN COLLEGE VISITS WITHOUT LETTING THEM CONSUME YOUR SUMMER

1. Take that family trip you've put off because of money, time, or inertia while your kid still wants to join you. If you happen to be near a college, sneak a peek. (If not, the travel may spark ideas for your kid's college essay that, in the best of all possible worlds, he will write this summer.)

2. Prioritize yourself for a change! If you've wanted to take that figure-drawing class offered at a local college, don't wait. Invite your kid to join you for the artistic experience, the human anatomy lesson, and perhaps the tour of the campus (especially if you'd like her to stay near home for college).

3. If you're at the beach, visit a college near it.

4. If you're in the mountains, visit a college near them.

5. If you're nowhere near a college and your teenager is content, *don't budge*. Revel in the rare sight of the content teenager. You are passively helping with your kid's college transition by reminding her of her strong foundation at home, and you are helping yourself by not rocking the boat. Win-win!

Chapter 7

June and July

SUMMER CAMPUS VISITS: A CAUTIONARY TALE

Summer is not the best time to visit a college. The flora and fauna there are not representative of the academic year. Campuses either resemble ghost towns or teem with kids participating in summer programs who will not be the same kids in classes in the fall. Summer is also not the worst time to visit a college. Strolling around a lush groomed campus on a summer day can make you feel like a character straight out of a Jane Austen novel, minus the parasol. (Can you imagine the expression on your kid's face if you whipped out a parasol during a college tour?)

My daughter wanted to see a college in Minnesota, so in July, when we both had a little more time on our hands, we flew from Boston to Minneapolis–Saint Paul. Then we rented a car and drove through the Midwestern countryside. If you live on a coast and have ever referred to the Midwest as "fly-over country," repent! There's nothing more beautiful than cornfields, pastures, lakes, and Dutch-style windmills on a sunny, temperate July day in rural Minnesota.

When we arrived at the college, not one drop of humidity hung in the air. Flowers sprouted everywhere. In town, on campus, you could spit anywhere and you'd hit a flower. Our student tour guide led us through deserted buildings on the vacated campus. We were left to imagine the classrooms and student center when colonized. My daughter told me that she liked the school, but in her estimation, it was not worth flying halfway across the country to attend a college so similar to the colleges near home. In my estimation, it was not worth traveling this far to visit only one college, so I'd booked a tour and an information session at a second one.

My daughter humored me and capitulated to this second college visit — and I may have reminded her that I had paid for the plane tickets. We sat through the info session, which sounded similar to all the other info sessions to me, but my daughter latched on to their exceptional emphasis on study abroad, as if Minnesota wasn't far enough away. This college insisted prospective students and their parents take separate tours, so my kid went off on her tour and I went on mine (even more flowers). Notably, all the buildings connected via indoor walkways and tunnels so students would never have to venture outside during the harsh Minnesota winter.

When we reconvened, my daughter stood before a botanical garden, her hair gleaming in the sunlight, and said, "I *like* this school. I can see myself here."

I pictured her standing before the alternative brutal dystopian landscape she'd find here during the academic year, with biting winds whipping swirls of snow. I don't think it had registered with my kid that the whole campus was designed like a hamster's Habitrail for a reason.

Back in the Office of Admission, my daughter's young interviewer bounded into the waiting room and announced, "I'm from Massachusetts too! But after graduation, I stayed here because it's friendlier, with smart people, but more *chill*." I refrained from pointing out that "chill" had multiple meanings. I could hear the two of them chatting happily along the corridor, their voices fading, until an office door clicked shut.

I thought about a lot of things during the forty minutes I sat alone in that waiting room. I thought about how I'd led my kid right into the hands of this charming Massachusetts-native interviewer, who at that very moment could be wooing her to another part of the country, potentially forever. I calculated the money and time we'd need to invest in transportation. I added both the perk and the supplementary cost of frequenting the nearby Mall of America when I came to visit. Mostly, I thought about how my kid hadn't even asked to see this college, and I'd tacked it on to the trip on the most beautiful day of the year. If I'd brought her here in February, this turn of events might never have happened.

Our return trip took sixteen hours if you include the flight delay, and we didn't arrive home until two o'clock in the morning. My daughter, undaunted, added the second Minnesota college plus a college in Colorado to her list. I had no intention whatsoever of risking a Rocky Mountain high after witnessing the Minnesota botanical gardens effect. I told her she could visit the college in Colorado, and revisit the one in Minnesota under different barometric conditions, if she was admitted.

By the end of the summer, I had found some peace. I reminded myself my daughter's college journey wasn't about me. Though I'd miss her, these would both be excellent schools for her, and if we gave up meat and our gym membership, we could cover the cost of plane tickets to either of them. I began preparing emotionally for this possibility.

The point is that wherever you bring your child to visit this summer provides her with your tacit approval to enroll there. I am writing this from a hotel room in Colorado with a sublime mountain view the night before a college tour with my *son*. You'd think I would've learned. As I've said before, we are all in this together.

TESTING YOUR PATIENCE

June means summer break for some lucky kids, while most have to sweat through a few more weeks of school without sufficient air conditioning. But chances are both the rising seniors and perspiring juniors will take a standardized test in June, which has the dubious distinction as one of the few months both the SAT and ACT are offered.

As for the other summer test dates…

- In 2017, the College Board started offering an extra annual SAT test in August. (Bonus!)

- The ACT added an extra July test to their repertoire for 2018. (Take that, College Board!)
- Now there is not a single month during the whole year that your child cannot sign up to take one of these tests. (Huzzah!)

I remember the days when summer meant a break from testing, but sadly, my kids don't and neither will yours. It's no secret by now that I have feelings about the standardized testing scourge upon us. I'd let it go, I really would, but professor after professor in my college town and beyond tells me that those tests that help our kids get into college *hinder* them when they arrive in college classrooms. Many new students enter real college classes unprepared for and initially frustrated by the depth of critical analysis required. They want to get the right answer and then move on quickly without stopping to think, as they've been trained to do for multiple-choice tests. Using standardized testing as the educational metric for our students has become a frightening ritual embedded in our culture. The worst of it, in my opinion, is that all this test prep—studying tricks to outwit the SAT and memorizing and regurgitating facts for AP exams—flattens learning and makes school *drop dead boring* for our kids.

Well, that's terrible that my kid's bored and only learning to memorize and think shallowly, but he still has to take and retake tests to get into a good college, and take more tests to get into a good graduate school, so he can have a shot at the best career that will probably require more tests to rise up the ranks to make the highest income to support his family, so his kids (my future grandkids) can afford test prep to have a shot at a spot at my kid's alma mater, which, by the time they apply, will have an admission rate of .005%...

I know! It's crazy-making. It's virtually impossible not to get stuck in this cycle. Then again, over a thousand colleges have become unstuck with test-optional or test-flexible application requirements. We parents can also jump off that testing conveyer belt when we've had enough. I'm empowering you not to let those pesky tests hijack your summer fun, even if your child has to take them. Let other parents cancel family beach vacations so their kids can attend test prep boot camp for six weeks this summer. (Don't judge them. They're doing their best.) I grant you full permission to do the following:

- Spend exactly the amount of time necessary discussing where, when, and if your child will take tests this summer or fall, and how he will study for them. No more, and no less.
- Spend every minute you are not having this conversation enjoying your summer without any SAT or ACT interference.
- Once you've helped to set everything up, let your child deal with studying for any test he's decided to take. You can't study for him, so why let it suck up any more of your time?
- Whenever you see your child tossing a Frisbee with his brother in the surf instead of taking practice tests, remind yourself that what he's doing—enjoying his life and the relationships in it—will matter more in his future than his score on the July ACT.

TIME TO WRITE (OR PLAN TO WRITE, OR THINK ABOUT WRITING) THE PERSONAL ESSAY

Strategies for Motivating Your Kid to Just Write the Thing

If you didn't already know, I'm telling you now that it's a good idea for students to write college essays over the summer. Many have the best of intentions to write them, but the weather is *so lovely*. The swimming pool has opened for the season, and every distraction under the sun (literally) entices our kids—swimming, kayaking, hiking up a mountain, hanging out on a park bench finally reading that juicy novel…Trying to pump your kid up to write essays may not go over so well.

You have three options here:

1. Try to convince your kid that if she gets this thing done, her senior fall will be tolerable.

2. Find someone else to convince her.
3. Let nature take its course.

Strategy #1: Do-It-Yourself Nagging

When my daughter told me she wanted to work with me on her personal essay, I said, "Yes!" because the optimist in me thought, *I coach kids internationally writing these essays. I get along great with other people's teenagers. Why shouldn't I apply my skills and experience to working with my own child?* I thought, *Maybe the two of us are different from almost EVERY SINGLE MOTHER AND TEENAGER SINCE THE BEGINNING OF TIME.*

I suspect you have also had this delusion at least once in your parenting life. As I'm sure you've guessed, my daughter and I were *not* different. Despite my expertise, the nagging began, as it does in households across America. Then the pushback followed, resulting in the gatherings of parents around a wine bottle, where we admitted (not without guilt) that we could not wait until our kids left for college, if only to stop hearing ourselves nag. Then we teared up, lamenting our children's imminent departure. We leaped across the emotional spectrum, often within a few seconds, feeling certifiably wacko.

Are you experiencing any of this? If so, Dr. Appy assures us these push-pull feelings are perfectly normal. You may be dealing with the same separation anxiety as your angst-ridden teen, but part of being the adult is holding it together for your kid at home and finding appropriate outlets to vent your feelings elsewhere. The impulse to complain to friends over wine or cocktails (a Shirley Temple counts) is *healthy.* In case I haven't made myself clear, Dr. Appy and I are prescribing an adult playdate for you. (You're welcome.)

You can try the DIY nagging strategy. Some parents have more luck than I did motivating and helping their kids through college essays, and if you are one of them, more power to you. If you try and it doesn't work out, know the forces of the universe are working against this writing partnership. Know that your child still loves you no matter how much he resists. Know that if you face defeat, we are right here to comfort you, with arms open wide, beverage of choice in hand. Take no more than five minutes to wallow in this failure because it will not matter five years from now, when many of our children will have *graduated* from college.

Strategy #2: Outside Intervention

As I've mentioned before, teachers (see p. 135) and friends can help for free. College admissions professionals are available for hire (see p. 136). There is no shame in asking one or more of them for help. Not now. Not ever.

Strategy #3: Letting Nature Take Its Course

You probably think I'm going to tell you your child should without a doubt get his essay written this summer, but I will say no such thing. If you know your kid will remain a nervous wreck until he stops anticipating and starts writing, then by all means, encourage him to get started. However, letting nature take its course is the right path for some students. You saw what happened with my friend Karen and her daughter, Min (who wrote her essays at the last minute and everything turned out okay). If your kid really needs a vacation, and you know he works best under pressure (no matter how much suffering it causes you), let him prioritize whittling that fishing pole over getting down to this college application business, especially if it will prevent the nag-fest your summer could otherwise become.

The Point of the Personal Essay

What should this 250–650-word, time-consuming, fear-inducing personal essay accomplish?

I'm going to warn you right now that you won't find a secret formula for writing the perfect essay in these pages. Any formula would generate a boring, generic essay that would not represent your kid well, but I can share what a successful finished essay should accomplish.

- The essay should tell an engaging story.
- It should hook the reader's attention at the beginning.
- It should keep the reader interested in the middle.

- The protagonist of the essay (your child) should be likable.
- It should show the reader that your kid has reflected upon her topic with some depth.
- It should sound like your kid sounds when speaking casually, to capture a snippet of his personality.
- The ending should leave the reader thinking, feeling, or understanding something about your kid that he didn't think, feel, or understand before he read the essay.
- There should be no typos.

I can also share with you some common mistakes that can cause a personal essay to crash and burn:

- The essay should not read like a list of accomplishments (making your child sound like an obnoxious braggart).
- It should not look like a formal cover letter loaded with thesaurus words (making your child sound stiff and pretentious).
- It should not contain loads of grammar, syntax, and spelling errors (making your kid look like he has a shoddy work ethic).

Myth: The essay is the golden ticket that will get your kid into college.

Truth: If your child's application progresses as far as the "maybe" pile at a target or reach school for her, it means the admission evaluators think she's a viable candidate. Then her essay matters in the following ways:

- If your child puts zero or little effort into her essay and it's a careless, incompetent piece of writing, it can knock her down into the "no" pile. This rarely happens.
- If her essay is perfectly fine, with no red flags but nothing special, either, it will show she's a competent writer and won't count against her, but it won't help her case.
- If she works hard and submits a sensational personal essay, it can bump her file from the "maybe" to the "yes" pile.

A Glimpse into Your Child's Fears About Writing
the Personal Essay

I don't know which prompt to choose (a.k.a. prompt paralysis).

Some students stare at the essay prompts on a college application and panic, *I might choose the wrong prompt and then write the wrong essay and then never get into college.* If yours is one of those worried kids, you can deliver this great news: *It is impossible to choose the wrong prompt.*

Prompt: *to move to action...assist by suggesting.*

Prompts are meant to help your kid get started, not limit her. "Topic of your choice" is one of the options on both of the most common applications required by colleges, making choosing any of the other essay prompts they offer *optional.* Whichever essay prompt your kid chooses will be fine.

I have nothing important to say about my normal, boring life.

Fitting in is the modus operandi of teenage existence. Your child might have spent his entire school career trying to cover up differences, even to himself. When asked what *makes* him different from his peers, it might be the first time he's thought of difference as a positive thing. Everyone has extraordinary qualities, but most of us don't recognize them, or we take them for granted. You can tell your kid what you think makes him special, which might only irritate him, or it might supply a little morale boost and the germ of an idea for his essay.

I have to cram my entire life into 650 words.

Many students start out with a topic that's too broad, trying to stuff seventeen years into a one-page essay. Then they complain they don't feel like they have much original to say about their topic. It sounds counterintuitive, but if your kid can narrow down her topic, she'll have more to write about it. As an example, your kid might desperately want world peace, but if she tries to summarize such a voluminous topic, the essay will emerge vague, generic, and as something anyone could've written. If your child writes about the moment she stood on the steps of the city hall with her hand-painted rainbow peace sign, she'll better convey her zeal for world peace and how personal the topic is to her.

I have writer's block.

Professional writers fall into two camps: those who believe in writer's block, and those who don't. I am not a believer. I believe the paralyzed feeling comes directly from fear and doubt, and of *course* your kid feels fear and doubt about this essay. These essays are built up to be the end-all-be-all, make-or-break moment of the college admissions process, and yet not everybody is comfortable with writing. If your child feels most competent in the world of numbers and finds this assignment to write about herself daunting, who can blame her? Great writers can become paralyzed too, thinking this has to be their very best work ever. Students tend to give the college admissions process in general, and the personal essay specifically, way too much mystical power.

To snag that power back, you can tell your child that this is not life or death. She's got this, and no matter what she writes, she'll get into college. For added encouragement to help her start writing, tell her no one, not the admissions staff of any college or anyone else, ever has to see her first draft.

A CURE FOR WRITER'S BLOCK

1. Set an appointment with yourself.
2. Keep the appointment.
3. Plant your butt in a chair in front of a computer.
4. Start typing. (It might feel stiff at first, but no one ever has to see this.)

5. Try to refrain from judging anything that emerges as you're writing. (If your inner editor comes out too soon, she will stir up doubt and fear that you're doing everything wrong, and that's what causes writer's block.)

6. Keep typing, no matter what comes out. (Even if it's crappy, it will be a relief to have something on the page. Consider it a warmup, never a failure.)

7. Sometimes it helps to set a timer for five or ten minutes and write down everything that pops into your head until the timer dings. (You might be surprised at how many words you can blurt out in the same amount of time it takes to complain about writer's block.)

I have to find the perfect, most original topic.

I have read thousands of college applications, and let me tell you, if your kid is fixated on finding an essay topic I've never seen before, she's wasting her time. There are no new topics. Instead of aiming to impress with some mind-blowing, never-before-encountered topic, your kid should *write what she wants to say instead of what she thinks someone else wants to hear.* If your kid writes about a topic that matters to her, it will matter to readers. The topic does not have to be exotic. What your kid loves most might be something almost every kid in the world loves too, but only *your* kid can articulate her personal experience of loving it, and why.

I have to avoid taboo topics.

You'll hear that your kid shouldn't write about sports because *everybody* writes about sports. She *obviously* can't write about her service trip, or religion, or anything political. I am here to tell you that advice is bogus. Your kid can write on any topic. It's her *approach* to that topic that will influence how fresh, commonplace, fascinating, or offensive her essay will turn out.

For example, lots of kids love to bake. Only one kid made me laugh out loud when he described how he botched the family Christmas cake recipe and had to serve it anyway to his uncle Joe, the foodie, at Christmas dinner. That kid displayed his resourcefulness and humility in the way he salvaged his cake and his pride.

Lots of kids love to play hockey. Only one kid's essay moved me as he described everything that passed through his mind in the three seconds before stepping onto the ice for his first varsity game. His personality flooded onto the page.

Lots of kids go to church. Only one kid brought her brother who suffers from Tourette's syndrome and told a tale about it with such love, compassion, and humor that I remember her essay to this day. (You can imagine what her brother shouted during the sermon.)

My essay has to be funny to be memorable.

If your child is a soulful kid but tries to be funny in his essay because he thinks he's supposed to, the following will happen:

- His essay will come out sounding forced.
- It won't sound like your child.
- It won't be funny.

If he writes from the heart, his essay will emerge genuine and memorable, whether it's funny or not.

I'm not feeling inspired yet.

If your child's sitting there in front of a computer waiting for lightning to strike, I have news for her. According to the National Weather Service, there's a 1/13,000 chance of that happening in her lifetime (lower if she's sitting indoors). Tell her to remain seated and follow my instructions for overcoming writer's block (p. 152). Fingers scurrying across the keyboard will create the perfect climate for inspiration to pay her a visit.

There's no point to this essay, so why bother?

Rarely are seventeen-year-olds handed the power to say what they want to say about themselves, unplugged, to a captive audience. For every teenager who has ever said that no one understands him or listens to him, this is his chance to be heard. Hidden within the college admissions process are opportunities to find meaning, and this is one of them.

In my role as a college essay coach, so often when I meet a student, he feels defeated before he's even started. He has internalized the voices of all those people who have told him that the college admissions process is totally arbitrary, so no matter how hard he works on the formidable task of representing himself in 650 words, it's futile. Then we begin talking. We find little stories from his life, funny ones he hasn't thought about in years, or poignant ones he's never dissected. He opens his mind to reflection and finds it fascinating to think about how these small moments have combined to shape him, which leads him to wonder who he is, and why, and who he wants to become. He sees that this personal essay is not a pointless assignment at all. It could actually be useful in his growth.

As he focuses inward on the qualities that make him unique, those pessimistic, fearful, defeatist internal voices begin to fade. By the time he finishes an essay he's proud to submit, he's a better writer, he's a stronger analytical thinker, and he's found a sense of self-worth. He feels in control and emboldened to represent himself in his own way. The story he tells in his essay may be different from the story others have been telling about him or that he's been telling himself. It's not unusual for students to rethink their college list or potential major as they go through the writing process. Many have the epiphany that maybe getting into college is not the endgame they've been working toward. Maybe the endgame is becoming the person they want to be.

The thinking that goes into the essay can become more valuable than the finished product itself. Writing a personal essay can work like therapy, arouse self-awareness, and empower the writer. Writing *this* personal essay has the potential to effect real change in your child at a time when his life is in flux. As a sidebar, it may even help your kid get into college.

Parents as Proofreaders: Proceed with Caution

The Load You Carry

When your vulnerable teenager, who has written something personal about himself, hands his essay to you and asks you to "read" it, he might be asking for anything from grammar help to a proclamation of your undying approval and love. He may not tell you so, but your opinion of his essay, and of him, deeply matters. If you dive into your child's essay with a red pen, your kid could easily interpret even your smallest suggestion as disapproval and a directive to rewrite the whole thing.

Before you read the first word, ask him what kind of feedback he would like from you. If it's his first draft, he may have questions about the topic he chose or the examples he used. If it's his seventh draft, he may only want you to catch sentence fragments. If he's not sure what he wants from you, focusing on writing mechanics, not content, will generally help your kid the most.

GUIDELINES FOR APPROPRIATE PROOFREADING

1. Start by saying something positive about the topic idea, a particularly compelling sentence, or one great word choice, if that's all you can find. If nothing else, praise your child's effort.

2. Point out anything that you found confusing as you were reading along, and explain why.

3. Point out anything off-topic or extraneous that wouldn't be missed if it were cut.

4. If you spot an awkward sentence or "overshare" that might convey something to the reader your child had not intended, tell him how someone who doesn't know him could interpret what he wrote, and ask if that's what he meant.

5. Explain his grammar, spelling, and punctuation mistakes, including any typos, misused words, misstated facts, or other *objective* errors. You will give him a great gift if you have time to work through the corrections with him, so he can find and fix those sorts of mistakes himself next time. (If you are both strapped for time and you add one little comma for him, no one will die.)

6. Remind him that if he consults a thesaurus, he should look for the *correct* word that most accurately and simply says what he wants to say, *not the million-dollar word*.

7. Point out where added details could make the essay clearer, more colorful, and even better than it already is. (Use this sort of encouraging language to keep that positive vibe going.)

8. If you have any tips that might enhance the essay's message, it's okay to share them *if that's the kind of feedback he asked for*.

9. End by saying something upbeat like "Great job!" or "I love the way you described that pig roast; I could really smell it." Or the ultimate praise: "This essay is so 'you'!"

What if I read my child's essay and it's atrocious?

He voluntarily showed it to you, and he's awaiting your response. You don't want to lie to your child. Well, this is awkward. I cannot decide for you whether or not calling attention to the essay's failure is worthwhile. I haven't seen how bad your kid's essay really is.

If you do go the brutal honesty route, you have my support. Your child has my support, too, because if it's *that* bad, he probably secretly knows it. He probably wanted this essay over and done with already and he hoped no one would notice its cavernous flaws. (Now that you've noticed, don't be surprised if your child blames you for them.)

If it's not that bad, the greatest service you can provide is to proofread as carefully and tenderly as you scraped that splinter out of his finger when he was a toddler. If the essay sounds like your child, warts and all, honest and unpretentious and real, that is the best kind of essay. Don't polish it up into something he's not. Show him where he's got a run-on sentence and where the verb tense is confusing. Then, after he makes changes, offer to proofread it again to catch any last typos. This restraint you have shown will go miles and miles toward gaining his trust and helping both of you adjust to your shifting parental role.

How Letting Go of Your Kid's Essay Can Help Both of You

I'll let Dr. Appy take this one. Here are her insights:

- *It can help the child feel as though he is truly presenting himself and not his parents' version of him.*
- *It can help the child's self-esteem and sense of accomplishment.*
- *It helps parents truly appreciate that applying to college is not their job.*
- *It can help parents remain calm and soothing in the face of their child's emotional ride.*
- *It helps with the separation process for you both.*

A GAP YEAR, OR NO GAP YEAR? THAT IS THE QUESTION

The meaning of the word *gap* runs the gamut from "intermission" to "chasm." In the context of a person's education, taking a year off between high school and college, a.k.a. a gap year, is a break, not a deep dive into a bottomless pit. I want to make one thing clear: *Your kid does not have to go to college at the exact same time or in the exact same way as everyone else.*

Good Reasons to Consider a Gap Year

- If your "oblivious child" can muster zero enthusiasm about college, despite your elaborate spreadsheet and updated calendar, she might need an extra year to mature into a college student.
- A gap year provides a year away from the pressures of academia for the "volcanic child" to unwind, so she can enter college calmer and more focused.
- If she's itching to travel more than she's itching for more school, programs like Workaway (see Resources) offer affordable opportunities for your child to explore the world and gain perspective before attending college.

- Some kids are just plain young. If your kid's the youngest in her class, or not as socially or physically developed as her peers, starting college a year later can boost her confidence and help her feel "caught up."
- If your child needs another year of high school to prove herself, either academically or athletically, a post-graduate or "PG" year at a private school, if you can afford it, might help enhance her profile before applying to college.
- If someone has fallen ill, health comes before college, which will still be there when the person recovers. If it's the student, she'll need time to convalesce (often from a concussion — a topic for another time over a hot beverage). If it's a loved one, the student may be needed for caretaking right now.
- It's worth it for your child to work full-time for one year if the additional income could help your family afford college tuition for her the next.

Bad Reasons to Consider a Gap Year

- Your child, who was previously eager for college, suddenly has cold feet when it's time to start writing his applications. That could be fear of rejection talking. If he's a "volcanic child," a gap year would set him back a year behind his high school classmates, and for him, feeling behind on *anything* might not be worth the stress it will cause. It won't hurt his college prospects if he waits a year to apply, but you might want to hold off on telling him that.
- For the "oblivious child," getting out of the school groove can lead to a year without structure, resulting in procrastination on an epic scale. Playing video games in your basement does not a productive gap year make. Plus it could add significant stress for you, wondering if you'll ever get your kid out of your house.
- Then again, if your child is not ready to leave home, that doesn't necessarily mean he's not ready to start college. If you're okay with it, he can remain in his own room, enjoying home-cooked meals, while attending a local two- or four-year college.

- It's summer. Your kid lounging in the sunshine might look like a candidate for a gap year now, but when senior year begins, seeing all his friends applying to college could be motivation enough.

Some kids need a year's respite from school, and others need to do college in a less traditional way. Communicate with your kid and listen closely. Determine if a gap year is precisely what he needs before embarking on his next educational undertaking, or if he just needs a little TLC from his loving parent before venturing forward.

TO-DO LIST

- ☐ Complete or register for more standardized testing (for some). (This too shall pass.)
- ☐ Let the summer college visits commence, but don't let them take over your summer.
- ☐ Encourage your child to write his personal essay (and let it go if he doesn't).
- ☐ Reflect on whether or not your child's a candidate for a gap year. If so, explore options, but instruct her to fill out college applications anyway. It's easiest for her to collect materials and apply to colleges now, then defer the starting date once admitted.
- ☐ If your kid's a science whiz, some prestigious, big-ticket scholarship contests—such as the Siemens Foundation Competition and the Regeneron Science Talent Search—have deadlines in the fall, so it's worth researching this summer.
- ☐ Spend much more time enjoying activities with your child while he still resides at home than worrying about college. It's called summer *vacation*, people.

Chapter 8

August

If you recall, we left off last month after my unsuccessful attempt to apply the do-it-yourself nagging strategy to motivate my daughter to write her personal essay. By mid-July, some of my students had finished their essays, others had begun them, and I could not stand the sound of my own nagging voice reverberating through my home any longer. That's when my daughter took off for a summer writing workshop in another state. A *writing workshop*.

Still no essay.

When she returned home, she needed to see her long-lost (for two weeks) friends and lobby for extra shifts at her job at the local stationery store to earn money for college. I reminded her that college wasn't going to happen if she didn't write an essay to apply for it. Then I gritted my teeth and suggested outside intervention (not for the first time). I vowed to myself I would remain the calm adult in the room no matter what my kid did or didn't do.

There is something to be said for waiting until your child is ready. Mid-August, my girl sat down and took a stab at her essay. She wrote drafts of two very different essays and asked me to choose which one I liked better. They were both good. I chose one, as she had asked.

She showed both of her essay drafts to my husband, an outstanding writer in his own right, and very, very smart and handsome. (He will read this at some point.) He told her he liked the other essay better.

I tempered my initial, effusive praise for the essay I'd chosen to show respect for my husband's opinion. After all, both essay drafts were good, and I would have to continue to live with my husband after my daughter departed for college.

My daughter accused me of being indecisive.

I suggested *again* that she consult someone outside of our family.

I will leave you here, at exactly the unresolved place I was left that sweltering August, while I tackle the backlog of emails in my inbox appealing for essay-writing help for other people's children.

APPLICATION INTEL

The Common Application

What exactly is the Common Application?

The Common Application is an electronic platform for submitting college applications. A paper version was first introduced and accepted by a handful of private colleges in 1975. It became available online in 1998, more colleges signed on, and the Common Application eventually made paper applications obsolete. More than 800 public and private colleges now accept the Common Application, including most if not all of the colleges where your child will apply. The company that created it is called "The Common Application." The website your kid will visit to access it is called "The Common Application." It's easy to find.

The beauty of the Common Application is that your child only has to fill out information once rather than retyping it on multiple applications. This convenience also leads to its downside. Because this platform makes it simple to apply to more schools without expending extra effort, kids say, "Why not?" and submit a few extra applications. This practice contributes to the escalating competition nightmare that afflicts college admissions today.

When can my kid start the application?

On August 1, the buzz begins that the Common Application has gone live, which means students can start filling it out online. The operative word is "students." Let your kid ask all the questions she wants along the way. (What's dad's job title again? What if I don't know my future major? What's your credit card number?) But hands off the keyboard. Little acknowledged fact: *Your teenager, who is a digital native, is better at using a computer than you are.*

The Common Application Hokey-Pokey

The Common Application consists of seven sections totaling about seven to ten pages. I'll cover all of it in detail, but for now, here's an overview, including your role as your kid completes it (lean in to help vs. lean out to butt out):

1. If the student is incapable of filling out the Personal Information section on his own (name, address, birthday, etc.) then he has no business going to college. *Lean out.*
2. Here's the lowdown on the Testing section. Most colleges require scores to come directly from the College Board or ACT. For those schools, you can *lean in* to tell your kid he can skip filling out this section, since scores will be reported elsewhere. Recently, more colleges allow students to self-report scores. For those schools, *lean in* even harder and advise your kid to triple-check that there's no need to pay the College Board for a score report, have him self-report his test scores, and save yourself some dough (until spring, when you'll need to pay to send an official score report to the one school he chooses).
3. Most students don't need to use the Additional Information section, as you'll see in The Additional Information Opportunity (or Temptation) at the end of this chapter, but if your child decides she needs it, *lean out.*
4. Your child might need your help to complete the Family section because that's the part about you. If he's a typical teenager, he has no idea where you came from or what you do for a living that pays for the roof over his room from which he locks you out while he does God knows what. *Lean in.*

5. He should be able to fill out most of the Education section without help. I mean, he walks past the sign with the name of his school on it every single day. *Lean out.* In the Honors part of that section, he may need a little help remembering what happened four years ago because for him that was another lifetime. *Lean in* to jog his memory. *Lean out* while he types.

6. He surely knows which Activities he's doing now, but he might need your help remembering those past activities to which you spent hours (and hours) driving him. *Lean in* for the brainstorming. *Lean out* for the writing. *Lean back in* for the proofreading, if he asks. This is fun, right? It's like doing the Hokey Pokey.

7. We have already dealt with the section that spooks families most: the Writing of the personal essay. *Lean out* for the writing. *Lean in* to help proofread if your help is requested.

The Other Applications

Are the Coalition Application and the Common Application the same thing?

Like the Ohio State–Michigan and SAT-ACT rivalries, popular college application delivery vehicles battle for the top spot. The Common Application is the frontrunner, but the Coalition Application, short for the Coalition for Access, Affordability, and Success, challenged the Common Application in 2015, and it's gaining steam. Now about 140 selective colleges accept the Coalition Application.

A comparison:

- Almost all colleges that accept the Coalition Application will also accept the Common Application. As of this writing, only three schools require the Coalition Application exclusively.
- The Coalition Application offers five essay prompts, while the Common Application offers seven essay prompts. Both include "topic of your choice."

- The Coalition Application suggests aiming for 500–550 words on the personal essay, while the Common Application's personal essay instructions request 250–650 words.
- The Common Application offers ten slots for activities, while the Coalition Application allots eight slots.
- The Coalition Application invites students to use a "locker" to begin uploading and storing college-related documents and guiding them to think about college starting freshman year of high school. Most people don't access the Common Application until it's time to apply.

Unless your kid plans to apply to one of the three colleges that requires the Coalition Application, I'd say why bother with it? If your kid applies to one of those three colleges, she can lop off about 100 words from her 650-word personal essay, remove two activities, and copy all the information from her Common Application onto the Coalition Application form. Done. Don't get me started on how beginning the college-application process freshman year in high school could affect families in communities already obsessed with college admissions.

Are there other applications to worry about?

Have you heard of the Universal College Application (UCA)? Neither has anybody else. The Universal College Application took a shot at breaking up the Common Application's monopoly in 2007, and it's still hanging in there, but just barely, with only a small handful of schools accepting it (so not universal at all).

Some colleges and universities, such as Georgetown and the University of California system, only accept their own applications, but they're nothing to worry about. Your child can tweak the advice that follows for the Common Application to suit any application on the screen in front of her.

ANSWERS TO MY CLIENTS' FAQS ABOUT THE COMMON APPLICATION

The Personal Profile Section

Will checking the wrong (or right) ethnicity box reduce (or increase) my kid's chances for admission?

After filling out her name, address, and the usual rote information requested on forms, a screen will appear entitled Demographics. As in the doctor's office, this section is optional. It's always optional. I'm sure you've instilled in your child that she should be proud of who she is. Whether or not she answers the demographics questions will not change that. Some guidelines:

- If your child feels like this question is racist or nobody's business, leaving it blank will not affect her chances for admission.
- If your kid checks the box in front of "white," she is part of the majority of students admitted to colleges every year.
- If your child checks one of the other boxes in this section or reports religious identity or participation in the armed forces, *and* there's evidence of a cultural connection elsewhere in her application, it alerts readers that your child may have a perspective to offer that's unique on their campus. Many colleges value this type of diversity, yet they will not admit otherwise unqualified students because of it.
- If your child's applying to one of the 101 Historically Black Colleges and Universities (HBCUs) and checks the box indicating he's "Black or African American," he will be in the racial majority of applicants and students on that campus. In the same way, students who identify as Catholic applying to Jesuit colleges and students who identify as women applying to women's colleges will be in the majority.

- I've heard about students afraid to mark the "Asian" box, fearing discrimination. There's a lawsuit on this topic happening at this writing, and I'll leave it to the courts to rule on it. That said, from an admissions perspective, Asia is a huge continent containing numerous disparate countries and cultures. Applications from students whose families come from some of those countries, such as Vietnam and Cambodia, are sorely lacking in applicant pools at many colleges.

- If anyone in the student's immediate family is an undocumented immigrant, please check with someone in the know, like a high school counselor or a lawyer, before reporting anything on the Common Application, but don't let that prevent your child from applying to colleges.

Much controversy surrounds the topic of diversity in higher education. Working in admissions offices, I have seen firsthand the earnest efforts of many colleges to include students who might have been discriminated against or overlooked in the past. At the end of the day, your child's application will be thoroughly reviewed based on merit within her school and environmental circumstances and not through the lens of her race or religion. Despite all of the other flaws in the college admissions process, this, to me, feels like progress.

Does high school French count as language proficiency?

If your child can speak, read, and write French fairly fluently after five years of French class, it can't hurt to declare fluency. It won't interest admission evaluators much unless she also has lived in a French-speaking country, speaks French at home, or has gained fluency some other way that would add an interesting dynamic to conversations in the college dining hall. If she memorized her Torah portion for her bat mitzvah and can sound out Hebrew letters, that does not count as language proficiency.

Does marking the box for "needs financial aid" hurt my kid's admission chances?

- If a college claims to be "need blind," whether or not you check that box will have zero impact on admissions.
- If the college is "need aware," it can be a factor for admissions; however, how large of a factor depends on the institution.
- For colleges with large endowments, their "need aware" policy can work in favor of students applying for aid. Some scholarships are only available to applicants who cannot afford full tuition.
- Other colleges with less sizable endowments may need more students paying full freight to cover expenses, so marking that box could make a negative difference for your kid.

If you need financial aid, your child should mark the box. If she is admitted but she can't afford to attend, that edge she thought she had by not marking the box was nonexistent from the get-go.

Does the two-week summer program on the Brown University campus count as a college my kid has attended?

If your child attended a summer academic program, she can include it along with the dates she attended, and/or she can include it in another section as an activity. However, this section is really intended for kids who have taken a semester-long in-person or online college class.

My child can't think of any honors to fill in; what should she do?

Most kids have some honors, but many don't realize those honors count. As an admission evaluator, I've noticed that often students skip this section, and then as I read further into their application, a recommendation reveals the student was National Merit Commended or made the honor roll. Sometimes our kids have no idea of their achievements (or lovability). Teenagers.

Some guidelines for the Honors section:

- There are five slots for honors, for which students are allotted 100 characters (not words) each. Spaces between words count as characters.
- Students should log academic honors at the school, regional, and national level. As examples, AP Scholar, National Merit Finalist, dean's list, and book awards belong here.
- Some students don't realize that non-school-related academic honors should also appear here. For example, local scholar-athlete recognition or a National History Day award.
- Honors for electives, such as Scholastic Gold and Silver Key art awards, are legit honors to note here.
- Any academic departmental recognition at the school, even if it's for effort, is an honor.

If your child can't think of honors, she should brainstorm everything she's ever done in high school beginning in ninth grade. If academic honors don't appear on that list, certainly activities will turn up for inclusion in her Activities section (we'll cover that next). Maybe you remember honors your kid forgot because you devoted time, energy, and the funds to celebrate them. Feel free to remind her.

How can a teenager possibly know her future career and highest degree?

The Future Career section on the Common Application includes a drop-down menu, and one of the options is "Optometrist." I have never seen an application with that profession chosen. Who knows at seventeen that she wants to specialize in optometry? This question just feeds into a kid's misconception that she is the only high school student alive who has no freaking clue what she wants to do when she grows up.

In the privacy of their own homes, most students choose "Undecided" from that drop-down menu, which makes sense to me. Many of our children's future careers don't even exist yet. However, if your child does have a sense of a career she might want to pursue, she can go ahead and select it. It could work in her favor if the reader sees that her lowest grades are always in math but she wants to become an actor (a future career for which math genius is not a prerequisite).

As far as the Highest Degree goes, that depends on the future career, doesn't it? Why not go for the fantasy Ph.D.? Your kid can always scale back later, IRL.

The Activities Section (a.k.a. "the Brag Sheet")

Even if your kid is very humble, she shouldn't hold back here. This section is for her sales pitch (as its nickname suggests).

Are some activities better to include than others?

Rule #1: Do not lie in any part of the application, including this section. A student can get caught when her well-meaning counselor describes, with admiration, that the student wasn't afraid to try something new and joined a knitting club senior year when the student has checked boxes indicating she's been a member since freshman year. Your child will sleep better at night if she tells the truth, gets into college on her own merit, and then channels her newfound enthusiasm into starting a knitting club once she arrives.

Rule #2: Your child should not downplay what she's done. Your kid may not have won first prize for her painting in the juried art show, but her decade of dedication to art, culminating in her artwork appearing in that show, will impress evaluators nonetheless.

Rule #3: Everything your child does counts. By "everything," I mean every activity in which she has participated since the summer before ninth grade (except video games—see Rule #5). Hobbies that took up significant time and energy, employment, and activities organized by the school or not organized at all count. Some students don't include such activities as babysitting, self-taught guitar, learning computer coding outside of school, or running a marathon. They should.

Family and work responsibilities also count. If your child is not involved in activities organized by the school, but she takes care of her younger siblings or works after school every day, no one will hold against her that she wasn't captain of three sports. She is captain of her own life. Taking on all that responsibility shows accountability, genuine leadership, and all the things admission evaluators seek.

Rule #4: Sustained interest over time impresses admission evaluators more than short-term commitments. Every activity your child does counts, but the longer she's done an activity, the more impact it's likely had on her development and on other people. In admissions-speak, "sustained interest" means the student has developed a skill, talent, or interest over time and stuck with it.

Rule #5: Video-game playing or doing anything illegal, even if it seems harmless, doesn't count. Reaching the top level in Super Mario Bros. will impress no one evaluating a college application. Nor will the report that your child has built a sizable stock portfolio when twenty-one is the state's legal minimum age for investing (though it may help you pay college tuition).

Rule #6: If your kid's activities skew disproportionately toward one area, she should own it, not try to hide it. Some students worry that they won't look well rounded because their résumé tilts in one direction, such as STEM or music. On the contrary, sometimes passion for one or two activities will make your kid stand out. If she only has space for yet another math club she loves versus that yearbook camp she attended for a week freshman year, the math club wins.

Rule #7: It's okay for your child to estimate how many hours she spent on each activity. I bring this up because some dormant quirk in many a teenage brain springs awake when the Common Application asks them to report hours spent on activities. We all know your kid did not keep a time sheet, but a critical mass of teenagers are sticklers on these numbers. You can tell your child that the best anyone can do is estimate, and she can put her calculator away. If your kid argues that you couldn't possibly know this because you don't know *anything*, she wouldn't be the first.

How much space does my child have to describe each activity?

Your kid will be adept and practiced at squeezing activity descriptions into limited space because: Twitter.

- There are ten slots under Activities on the Common Application.
- Each slot allows 50 characters (not words) for the title of the activity and the role your child plays in it. Spaces between words count as characters.
- She's also allotted 150 characters for a description.

Your child can present each activity in résumé format using résumé verbs, incomplete sentences, and ampersands to save space. Example:

Math & Engineering Team, Captain
Recruited to compete in Test of Engineering Aptitude (TEAMS). Earned top 3 in state 2017 & 2018. As captain, mentor new teammates in math & biology.

What if she participates in more than ten activities?

Every year, students upload résumés onto the Common Application and don't take the time to fill in the Activities grid, usually because they have many more than ten activities to include. Bad idea. Every admission evaluator will carefully read through the Activities section on your child's Common Application. Some evaluators might read the attached résumé. Some might skim it. It will annoy evaluators when they see that your kid attached a six-page résumé when she is only seventeen years old, yet the reader is fifty years old and has managed to squeeze the summary of her life's work onto a one-page résumé.

If she has participated in more than ten activities, your child should include the most recent, relevant, and important to her on her Common Application. Sometimes, a student can group activities into categories to squeeze more into the designated space. For example, if she's devoted small amounts of time to several community service organizations, she can cluster them into one item—"Local Community Service, Volunteer"—and then list them in her description. If a college explicitly suggests attaching a résumé, it's appropriate to submit it in addition to (but not in lieu of) completing the Activities section.

What if my kid has done only, say, four activities?

If she lives for the theater and served on tech crew for three plays, as stage manager for one, sang in the chorus for two, and played a leading role in one, theater alone could fill up four to seven spaces on her activities roster. Splitting up one activity, "theater," into its component parts, and providing more description and detail in each, can help give readers a fuller picture of your kid's world.

I heard they want "leadership," but my kid's not president or captain of anything. What to do?

Some kids were not born to found and preside over a game club at their school. Yet sometimes one of those kids becomes that awkward teenager who enters the high school office and sheepishly says to the front desk secretary, "I want to start a game club."

The office secretary has never noticed this kid because he likes to stay under the radar, but she gives the student the forms to start his club.

He brings the forms home for his mom to sign and says, "There. I founded a club. Are you happy?"

His mom says, "Now you have to advertise for members."

This kid refuses to post the flyers his mom made for him on her office photocopier. Instead, he and his friends sit in the math teacher/club advisor's classroom after school for three Thursdays while the math teacher grades homework. They play the same card game they've played together since seventh grade. On the fourth Thursday, they decide to go to one of the friends' houses instead because there are snacks. Our hero includes "Founder and Coordinator of Game Club" on his Common Application activities section and claims it continued through senior year, which is not a lie, since its three members did keep their card games going, though it's a stretch.

Who is responsible for this silliness?

I can't blame the kid. He was trying to beat the system, please his mom, and play his favorite game with his friends in peace.

I can't begrudge the Common Application for its attempt to provide colleges with a more complete picture of a student outside of the classroom.

Even though I've painted a picture of a ridiculous situation perpetrated by a parent, I cannot blame this mother either. Sure, her request went totally against the nature of her introverted child, but her motivation — as is our motivation for everything — was love. A deep, burning love seared right through her prefrontal cortex and temporarily incinerated her rational decision-making abilities.

Your child does not have to found a game club or captain a sport to be a leader. Leadership comes in many forms and often occurs naturally when two stars align: 1) sustained interest over time, and 2) sincere commitment.

Some kids love the spotlight and lead as president of their favorite club. Others quietly attend every single meeting, always volunteer for cleanup duty, and naturally become a senior leader and role model for younger members. Still others take on the job of event coordinator and enthusiastically organize one club function — like a political rally, monthly recycling collection, or an open-mike night. Any of these forms of leadership require devotion and initiative and should appear as a title in the Activities section of your child's application.

Does the order my kid lists activities matter?

Let's put it this way. I'm the admission evaluator. I've read twenty applications today, and I'm tired. I am *so* tired. I'm drinking caffeinated tea at ten thirty p.m., so I can fairly assess one more application — your child's application — before I fall asleep. I come to the Activities section and read the first couple of entries, about her ten years of private violin lessons and her four years as first chair violinist in the high school orchestra. By the time I get to the third entry on her activities list, and it's about earning accolades as a soloist in the school's select chorus, I understand. Your child is musical. When the tenth entry on her activities list reveals that she's also a co-captain of the JV soccer team, I think that's great, but I've already determined that music is her main thing. Adding her soccer leadership makes her well rounded, and it supplements her music. I prioritize her activities this way because of the order she chose to list them.

Activities most important to your child belong at the top of her list to cement them in my brain no matter how tired I am. If she didn't discover her most important activity until junior year, your child can still include that activity first and write an essay about it. Then the reader will know all about her newfound enthusiasm, which she'll continue in college.

The Writing Supplement FAQs

What exactly is a "supplement"?

If a college requires a "writing supplement," it means that after the student completes his Common Application he'll need to fill out a second application for that college. On that second application, he'll answer questions such as "What's your first choice major?" or "Is a parent or grandparent an alumnus?" Some writing supplements end there, but many request that applicants write one or more new essays specific to that individual college. When people refer to supplements, they usually mean those additional essays their kid needs to write.

- Some colleges, such as the University of Colorado, Boulder, require an additional essay about the same length as the Common Application personal essay.
- Other schools, such as Chapman University, require a handful of shorter essays.
- The majority of colleges that require a supplemental essay request one additional, school-specific essay of about 250–500 words.
- The most common supplemental essay prompt asks, "Why this college?" For example, "How did you learn about Vassar and what aspect of our college do you find appealing?"

- Some supplemental essay prompts are meant to inspire creativity. For example, a University of Texas supplemental essay prompt: "You've got a ticket in your hand—Where will you go? What will you do? What will happen when you get there?"

Some colleges don't require a writing supplement. The pro: Your child can fire off his completed Common Application to that college without any extra effort beyond signing the check for the application fee. The con: It's as easy for every other student. More students will apply just to see if they can get in, making admission statistically more competitive for your kid.

Should the writing be more formal on a supplemental essay?

All essays on an application should read like the same person wrote them, and that person should sound like your child sounds when she's having a conversation. The goal of all writing on college applications is to help the admission evaluators understand the human being behind the data.

Why bother with all the extra work of writing supplements my kid might never need?

I get it. Your kid hasn't even finalized her college list yet. By the time application deadlines come, you'll be shivering in your parka, which seems so far away on this sun-kissed summer day. So many students make the same gigantic blunder of blowing off their supplemental essays until the last minute that I feel the need to dwell on this for a moment, POV college admission evaluator. To help you understand where I'm coming from, we're going to do this *A Christmas Carol* style.

I am the Ghost of College Admissions Future, transporting you from your living room into the home office of a college admission evaluator, who sits at his Ikea desk, still wearing his pajamas at noon. On his computer screen is your child's application, which the evaluator has read all the way through, including your child's thoughtful, polished personal essay that she toiled over through nine drafts. The application concludes with a sloppy supplemental essay your kid whipped off the night of the deadline.

I'm transporting you deeper into this image, into the admission evaluator's mind. The glaring discrepancy between the two essays has given this reader pause. *Which essay reflects the student's true writing ability?* he wonders. He knows that many students solicit some form of help on their personal essays, but he thinks, *Maybe someone else altogether wrote the personal essay for this applicant. Maybe that awkward, hurried supplemental essay riddled with typos is a more accurate depiction of this student's writing and work ethic.*

I'm snapping my fingers to transport you back to your own home. Please take out a highlighter, highlight the following sentence, and stick it under your child's nose: *The supplemental essay will probably be the last part of the application the evaluator reads before making an admission decision about you.*

The evaluator you've just visited will determine whether or not your kid makes it to the Admissions Committee. It will be much easier for him to focus on the glittering gemstones in the application if your kid doesn't plop a big lump of coal where the supplemental essay should be.

Are you game for a second nocturnal visit from a Ghost of College Admissions Even Further into the Future? Here we go. I'm transporting you from your home (where your teenager scowled at that highlighted sentence you just showed him) to the room where the entire Admissions Committee is in the process of discussing your kid's application. This is where the "maybe" pile gets sorted into "yes" and "no," and where your child's supplemental essay matters much more than you may realize. Your kid is "on the bubble," meaning the committee is on the fence about him. Someone suggests, "Let's read an essay out loud to hear the student's voice." With time of the essence, guess which essay they will read right there during the committee session? The supplemental essay is usually shorter, and it's written with their specific college in mind, so you tell me.

Enough with the ghosts. Back at home, even if he doesn't plow through all of his supplements this summer, please give your child my Student Checklist for Supplemental Essay Prep (p. 178) and "suggest" (in whatever way this works in your household) that he progresses through step five before school begins.

But it's summer, and he's got a ton of AP prep work, and the pool will close soon.

Writing or preparing to write supplements now is like filling up your basement with canned goods as a safeguard before a storm. If your child's list includes colleges where he already knows he wants to apply, wouldn't it be nice to get the supplements out of the way before his senior classes ramp up into high gear?

STUDENT CHECKLIST FOR SUPPLEMENTAL ESSAY PREP

1. Log on to the website of a college to which you might apply or find the school-specific supplement requirements on the Common Application. No one is asking you to commit right now.

2. Copy the essay instructions, prompt(s), and maximum-word count for any supplemental writing required (even if it only asks you to describe an extracurricular activity in 150 words or less).

3. Paste it into a fresh Word or Google document.

4. Repeat steps 1–3 for every college you are considering. Collect all the supplemental prompts and paste them into the same doc you just created, so they exist in one place that's easily accessible. You might feel immediate relief when you see there's some overlap among the prompts.

5. Brainstorm a few ideas for essay topics for each and jot them down beneath the prompts. No matter what frame of mind you're in when you return to this document, you'll have a place to start.

6. Ideally, write a draft of one "Why this college?" essay to use as a guideline for others, since it's the most common prompt.

7. In my wildest dreams, write a draft of an essay in response to one of the more creative prompts on the list, as a template. The topic should highlight something new about you that doesn't appear in other parts of your application.

8. I will perform cartwheels in celebration if you carve out enough time to complete all your supplemental essays this summer. (I will do some hopeful stretching.) You'll turn cartwheels too when you see your classmates cranking out their supplements while in the midst of midterm exams in the fall.

What's the difference between an Arts Supplement and a Writing Supplement?

The Arts Supplement is designed to showcase a student's talent in music, art, film, theater, dance, or creative writing. Preparing one can take some effort, especially if it requires photos for visual arts, or recordings or videos for performing arts. Colleges' guidelines differ, and they use various submission platforms. Learn requirements from the Common Application and college websites, and if possible, start pulling those materials together now. If not, once school begins, your kid can request his teachers' help.

The Additional Information Opportunity (or Temptation)

In the Additional Information section, the Common Application invites students to submit whatever information they couldn't fit anywhere else, and it causes all sorts of confusion. If your child does include something in this section, he should do so as succinctly as possible. Guidelines for using this space:

- *Leaving this section blank will not count against a student in admissions.* It is not a missed opportunity if she has nothing substantive to add. More is not always better.
- This section provides space for a maximum of 650 words, but it's not an invitation to upload a second personal essay because your child is nervous that leaving something blank will count against her (it will not), or she wrote two essays and couldn't decide which one to submit (a supplement might present an opportunity to use parts of it).
- Up to 300 words should be sufficient to describe anything important to your kid that she couldn't convey elsewhere. As an example, if a college doesn't require a supplemental essay and offers a specific program that intrigues your child, she can

convey that in Additional Information (as long as she remembers to delete it before sending details written exclusively for one college to another).

- We've already covered that exhaustive résumés are not encouraged or helpful here. However, if a college requests or suggests an added résumé, that's different. Upload one of a reasonable length for a seventeen-year-old here if the college does not offer a space for it elsewhere.

- Explain why the college received numerous transcripts, and their chronology. It will save the admission evaluator time figuring out that the student participates in dual enrollment with a local college or that he switched schools, and why. The evaluator will dedicate that extra time to reading other parts of the application more carefully, while in the background, good vibes about your kid for making the reader's job easier will play like euphonious strings on an angel's harp.

- If disciplinary action was taken against your kid, an explanation is required. The place to upload this explanation appears in the Writing section of the Common Application, under the subhead of Disciplinary History, not here. However, while we're on the subject, if your child committed a serious crime or blatantly plagiarized, she can express remorse and vow never to do it again. If she was caught with beer in the mini-fridge in her boarding school dorm room (with no intention of drinking it, as I've read on multiple applications), the misdemeanor will require an explanation, but it will not figure heavily into an admission decision at most colleges unless your kid blames others instead of owning her mistake.

- Scheduling conflicts are common and worth noting. As an example, your child might have dropped down a level in Spanish junior year because the only Spanish honors section met at the same time as AP Calculus, not because she desired less academic rigor.

- Your child can upload a scientific abstract here if she participated in scientific research.

- Using this section to explain a poor grade will rarely reflect well on your child. Even if that C– in English sophomore year haunts her, and even if that teacher was a notoriously hard grader, highlighting it here will only draw attention to it. Your kid's guidance counselor can explain a blemish on a student's academic record without sounding whiny. If applicable, add this to your list of topics to bring up when you meet with the counselor in the fall.

SUMMER'S END

In August, as the light changes from bright yellow to gold, you can feel the summer winding down. The longest day of the year has passed, but with camps done, and the lake water at its warmest, it's family time. Enjoy the last hurrah of barbecues, beach days, and walking to the end of the driveway barefoot to collect the newspaper. If you feel sorry for your kid (and yourself) because she has to go back to school so soon, pity the poor kids in Texas, whose school started weeks ago. Remember to relish the small pleasures—cutting flowers in the garden, cooking with fresh, ripe local tomatoes, a dip in the swimming pool. Savor it all before the gates of hell swing open in the fall of senior year. Scout's honor, we will prevent you from entering the seventh circle.

TO-DO LIST

- ☐ Help your teenager budget time for indoor activities such as taking that August SAT, finishing that AP summer work, and filling out the Common Application even though it's the last thing either of you wants to do on an eighty-degree beach day.
- ☐ After you've budgeted time for college-related activities, relinquish the responsibility of completing them to your

kid. She has access to the same calendar you do, and your constant needling will ruin what's left of the summer for both of you. (See Strategy #1: Do-It-Yourself Nagging on p. 148 as a reminder that trial and big honking error make me the best possible person to impart this advice.)

- ☐ When she's not working, let her play.
- ☐ Let yourself play.
- ☐ Alert your child that now is a good time to ask for that recommendation from her summer boss to show colleges how responsible and personable she is.
- ☐ Help your child pull together her art portfolio, athletic reel, or other supplementary materials, if she asks.
- ☐ If she doesn't ask, have another cocktail, and encourage her to work with school staff when the school year begins.
- ☐ Stock up on your beverage of choice for fall of senior year.

PART V

FALL OF SENIOR YEAR

FIVE DINNER TABLE TOPICS OTHER THAN COLLEGE

1. If you could take part in one historical event, which would you choose? (Educational)

2. What circus act would you most want to perform? (Self-esteem building, especially if your kid chooses lion tamer.)

3. What sentimental item would you rescue if the house caught on fire? (Reassure your kid this is hypothetical.)

4. If you had a windfall of $250,000, what would you do with it? (Do not mention that this is the amount you'd save if he chose not to attend college, after all.)

5. Is kindness learned or genetic? (Feel free to take credit no matter what the consensus.)

Chapter 9

September

Your kid enters the house after her first day of school as a high school senior, and you ask, "How was your day?"

This sets off a five-alarm fire of "OMG, Muh-ther, can't you just leave me in peace for one minute?" Your kid grabs the jar of peanut butter and a spoon, stomps upstairs, disappears into her room, and the door slams shut.

If you are anything like me, you're left alone in the kitchen, staring at the refrigerator, trying to figure out *What just happened? Have I failed as a parent?*

You have not failed! You've done so many things right to raise this healthy, spirited child for no compensatory paycheck or even a thank-you much of the time. At the start of the thirteenth and final academic year your kid will spend under your roof, I think recognition is in order and long overdue.

I hereby present you with the Medal of Parenting Valor. While your child sulks upstairs behind the locked door of her room, envision yourself mounting an Olympic podium. The American flag unfurls above you. You bow your head as I drape the gleaming, golden Medal of Parenting Valor you've earned around your neck. Now lift your head and stand up straight and proud. That's right. Chin up, shoulders back. Feel the weight of that medal tug at your neck, and wave at the cheering crowd as the first notes of "The Star-Spangled Banner" swell from the loudspeaker and Beyoncé starts singing. Place a hand over your heart, the heart that you've more or less ripped out of your body and presented on so many occasions to that child upstairs splayed on her unmade bed, probably tweeting about how you *interrogated* her the *minute* she stepped into the house.

Yes, you have made mistakes, but you have done your best by your kid, who will have forgotten your annoying question by dinnertime.

Lift that Medal of Parenting Valor to your lips and kiss it periodically when the scene in the kitchen repeats itself and you feel worn out, which will surely happen often during the next several months.

'TIS THE APPLICATION SEASON

Jolliness is not usually the prevailing emotion.

Why am I feeling so anxious about college when I'm not the one applying?

Let's begin with the environmental stressors. Over the summer, you could surround yourself with safe people in the sanctuary of backyard barbecues. You could enjoy a three-month hiatus from Lucy's mom telling you (again) how Lucy was accepted to the most selective, prestigious, competitive, top-tier summer program ever to grace Planet Earth. Now that school has started up again, you cannot avoid the Lucy's moms of this world, or any of those other jittery parents at the school's open house. They will not stop humble-bragging about their kids, or dropping names of prestigious colleges they've visited, or asking, "Where is your kid applying to college?" You know they're only anxious, and you don't want to be mean, but they just will. Not. Stop.

The stress may be bad for you, but your kid's got it worse.

At those parent events, you can sidle into the back row and scoot out early. At work, you can look at your watch and say to that busybody co-worker obsessed with college rankings, "Oh gosh, look at the time! I'd better get going to my meeting." That meeting may be with yourself, locked in a bathroom stall, possibly crying, but still. When you've got to go, *you get to go.*

Not so for your poor child. She must take a deep breath, stride into the high school, where college talk has peaked, and remain there *by law* for almost seven hours every day. Parents at PTO meetings behave like Buddhist monks compared to the nervous kids assembled in AP classes. No matter what classes your kid takes, she's inside the fishbowl, sure to hear about that guy's perfect SAT scores, or that girl's perfect grades, or nonstop speculation about who will or won't get in where.

This might explain why your child performs some rendition of that kitchen drama I recently described, and why, though it's not fair to you, it's a compliment in its own distorted way. Creds to you that your child considers her home and family a safety zone for release after a harrowing day in the school building. When it feels like she's pushing you away, she probably needs your sympathy and support the most, so try your best not to take any of her histrionics personally. Apply the Zen (a.k.a. Don't Be a Hater) approach that we learned last spring (p. 112), and mentally resist your kid's advances. Remember that whatever abuse your kid flings at you has nothing to do with you or your parenting. If she won't tolerate your hugs and soothing words, offering ice cream is always an option. Or better yet:

Inhale.

Exhale.

Inhale.

Exhale.

Inhale.

Exhale.

Why is everyone so insanely competitive?

Competition: *active demand by two or more organisms for some environmental resource in short supply.*

We've already established that the USA alone houses more than 4,600 four-year colleges with plenty of thin, lumpy mattresses and mediocre dining hall food for all the kids who want to enroll. There's no shortage of resources. Yet an atmosphere of cutthroat competition permeates the air surrounding college admissions, fueled by too many sources to cover here. If I may, I'd like to address a couple of the biggest culprits because knowledge is power, and empowering you is the goal of this support group.

The Toxic Impact of College Rankings

Whether you've treated college rankings as gospel or feel like plugging your ears and screaming when someone brings up "top-tier" colleges, here's your public service announcement: The media *invented* those tiers.

The mother of all college rankings, the *U.S. News and World Report*, stopped circulating their weekly print news magazine a decade ago. ("Cash flow problems" were mentioned on their website.) Their "rankings products" (that's what they call them) are the only periodicals the *U.S. News and World Report* prints on paper anymore. I'm sure you've noticed that other print and online publications have also figured out that college-ranking lists sell magazines and attract eyeballs online.

The flaws in these rankings are widely documented. I invite you to Google this. You'll find volumes on the subject. Still, there's no avoiding the influence of rankings because people pay attention to them. How can they help it? I've seen the *U.S. News and World Report's* annual *Best Colleges* publication displayed in the grocery checkout line beside the *National Enquirer.* Colleges ranked in the "top 10" or "top 100" have achieved celebrity status right up there with the Kardashians. Your kid's senior year, with her applications looming, you may hear more about those top-ranked, top-tier "best colleges" than you'll hear about Kanye and Kim.

The Prestige Factor

Prestige: (the original French definition) *conjuror's trick, illusion.*

The clamor by many for acceptance to a few prestigious colleges, usually clustered at the top of those ranking lists, also compounds the college admissions frenzy. I can't possibly tackle all the reasons here. If you tell people you went to Stanford, you'll likely get a different reaction than if you'd told them you went to Humboldt State, and you might have feelings about that. If your father told you thirty years ago he refused to pay for college unless you went to MIT, your kid's college admissions process may stir up all sorts of emotions I can't even imagine. I cannot say that prestige doesn't matter or shouldn't matter to you, but I can highlight some realities that may make it matter a little less.

- *Your kid can get a top-quality or lousy education at a prestigious college.* Your child won't land at a prestigious university (or any university) and receive an intravenous drip of quality education. The quality of your kid's education is up to her.
- *All of the brightest minds do not congregate in only a few ivory towers.* The same adjunct professor might teach at a prestigious college one semester and a community college the next. (I did.) High-achieving and brilliant students attend a wide variety of colleges and universities for a wide variety of reasons.
- *Graduating from a top-tier college has little to do with admission into a top-tier graduate school in most fields.* As an example, the straight-A college student who scores highest on the MCAT will make the strongest candidate, no matter where she attended college as an undergraduate.
- *A prestigious college is not the only route to a successful career.* In most industries, and for all second (and third) jobs, experience and interpersonal skills are much more important than alma mater. "Education" sinks to the bottom of our résumés as work experience accumulates for a reason.
- *Getting into a prestigious college is not the only road to riches.* Many colleges you may never have heard of have strong alumni networks that can help your kid land a great job, and so can the network your child already has through your family.

Gauging the Effect of College Admissions Fever on You and Your Kid

The bombardment by college admissions mania started when our kids were born. We can't help but absorb at least some of it. If it has always felt important that your child attends a prestigious, highly ranked college, you are perfectly normal, but it's worth taking a moment to ask yourself why you want this so badly for your kid. Is it because...

- you know how badly your kid wants this for himself?
- he's worked so hard for all these years that he deserves it?
- you believe your child will get a better education at a prestigious university?
- you had a good experience and made great friends at a prestigious school and want the same for your child?
- you've heard how important college name recognition is for his future?
- you don't want people to think your kid's not smart because he attends a college no one has ever heard of?
- you can just picture the look on Aunt Birdie's face when you tell her your kid was accepted to a top-ranked school?

If prestige is deeply important to your child, that's totally out of your hands. If it is deeply important to *you*, you might not realize how badly your child wants to make this happen for you, even if it's totally out of *his* hands. What if he can't get in? What if he disappoints you, or *feels* like he's disappointing you?

Dr. Appy explains how this all plays out:

- *Students apply to colleges for the parents and not for themselves.*
- *They can often feel as though they are disappointing their parents if they don't get in.*
- *If they do get in, they feel pressure to go because it's what the parents want, but it is not necessarily the right fit.*
- *I hear in therapy sessions, "I am here at ABC University because my parents wanted me to come here, but I don't like it and I'm afraid to tell them."*

Even if you're pretty sure you've said nothing out loud about your lofty dreams and aspirations for your kid, he knows. And even if your kid has never said out loud that he cares what you think, or he's told you outright that he *doesn't* care what you think, he cares.

I care too. This is one of those times when I reassure you. We all know what you really want most is what's best for your child. I already gave you the Medal of Parenting Valor, and I meant it. No college's name is engraved upon it. The entire endeavor of parenting does not culminate in your kid's acceptance into the most prestigious, highest-tier college, despite the hype. I hope it provides you with some relief to know you have already crushed it, and your kid hasn't even applied to college yet.

The Six-Step Competition Detox Plan

Let's take these six simple steps to rid the country (or at least ourselves) of college admissions fever together!

1. *Forgive yourself.* Treat yourself with gentleness and compassion, the way you'd treat a dear, lifelong friend. No matter what you've been thinking, feeling, or doing since your child's college search began, you've caused no irreparable damage.
2. *Forgive other parents their trespasses.* Does this sound familiar?
3. *Build community with other parents* accompanying you on this path. Commiserate about the very real pain you feel, and then laugh about it. (I will not be offended if you use my gaffes as the butt of your jokes. I'm here to help.)
4. *Stay busy with your own life.* When you start to stress out, refocus on things you enjoy—whether they're healthy and sporty or lazy and decadent—as an antidote for that lonely, tense, ashamed, out of control feeling that consumes souls during the college admissions process.
5. *Practice self-care* to soothe yourself. Some people take a walk in the woods. Some meditate or pray. You do whatever helps relieve your own anxiety.
6. *Model calm, rational, supportive behavior for your kid.* Once you conquer the frenzy within, you will be in a better position to help

your child. Remind him that being himself and trying not to worry about what other people think is the most effective path toward thriving in college admissions and everything else.

ED OR EA OR RD, OH MY!

WHEN AND HOW STUDENTS SUBMIT COLLEGE APPLICATIONS

How to apply	Is admission binding?	When to apply (approximately)	When will the college notify my kid?	When must my kid decide if she will attend?	How many applications can my kid submit?
Early Decision (ED)	Yes	Nov 1–15	Mid-Dec	Upon application	1 ED, multiple EA
Early Action (EA)	No	Oct–mid-Nov	Mid-Dec	May 1	Multiple
Restrictive Early Action (REA)	No	Nov 1–15	Mid-Dec	May 1	1 REA, 0 ED, multiple *public* EA
Early Decision 2 (ED2)	Yes	Jan 1–15	Mid-Feb	Upon application	1 ED2, multiple RD
Regular Decision (RD)	No	Jan 1–15	Mid-March–April 1	May 1	Multiple
Rolling Admission (Rolling)	No	July–Feb (varies)	About 4–12 weeks after applying	Varies, often May 1	Multiple
Open Enrollment	No	Anytime	Immediately	Immediately	Multiple

Okay, now you have your chart of the whens and hows of application submission. All of the abbreviations can become confusing, so to simplify, your kid will only need to make two major decisions this fall:

1. Will she apply for an *early* deadline (around November 1) or on the *regular* deadline (around January 1)?
2. Will she make a *binding* commitment to a college the minute she applies, or not?

The Decisions Your Kid Will Need to Make
in September and October

Early Decision (ED)

If your kid prefers one college she's positive she would love to attend over all others, she can apply ED. Once she signs an ED agreement, there are no take-backs or second guesses. If she's accepted, she must enroll. It's all good if she's certain about this. Some colleges accept 30% or more of their class ED, so if your kid is all in, you know you can cover the cost, and she can manage the November deadline, she should go for it. Her greatest gift for the holidays will be decompression from college admissions stress, if she's admitted.

Stop her if your kid's only planning to apply ED because a friend, relative, counselor, or (gulp) you persuaded her that it would give her a better chance of getting into somewhere "good." Most students are not ready to pledge themselves to a college or to present a polished application so soon. So many ED applicants hail from specialized groups, such as legacy and athletes, that for most applicants, the acceptance rate is nearly the same as if they'd waited. Plus, the giant, controversial negative of ED: A financial aid offer (or estimate) arrives with the acceptance, and "You get what you get and you don't get upset," as my kids' preschool teachers used to say. Colleges are criticized because ED excludes many students who cannot afford to make a decision without comparing financial aid packages. The critics are not wrong.

Early Action (EA)

Your kid applies in September or October (early), and learns the outcome in December, but she can postpone her decision until May (not binding). Do not minimize the power of the warm, fuzzy feeling of being desired. Students have four months to envision themselves at the college that *wants* them as they wait for notifications from others, and they're more likely to enroll. It's awfully nice to have an acceptance in your pocket early on, but discourage your kid from applying to a college where she wouldn't apply if it weren't one of the few that offered EA. Some schools accept a very small percentage of applicants EA, and an early rejection can feel as bad as an early acceptance feels good.

Restrictive Early Action (REA, a.k.a. Single-Choice Early Action)

REA is offered by a handful of extremely selective universities. Your child can apply early and learn if he got in early, but it's not a binding decision. That's all the same as EA. Yet he cannot apply anywhere that *is* binding, or submit EA applications to any *private* colleges. No, your child cannot apply ED to one college and REA to another and hope no one notices. His high school will only submit his transcript to one ED or REA college choice.

Rolling Admission

The college welcomes applications as early as July and then continues to accept them, and respond to each within a few weeks, until the freshman class is full. Some colleges' admissions keep on rolling throughout the summer after your child's senior year. I hope it gives you a sense of security to know that no matter what happens, *there are always options.* The sooner your kid applies and decides to attend in this first-come-first-served process, the higher her placement in queues for scholarship consideration, the housing lottery, class registration, etc. The downside: Rolling admission is nonbinding, but if she applies too early, some schools will force your kid to decide whether or not she'll attend before she hears back from other colleges.

The Decisions Your Kid Won't Need to Make Until November and December

Regular Decision (RD)

Despite the uptick in early applications in recent years, *RD is still the way most students apply to college.* On or around January 1, students submit a handful of applications and hear back around April 1. Students then have a month to compare and contrast admission and financial aid offers until May 1, National College Decision Day, a great day to celebrate but, unfortunately, not a bank holiday. (You still have to go to work.) A big plus: Multiple acceptances with financial aid options will give you negotiating power (see p. 259). Another big plus: For the student who had a slow start to high school, adding a whole semester of senior-year grades to the transcript can help raise his GPA before colleges see it.

Early Decision 2 (ED2)

ED and ED2 are the only binding application options. The difference between them is the timing. The "early" part of ED2 is misleading because your kid actually applies on the regular deadline, at the same time RD applications are due. However, the notification comes early — in February, about a month and a half before colleges release RD notifications. This might not sound like a big deal to you, but remember, we're operating on teenager time.

Beware: After a deferral or denial from their ED choice, some students become so fearful that they pick an ED2 option at random, without thinking through the binding nature of the commitment. This happened to one of my students who felt coerced by a pushy high school guidance counselor. After she was admitted ED 2, this kid could not turn back.

FALL MEETINGS

How to Milk the Counselor for All She's Worth (and She's Worth a Lot!) at the Fall Meeting

- The counselor's expertise can help your child revise her college list based on new grades and test scores since last spring.
- If your kid's college list is still not realistic, *let the counselor be the bad guy.*

- Gather information about available financial help. The counselor might know which colleges are usually generous with merit aid; or she might know about unusual scholarships, like the Tall Club's Scholarship or the one for the best duct-tape prom dress. (I swear on my life these exist.)
- Learn if the high school offers application writing help, such as essay workshops (or a direct line to a local therapist).
- Bring up your kid's unique qualities for the counselor's recommendation. The counselor's busy, and she'll appreciate information that saves her time, but tread lightly. She'll become justifiably annoyed if she intuits you're stepping over the line from helpful to telling her what to write.
- Now's the time to bring up concerns like an aberrant poor grade, a class scheduling conflict, or anything else you hope the counselor will address in her letter.

The Fall Family Meeting

True to form, my daughter announced an hour before our fall family college-planning meeting (scheduled two weeks in advance) that she had a conflict. Her need to meet her friend Lydia at the frozen yogurt shop had conflicted with our family meeting the previous spring, and now we were working around Lydia's tight window of opportunity to go for a run. After the run, my daughter would need to take a quick shower and rush to a party (that she'd learned about through Snapchat four and a half minutes prior). She was sure I could understand our meeting would need to be postponed. It was a tight turnaround.

Of course, I understood the allure of a run and a party, I assured her, but her father and I did not have mental telepathy regarding her college plans. I stood my ground. With the phones in airplane mode and wine chilling in the fridge for afterward, we powered on with our disgruntled teenager and our originally scheduled programming and charted the course for the rest of her application process.

AGENDA FOR A SENIOR FALL FAMILY MEETING

The tools you will need: your college-planning spreadsheet or worksheet, calendar, computer search engine, patience, and sense of humor. Questions to ask your child:

WHERE TO APPLY: REVIEW THE COLLEGE LIST

- Are any colleges a definite no? If so, press the delete key.
- Can you share good reasons for colleges to remain on your list? Fill them in on the spreadsheet.
- Do you have a broad enough range of foundation, target, and reach schools?
- Would you be happy to attend any of these colleges?

WHEN TO APPLY

- Do some colleges stand out more than others for you? Rank colleges in terms of *your* criteria, not the *U.S. News and World Report*'s.
- If you're thinking about applying ED to a college, would you like to visit again to make sure? If so, let's register for a visit right now.

SCHEDULING

- Do you know if representatives from colleges you're thinking about will visit your high school this fall? Check the school's website now, and add those visits to the calendar.
- Do any colleges of interest require or recommend an interview? If so, let's schedule one!
- Are you happy with your standardized test scores in light of your college list, or would you like to try testing one last time? If so, let's schedule a test.
- Have you recorded on our calendar every deadline your school has supplied for requesting and submitting application materials? If not, let's do that now.

PLANNING A UNITED RESPONSE TO THE QUESTION

- People will ask with increased frequency where you're applying to college. What should we share? If you're not sure, we can go over some options.

FALL COLLEGE VISIT AND REVISIT FAQS

In fall, college tourism fires up again—round two of the tours, info sessions, cookies, and anxious parents and kids side-eyeing each other. Admissions offices open on Saturdays to accommodate the crowds. That's all fine and good, but it's not like your kid has nothing better to do than college shop. Even missing one class period could mean hours of catch-up.

Is it worth my child missing a whole day of school for college visits?

If he has to miss something important like a test, forget about it. By now, all of the campuses are starting to blend together, right? I mean, they all have a library, a gym, and that recently renovated dorm they make sure to include on the tour. It's a different story if your kid visited during the summer and he thinks he might want to apply ED. Then it makes good sense to visit while the campus is populated and he can sit in on a class, but it is still not worth skipping school to visit a campus close enough for your kid to visit on a Saturday.

Is it worth it for my kid to miss a class when a college representative visits the high school?

During the fall semester, colleges send representatives to high schools across the country. They present sales pitches in the form of mini–info sessions to seniors deciding where to apply. It is absolutely worth your kid missing C period this one time if a representative from a college of interest visits his school. Demonstrated interest? Check. Scootch a little closer for the inside scoop. That regional representative visiting your kid's school will almost certainly be one of the evaluators of your child's application. It's worth your kid missing one class period to meet him.

Is an overnight visit worth the potentially awkward sleepover with a stranger or premature introduction to who knows what?

Many people I respect believe overnight visits are a great idea. Your child can eat in the dining hall, attend a class, speak with a professor, experience the social scene, cheer at a sporting event, and develop a more in-depth feel for the school. I can see the benefits and allure of roaming a campus like a native for a full twenty-four hours.

Though a good litmus test for some, overnight visits are not for everyone. A shy kid set up through an admissions office with some stranger could feel very uncomfortable. If it's a weekend, we all know what many teenagers do to blow off steam and loosen themselves up to socialize. I'm not saying your teenager would party hardy during an unsupervised overnight, but she will have no control whatsoever over what those other students do. And what exactly are the accommodations when your kid sleeps over in a double or triple dorm room in the freshman quad? A sleeping bag on the floor? At the foot of the bed, stuffed between desk legs and a beer keg? For the reluctant kid, a full day's visit might be enough.

Should I indulge in or put the kibosh on that plane trip to a distant college?

I wanted to hug my daughter's high school counselor when she suggested my kid pay a February visit to that college in Minnesota she'd adored in July. I would've shelled out the money for my daughter's plane fare in this case, but that doesn't mean you have to. Here's the rule of thumb. If you're within a few hours' drive of a college, your kid should show up if at all possible. If a college visit requires a plane flight, no one will expect her to splurge on the travel. Follow your gut. Let her go if you can afford it and believe a visit is important. If not, refuse to pay for the plane ticket.

FINALIZING THE COLLEGE LIST

How many are too many? How many are enough?

Clients ask me all the time how many colleges should end up on a final list. Ultimately, it depends on the kid and it doesn't really matter what I think, but I'm not one to hold back. So let's do the numbers.

Stating the Obvious

In 2018, a North Carolina senior was accepted to 113 colleges. For this kid, applying to college must have been a full-time job, likely with an entourage of support staff. I can't even imagine what her poor parents must have gone through. I hope it's obvious that applying to this many colleges is over the top. On the other end of the spectrum, applying to one college, assuming your child will be admitted there, is a risky plan. So somewhere in between 1 and 113 is a good place to start.

The Numbers from Professionals and Parents Who Have Been There

As a reminder, the three categories we're using for your kid's college list are foundation, target, and reach schools (see p. 99).

- My friend whose child included the least number of colleges on his list: 3 EA (2 foundation + 1 reach) + 1 rolling (foundation) = **4 total.** She reported that her child's senior year was very relaxing, with the exception of AP Calculus.
- Suzanne Buchsbaum, a private educational planner (formerly of the Lawrenceville School, and part-time at Princeton University and Williams College admissions), tailors all her advice to each individual student but generally advises 3 foundation + 3 target + 3 reach = **9 total.**
- I'm both a professional and a parent, and I'm with Buchsbaum — the numbers vary from student to student. Overall, I've found

that **6–10 total** hits the sweet spot for many students, broken down into 2–3 foundation + 2–4 target + 2–3 reach.

- The public school college counselor and revered guru at my kids' school told a crowd of parents she used to say 8 college applications were plenty, but she'd upped that number to **12 total.**
- My friend whose child applied to the most colleges: 1 ED (reach/denied) + 25 RD (1 foundation + 24 reach) = **26 total.** Want to guess where her child ended up attending college? She shared that all those last-minute supplements almost killed the family. Her advice: "Narrow down the list to realistic options, and then don't wait to see what happens before completing RD applications."

The Dos and Don'ts of Parent Input When Building a College List

The cardinal rule for parent input: *Always remember who is going to college.*

- Do make sure all colleges that captivate your kid are on that list. No secret wishes. No would've or could've regrets.
- Do suggest any additional colleges you think should go on the list. Then if your kid vetoes them, let them go.
- Do listen to her reasoning but try to talk her out of applying to a disproportionate number of reach schools she's heard are "good." If she insists, add them to the list anyway because this is not a battle worth fighting. When she sees how much work she'll have to put into the writing supplements, she'll probably eliminate half of them anyway.
- Do make sure to record all application deadlines on the college calendar. Your kid really should do this herself, but it won't hurt anyone if you help with time management a little bit longer.
- Do feel free to call the financial aid office with your questions. They're expecting you.

- Do remind your child to share her college list with her recommenders. She should make it easy for them to submit their recommendations. Teach her to treat recommenders well (see p. 203), so when she needs to request recommendations for that big internship or her first job, she'll know exactly what to do.
- Don't call college admissions offices as your kid's representative. Your kid may be shy, but colleges expect students to be in charge of their own college application process by now.
- Don't make the mistake of encouraging your kid to apply to a school you can't afford because you think she (or you) will feel good if she gets in. This will backfire. Whether she gets in and can't go or doesn't get in and feels bad, it's a lose-lose situation.
- Don't err on the side of letting your kid apply to 113 colleges. It's masochistic.
- Don't try to control whether or where she'll apply ED. If you think you cannot resist, recall the cardinal rule and try harder.

Dr. Appy's advice:

It is so important that students take ownership and feel good about their choice. If it's successful and they choose the perfect school for them, great! What a wonderful self-esteem builder. If they make a mistake and don't really like it, that's fine too. What a wonderful opportunity to learn that you can make mistakes and then, with help, figure out how to fix them.

The college admissions officer Erika Blauth explains:

It's important for parents to engage in the process but to stay securely in the passenger's seat, coming along for the student's ride and providing support only as needed. If the student isn't taking ownership of the process, then the best thing parents can do is find some ways to help their student climb more squarely into the driver's seat instead of simply grabbing the wheel when their child swerves a little.

STUDENT CHECKLIST FOR TREATING RECOMMENDERS RIGHT

1. Input your college list onto whatever computer platform your high school uses to show the guidance counselor where to send your transcript and recommendations.

2. If you asked an additional recommender to write a letter on your behalf, research on each college's website if and in what form the college will accept recommendations beyond those required.

3. Gather a list of email addresses or prepare stamped envelopes addressed to the proper recipient at each college, *with their names spelled correctly,* and hand deliver the email list or envelopes to the additional recommender.

4. Ask your recommenders if they need anything from you, like a résumé or info about other classes you're taking, to make their job easier. (As an aside, you can also ask your parents if they need anything from you about a half an hour before dinner tonight to make *their* job easier.)

5. After you submit each application, check your student status page created by the college. If a recommendation has not landed there within a week after the deadline, send a polite reminder email to the recommender that sounds totally different from what you call "nagging" when it comes from your parents.

6. Thank your recommenders profusely every chance you get because that is likely all the compensation they'll receive for going to bat for you.

TO-DO LIST

☐ Talk about any topic except college at the dinner table.
☐ Back in the fishbowl of school, you and your kid must keep calm and carry on.

☐ If you feel the college admissions vortex sucking you in, do a competition detox (see p. 191).

☐ Missing a little school for college visits and revisits is okay, and sometimes advisable. Register now for those visits to colleges and info sessions when college representatives visit the high school.

☐ Communicate with your kid via meetings (or in whatever manner possible).

☐ ED/EA decisions need to be made in September and October for November first-ish deadlines.

☐ Beware sneaky, unusually early application deadlines (like October 1 for the University of Texas), and mark them on the calendar.

☐ You'll pay a late fee but can still sign your kid up for last-chance testing for ED/EA applications.

☐ Sign up for November or December testing for RD applications.

☐ Remind your kid to keep track of recommendations and to express gratitude for anyone aiding and abetting her college applications.

☐ Schedule time for sports, coffees with friends, and other distractions from your kid's college application process (daily, if possible).

Chapter 10

October

We left off in August, when I—as well as my beloved, valued, extremely debonair, and talented husband (who so graciously reads everything I write…did I mention he is handsome?)—had lost all credibility in our daughter's eyes after the inconsistent feedback on her essay attempts. By the time the school year had begun, my students had long since finished their essays, but not my daughter. I tried to appear calm, though I was not feeling it, all the way up to five days before her first application was due, when my daughter announced that her essay was done and asked me to do a final proofreading.

The lesson: I had watched my daughter throughout high school pound out papers the morning they were due, but she always submitted them on time. If I threatened she couldn't attend a party until she straightened up her room, she waited until twenty minutes before that party to rush around throwing balled-up sweaters into her closet, saying, "Now you are making me late for the party!" but she straightened it. When she had a doctor's appointment, I'd yell up the stairs, "Come on, we're going to be late!" until I thought the veins in my neck might burst, yet we still always made it to the doctor's office in the nick of time for every appointment. *So what made me think my kid would approach her college essays any differently?* Take heed. For some people, racing a deadline is as exhilarating as an adventure sport. By now you know if your child is one of those people. Adjust expectations accordingly.

SUBMITTING APPLICATIONS

Nailing Deadlines

If your kid plans to apply anywhere early, we're nearing his deadlines, but *you are not behind.* If he's not planning to apply anywhere until January 1, your child's deadlines will appear soon enough, and this is your preview.

It's just business.

Do I enjoy filling out forms and sending money to the College Board? I most certainly do not, but I also don't enjoy paying my electric bill on deadline or filling out my tax forms (then paying the taxes). I do it because it's part of the imperfect infrastructure in place to make my lights turn on and to clear the snow off the roads I must travel to pick up my son from school because he did not wear boots, even though I told him explicitly, "Wear boots! It's going to snow!" before he left for school in the morning.

We are dealing with businesses here, with their requisite paper-work, money exchanges, and deadlines. Think of college applications as your kid's first major business transaction. You preside as his first boss. Good bosses patiently mentor. Good bosses don't lose their temper, grab their employee's pen, and do the work for him.

Keeping Track of Everything (and I Mean Everything)

It boggles the mind to think about how busy your kid must feel right now, but application deadlines wait for no one. We've introduced tools to help you keep track of all the moving parts, including ideas for a shared college calendar (see p. 95), a worksheet template (see p. 98), and Debbie's Dazzling Spreadsheet (see jillshulman.com). I'm adding a simple college application checklist (see p. 208). Personally, I am proud to report that I've completely converted from the paper calendar I used for my daughter's college admissions process to a shared Google calendar for my son's. I am a Luddite no more, though I still use paper for some tasks. Regardless of your chosen tool(s), add the following dates now:

- Scheduled college visits and interviews
- The last possible day to visit or interview at a college of interest
- Deadlines for every application due ED, RD, or other
- *If your kid's a last-minute Charlie, include warnings on the calendar a couple of days before each college's deadline*
- The deadline to *request* test scores so they make it to colleges on time (it takes testing companies about two seconds to accept your money but you'd better allow two weeks for those scores to arrive at their destinations)
- The high school's deadline for your kid to *request* a transcript and recommendations
- Deadlines for supplementary materials (transcript, recommendations, art portfolio, financial aid application, etc.) to *arrive* at each college, if it's different from the application deadline
- The date each college says they'll post notifications

Steps Students Must Take to Submit Applications (and When Parents Come in Handy)

1. The student will have his own password, and he'll log on to the Common Application (or another application site).
2. Your kid must make sure that he's input all his college choices to the Common Application, as well as whatever platform the high school uses to send out transcripts and recommendations. No typos on his social security number or variations on his name. If he included his middle initial on his SAT registration, he must include it on every form now. Not to sound alarmist, but any inconsistencies will send the system into chaos, and all of his applications will end up incomplete.
3. Hopefully, he's already filled in the information on the personal and family sections, but if not, he might call upon you to inform him where you went to college, what year you graduated, and how old is his sister again?

COLLEGE APPLICATION CHECKLIST

Here's my template using fake colleges as examples.

College	Utopia University (example)	Heavenly College (example)					
Deadline	11/1	11/15					
Common App	X	X					
Supplement	X	X					
Transcript	X						
Counselor rec	X						
Teacher rec 1	X						
Teacher rec 2	X						
Optional rec	X	X					
Test scores	X	X					
App fee	X $50.00	$75.00					
FAFSA	X	X					
CSS profile	X	X					

4. If he's written but hasn't uploaded his essays and activities and he uploads them now, he has to proofread them again once they're up on the Common Application site, where glitches occur regularly. Turn the page for horror stories. If he's wise, he will ask you or someone else to proofread them, too, at which point remember that *proofreading is not line editing* (see Guidelines for Appropriate Proofreading on p. 156).

5. The Common Application will lead your child to the Writing Supplement for each college that requires one. More uploading and proofreading ensues.

6. Before sending each application, your child can make changes on the Common Application (including the personal essay), if desired. As his trusty proofreader, you'll want to remind him to delete the part of his Additional Information paragraph directed at Rensselaer Polytechnic Institute before sending it to Georgia Tech.

7. Plan to remove your credit card from your wallet at this point and have it on hand for the last three steps.

8. The Common Application will require money in exchange for the privilege of submitting applications (anywhere from the average fee of $50 per application to $90, if your kid's applying to Stanford). At this point, you'll more fully understand why narrowing down the college list is a good idea.

9. If your child is submitting an art portfolio, the Common Application will direct you to Submittable or another submission platform that will provide separate instructions and charge a separate fee.

10. Next, your child will need to log on to either the College Board or the ACT website or both to access his test scores. He'll enter the information for each college where he wishes to send any scores (including SAT, ACT, SAT Subject Test, and AP scores), choose which scores he wants to send, and require your credit card again to make that happen.

If my kid waits until the last minute, what could possibly go wrong?

One year, on October 31, an ice storm ripped through all of New England, knocking out power in the entire region—including Internet access for seniors with November first deadlines.

"Happy Halloween!" shrieked Mother Nature.

Those seniors who had waited until the last possible minute freaked out. I heard one kid drove eight hours the next day to find a relative who still had electricity so he could submit his Common Application ED. When the power returned (almost a full week later, in my case), students moaned, whined, and begged colleges to accept their late applications. They were not met with much sympathy because *students had had since August 1, when the Common Application had gone live, to get this done.*

That year, the weather caused the snafu, but almost every year, the Common Application's website suffers some kind of technical glitch. Usually it overloads when students all over the world press "send" right before a deadline. It almost always messes up the formatting on essays, adding extra spaces or deleting spaces willy-nilly. Your kid might panic when she sees this new, creative formatting, but she can correct it on the screen. A couple of years ago, for some inexplicable reason, my students uploaded their 650-word essays and the Common Application lopped off the last paragraph. One student, who hadn't bothered to proofread again after uploading her essay, heard about this bug later and had to call every college to which she'd applied and ask them if she could resubmit her essay. This sucked up time she did not have, and it was not the first impression she'd wanted to make. Some colleges allowed her to resubmit, but for others, she was out of luck.

Another malfunction that can happen nestles deep within the teenage brain, which thinks anything—including completing a college application—will take less time than it really does. If this sounds like your kid, as previously noted, add to the calendar a warning for each deadline forty-eight hours before the real one to implant it in her brain a little bit earlier.

Last-Minute Help Without Helicoptering

Here we are, the night applications are due. We're in the throes of early applications now, but the situation will be the same on New Year's Day. Many students cutting it close will ask their parents to help. I know I said if your kid's smart, he'll ask you or someone else to proofread his work. I know you're probably the only one there at 11:45 p.m. on November 1. I know you have those Guidelines for Appropriate Proofreading handy (see p. 156 if you don't). I want to point out that I gave you those guidelines back in July, when proofreading your kid's essay did not oblige you to sacrifice sleep over it.

This is an opportunity to help your kid complete this task, but it's not a requirement. If you want to fly in for a rescue during this last push, then do it. No guilt. Remember that I made sandwiches for my grown kids' lunches when they were perfectly capable of doing it themselves, and for me, it was worth it. I also give you permission to say no and go to bed. Really. If your child has waited this long to get this done, your sleep deprivation will not save him. The panicked teenager might lead you to believe otherwise. He might accuse you of abandoning him at the highest-stakes moment of his life, when you are actually empowering him to take responsibility of his own destiny and to take pride in getting into college on his own.

It's a conundrum that I cannot decide for you — whether helping in this thankless endeavor will make a real difference for your kid and provide satisfaction for you, or letting your kid fend for himself could be the bigger gift. You're on your own here, but with my blessing however this night goes down. Godspeed.

Sending and Paying for Test-Score Reports

My daughter decided at the tenth hour to apply to one college EA, so I paid a rush fee for those scores to arrive in two days (because I was an enabler and horribly weak, though I have since forgiven myself, as per the cardinal rule). I paid...

$12 for the SAT test score report +
$31 rush fee +
$12 for 2 Subject Test scores +
$31 rush fee +
$15 for AP Exam reports +
$25 rush fee
for a grand total of $126 (I'm sure the prices have risen since.)

Three weeks later, at a time when those scores ostensibly would have arrived without paying any rush fees, *the score reports still hadn't arrived*. I attempted to retrieve my money, and it was worse than contesting a medical insurance bill. At least after thirty minutes on hold for the insurance company, someone picks up. Not so at the College Board. I never did manage to connect with a person or receive an answer about why the scores hadn't reached the college in the two days promised, but not for lack of trying through email and phone. Suffice it to say that from what I've seen, customer service is not the College Board's forte, but since the company generates over a billion dollars in annual revenue (well, if they didn't want me to see their tax returns, they should not have registered as a nonprofit), it seems to me they could have afforded to return that $126 to my Visa.

Regardless of whether your kid submits ACT scores or SAT scores, if he also submits AP or SAT Subject Test scores, or applies for financial aid for private colleges, you'll end up on the College Board website, credit card in hand. You might as well direct deposit your paycheck into the College Board's coffers during the fall of senior year to save you some time.

Breaking News! The College Board's website promised that my son's SAT scores would be released today, just in time to hit his EA deadlines. My son logged on to find the following notice (and I quote directly):

We apologize but your score is still being processed. You should get your score within a week; you'll get an email when your score is available. [Wait for it.]

> *If you still don't see your score more than three weeks after test day, contact Customer Service at 866-756-7346.*

I. Can't. Even.

After Applications Are Submitted

Check college websites, hound recommenders, repeat.

Once your child submits her application, the college will set up an applicant portal (or "student application status page," or whatever nomenclature that college uses) for her with a checklist of materials received and missing. Do not become flustered if your child does not receive the link to her portal right away. Some colleges take hours, while others take up to two weeks to set them up. Many pieces submitted by other people must land in one central location to complete the application, including the following:

- The guidance office at your child's high school must submit the transcript, high school profile, counselor recommendation, and teacher recommendations.
- Additional recommenders, such as employers, must send their letters under separate cover.
- Standardized test-score reports must come directly from the testing companies for many colleges.
- If your child switched high schools or completed college courses, all schools must send separate transcripts.

Though these materials come from other people, *it's on your kid to make sure the colleges receive them on time.*

In order for the high school staff to do their job, your child must inform them far enough in advance to gather this information and send it. Lest I remind you, what many teenagers consider "advance planning" might be considered "last minute" in the adult world. A guidance office needs weeks, not hours, to accommodate every student at the school applying to college, and with all that juggling to do, something will inevitably fall between the cracks. Your kid must check his portal for each college regularly, nudge anyone who hasn't submitted his portion of the application, and then check again, until the application is complete. Tell your kid that sometimes paranoia is a good thing. If she becomes too paranoid when a recommendation hasn't made it to the college a few days after the deadline, tell her to remain diligent but reassure her that late supporting materials will not count against her, as long as she did her part on time.

Another Chance to Learn to Let Go

Say your kid's transcript never made it to a college, and the application is due this week. She's *so* busy, and the opportunity to help is right there, staring you in the face. You want *so* badly to alleviate the tension for her. If you could make this one call to that one college, you could save her time and anxiety. Instead of calling, repeat as necessary:

> *Grant me the serenity to accept the things I cannot change; courage to change the things I can; and the wisdom to know the difference.*
> — *Serenity Prayer, Reinhold Niebuhr*

Celebrate the Small Victories

Your kid has completed applications and hit her early deadlines. I knew she could do it, and now you know too. You both deserve ice cream. (Mint chocolate chip is always a winner.) She needs sustenance for the next leg, which is happening right now. I know. You thought you could take a much-needed rest, but the minute your kid loads the ice cream dish into the dishwasher (because you have trained her to clean up her own messes), it's time to forge onward and deal with Regular Decision.

The Wisdom of Assuming Your Child Will Be Deferred

Suzy, a star swimmer from my town, was a top D3 swimming recruit. The coach at her first-choice college requested a "pre-read." That means admission evaluators looked at Suzy's transcript to make sure she was an academically viable candidate. After receiving a thumbs-up from admissions, Suzy and the swim coach shook hands and smiled, perhaps there was a hug involved, and it was settled. She would apply ED, the coach would support her, Suzy assumed she would receive an acceptance notification in mid-December, the unknown would become known, and she could enjoy her last high school swim season without the added strain of scrutiny by college coaches.

On December 15, Suzy logged on to her applicant portal and learned she was…deferred. Surprise! When a student is deferred, it means that she is not accepted or denied. Rather, her application moves to the RD pile, and months more waiting. Suzy was stunned. Had the admissions department not pre-read her transcript and deemed her worthy? Had the coach not shaken her hand and deemed her worthy? Had she dreamed the whole thing? Was she unworthy?

The exhausting process that she'd assumed would be done was anything but. Suzy scrambled to write a bunch of supplements for other colleges. It took superhuman energy to write anything at all, let alone good essays, while still reeling from disappointment. If Suzy's story does not prompt your child to prepare precautionary RD applications now, while the sugar rush from the ice cream celebration is still in her system, I don't know what will.

FACING THE DARK SIDE: THE FINANCIAL AID FORMS

Here I *just* advised you to start amping up your training for letting go, but when it comes to financial aid applications, scrap all that. It's okay for you to take over this piece of the application process. It's okay for parents to call the colleges' financial aid offices with questions, as I've mentioned. And about staying calm…I meant it…but not for this. It's okay to complain, grind your teeth, and scream (into a pillow if possible). Stock up the bar and buckle up for a bumpy ride, especially if your child is applying to any private colleges.

The Lesser of Two Evils: The FAFSA

The Free Application for Federal Student Aid (FAFSA) is the form to request money from the federal government to help pay for college. It really is free of charge to submit. The government has limited the form's length to six pages and has tried to keep it somewhat humane. The FAFSA is available online on October 1, and since it asks you to use your tax forms from the "prior prior" year (two years before your kid attends college), you won't have to estimate your future income the way you will on that other form (which I will get to in a moment; I have to gear myself up). If your income has changed significantly within the past two years, you can explain that later to the one college your kid chooses to attend and they'll often adjust their need-based award. If your child is applying to state-funded universities, you only have to fill out the FAFSA. If your child is applying to private colleges, you'll have to fill out the FAFSA and a whole lot more.

Pure, Unadulterated, Four-Martini Evil: The CSS Profile

When you see your best friend hasn't brushed her hair (or her teeth) in a week and her skin has broken out from stress, you can assume her child is applying for financial aid for private colleges, which requires filling out the CSS (College Scholarship Service) Profile. Sit her down at a table and offer her food and spirits to bring color back to her face, which has paled as if she has seen the devil. The devil has taken the form of…well, a form.

Whoever invented this form must enjoy persecuting us, we may be thinking. Then we learn it's distributed by the College Board. When you see the CSS Profile, you will understand that while torturing our children with the SAT and AP tests, the College Board was only sharpening its teeth.

The College Board has a monopoly on this application service, too, so there's no escaping CSS Profile hell if you need to request financial aid to afford a private college. You must once again visit the College Board's website to fill out and submit this beastly, time-consuming, invasive application, and they charge a fee to process it. I will pause for one moment to reflect on the ethics of charging you a fee to request money because you can't afford to pay for an upcoming massive purchase, especially when the federal government manages to process its forms for free.

The form is written as if the student will fill it out alone. As if. How could our children possibly know how much "deductible IRA and/or SEP, SIMPLE, or Keogh payments" his parents expect to make in the coming year? I completed college *and* graduate school, and I had to look up most of the acronyms and abbreviations thrown around on the CSS Profile. It is unduly lengthy. Did they really need to add a separate question about "black lung benefits" received by parents? Couldn't they have just lumped it in under the general category of "health" out of respect for our time? Some of the language barely makes sense. In one spot, it asked for the current market value of the student's assets, including "precious and strategic metals." What does that even mean? Jewelry? Ballistic missiles? Once you've figured out what they're asking for, it is difficult to find some of the information. Even projected income is difficult to figure out for independent contractors (one out of every ten adults), whose income fluctuates from month to month, let alone year to year. If you are divorced or part of a blended family, you'd better save personal days for the CSS Profile adventure.

Finally, the CSS Profile offers a space for "Explanations/Special Circumstances." Because the College Board can't help itself, it even gave *this* an abbreviation: ES. There's probably a character cutoff; I don't know. The space seemed to expand as I typed, like a mouth opening to swallow us (and our income) into inner darkness.

Help!

If your child is applying to private colleges or universities, you have to fill out both the FAFSA and the CSS Profile. Not a soul I know has ever enjoyed this, but there's help available, if you know where to look.

- My kids' high school holds a FAFSA Night! in an attempt to make festive what is not, as they walk families through this form. Your child's school might offer some similar free event.
- I've included some trustworthy free organizations that aren't government- or College Board–affiliated in Resources.
- College financial aid offices welcome parents' calls and emails when help is needed. They understand that filling out those unwieldy forms requires parental guidance.
- My family hired an expert who specialized in filling out college financial aid forms the first time we filled them out. (You're obligated to fill them out every year your kid is in college. Sorry. I'm just the messenger.) Yes, this kind of expert exists, though your everyday accountant might be able to help too. For us, it was money well spent.

The Urgency of Recording Financial Aid Deadlines on the Calendar in Red Sharpie

- Both the FAFSA and CSS Profile forms become available online on October 1.
- They are due the day each college says they are due, often at or around the same time as the application for early deadlines.
- Financial aid deadlines are very real, so burn them into your calendar.
- You'll already have accurate numbers from past tax returns for the FAFSA, but don't dawdle and wait for the exact numbers from new returns to fill out the CSS Profile. *Estimate* income and expenses if you have to and submit it on time. You can send updates later. The world helps those who help themselves.

TO-DO LIST

- ☐ When your nerves start to get the better of you, remind yourself applying to college is just the first of many business transactions for your kid. It's not life or death.
- ☐ Remind your kid to double-check *everything* before submitting each application.
- ☐ Students submit ED/EA Application(s) *on time.*
- ☐ If at all humanly possible, coax your child to deal with supplemental essays for RD applications now, even if he tells you he wants to wait and see what happens with the early applications he submitted.
- ☐ Whether your kid applies early or on the regular deadline, he will need to perform uncomfortable tasks like nagging high school staff and making phone calls to official places, and he'll need you to support him.
- ☐ Register for last chance testing for applications with RD deadlines.
- ☐ Face financial aid applications head-on. Try not to think about how you'll have to complete them again next year, and the year after that, and the year after that…

Chapter 11

November

THE THANKSGIVING CHALLENGE

We pick up our turkeys. We add extra leaves to dining tables and decorate with gourds and mums. For better or worse, families unite. It is there at that Thanksgiving table that you and your kid will experience your greatest test of strength fending off inquisitors.

Cousin Joe, the bachelor with no children, asks your kid, "Where are you applying to college?"

The planned response is in place: the Truth Without Apology strategy.

Your strong, competent girl sits up a little straighter. Her silver heart earring sways back and forth. She looks Joe in the eye and tells him where she's applied Early Decision.

Joe nods. "That's a fine school," he says.

Operation Truth Without Apology has gone smoothly until Aunt Minerva pipes up from across the centerpiece of arranged mini pumpkins. "That's a very competitive college," she says.

Your kid stabs a fork into the slab of turkey on her plate. Hey, better the turkey than Aunt Minerva.

Your niece, a junior in high school, looks terrified. The minute Aunt Minerva says the word "college," your niece's knife freezes midair.

Oblivious, Aunt Minerva keeps talking. "Do you really think you'll get in? I've heard it's impossible nowadays."

"We'll find out on December fifteenth," says your kid. Then she stuffs a roasted Brussels sprout into her mouth so she doesn't have to speak.

Note to self: Comfort your kid and your niece with extra whipped cream on their pumpkin pie. Next year at this time, your niece will be preparing applications, waiting, and hoping, as your kid is doing now. Also next year, one of the visiting relatives populating your Thanksgiving table will be *your kid,* home from her first semester of college. It's hard not to think ahead to the year after that, when she might bring a roommate home with her. Then junior year, she may study abroad and not come home at all, and senior year she might need to return to school a little early for a job interview. The next year—just four short years away—she will be out in the world. She may not manage enough time off work to travel home for Thanksgiving, especially if she lives far away. (Oh God, could she live far away?) Perhaps she'll have a family of her own, and then one year, it will be easier for you to skip the holiday traditions and travel to her than for her to travel home with your grandkids in tow. By then, your home won't be her home anymore. She'll have a home of her own somewhere else.

It puts this college search into perspective, doesn't it?

Aunt Minerva doesn't have the wherewithal to notice your niece slumping in her chair, praying the conversation about college doesn't turn to her, or that your daughter's sawing at her turkey more aggressively now. "Marjorie's granddaughter is at West Central State University. It's a very nice place. Will you apply there if that first choice doesn't work out?" Aunt Minerva says as casually as if she were asking your child to please pass the candied yams.

Breathe in.

Breathe out.

Smother your stuffing along with the choice words you have for Aunt Minerva with gravy and cranberry sauce (a surprisingly tasty combination). Fill your mouth, and chew. Listen to your kid repeat whatever canned speech she's planned for this moment. Wash down your food with a swig of wine. Watch your kid handle Aunt Minerva's interrogation with grace and kindness. Celebrate how well you've raised her with another swig of wine. Remember to tell your child how proud you are of her *before* her first college notifications roll in.

TO-DO LIST

- ☐ Nail mid-month ED/EA deadlines.
- ☐ Your kid should share her RD list with the high school guidance office by early December or the high school's deadline, whichever comes first.
- ☐ Root for your kid as she works on RD applications.
- ☐ Take time now to tell your child, either verbally or in writing, how much you love and admire her, and how much you will continue to love and admire her, no matter where she's admitted to college or where she ends up enrolling.
- ☐ Give thanks for loved ones, food, and the fact that the college application process is almost over.

Chapter 12

December

EARLY NOTIFICATIONS COMING IN

How College Notifications Happen

Your child will monitor the exact minute notifications will arrive.

The days of waiting for the mail carrier to deliver a thin or a fat envelope are over. My daughter learned through some unofficial website like College Confidential (a seedy black market of college admissions information and misinformation—don't believe everything you read there) that the college where she'd applied Early Decision would release notifications online at 6:00 p.m. on a Thursday. Her ED choice was an hour and a half drive from our house. She'd also applied EA to a college that was a four-and-a-half-hour airplane flight away (plus over two hours of driving). She'd have to wait another week for that notification.

At 4:00 p.m., my kid placed her laptop on the kitchen table and began obsessively refreshing her computer screen. She stared into the pixels, as if into a crystal ball, willing the notification to materialize sooner. Between computer refreshes, my kid announced, "If I'm not accepted ED today and I am accepted EA next week, I'll probably end up going to college far from home. Did you realize that?"

I did not. I had thought she'd apply RD to more colleges close to home, as well. The stakes had grown higher for me. I made up an excuse to stay in the kitchen stress-baking. I was balling chocolate chunk cookie dough at approximately 5:30 p.m. when my daughter started screaming, "I'm in. I'm in!"

"CONGRATULATIONS!" flashed on the screen in giant font. She let me hug her tight, even with my sticky fingers.

In New York City, ambulances troll the streets and arrive at the next emergency within seconds. Once, when we lived there, we needed to call 911, and we could hear the ambulance siren outside our apartment building while we were still on the phone with the dispatcher. It was like that with my daughter's friends. Within a few minutes, I could hear a car in the driveway, and two of my daughter's besties rushed in, screaming, hugging, and crying. My daughter had received the first college notification of the group, and it seemed this moment offered all of them an opportunity to release the built-up tension from the past months. I'd also like to believe that friendship is sometimes selfless. My daughter told me after her friends left that her own tears came partially from relief that she was going to a college close to home. Then she stayed up most of the night writing thank-you letters to her recommenders.

The next day, a glittering golden envelope with my daughter's name written in calligraphy arrived by mail. Inside, an invitation, as if to a gala event, read, "You are cordially invited to the class of 2020."

The Notification Varieties for Early Applications

My daughter received her golden ticket. My friend's son received an acceptance video with his name flashing on a Jumbotron in a sports arena as a sportscaster announced personalized congratulations. Some colleges go all out to make kids feel special when they are admitted, but not all kids are admitted. Online Early Decisions arrive in three distinct varieties:

- *Acceptance* is the optimum. "We love you as much as you love us!"
- *Denial* is the least desirable. The notification will look much like the rejection letter almost all of us have received at some point in our lifetimes. "The applicant pool was extremely strong... We wish you good luck" and so forth. This might be the first rejection your kid has ever received. (Tips for helping her handle it appear on p. 231.)
- *Deferral* is purgatory for many hopeful students. It's the college telling the applicant, "You're qualified, and we like you, but we

are not ready to make a decision about you yet." If your kid wants to be considered again in the RD applicant pool, he must write a "letter of continued interest" (see p. 235 for instructions) or fill out a form if the college provides one. Then you'll have to wait until spring to learn if the college loves your child (almost) as much as your child loves them.

Admitted!

Revel in every acceptance.

An acceptance, whether to a top-choice reach college or a foundation school, is a victory. No matter what happens from here on out, this is an enormous win! Ice cream, though not required, is recommended.

Some Etiquette If Your Kid Is Admitted ED (Because Most Are Not)

The air in your home will feel breathable again as the thickness of anticipation, fear, stress, and longing dissipates and elation and relief take its place. However, most of your kid's friends are either suffering disappointment or haven't applied to college yet. It's a time for celebration, but it's also a time for restraint and empathy because there but for the grace of God goes your kid. Here are some guidelines:

- *Think carefully before you post on social media.* It's a tone thing. You get one excited, multi-exclamation point post per social media platform before sharing your good news morphs into gloating.
- *Listen and observe before you speak.* Online, your friend's Facebook feed can clue you in by announcing an acceptance with fifteen exclamation points, or going radio silent. In person, your friend's face will register what happened before he utters a word. Expressing compassion for your friends whose kids were denied or deferred without coming across as smug is tricky business. Let them ask you college-related questions. If you ask first, you'll sound a lot like those "Where's your kid applying?" interrogators.

- *Do unto other parents as you'd want them to do unto you.* Some parents want to talk about college and some don't. Be as sensitive as you possibly can be to their needs, even if you want to shout your excitement from the rooftops.
- *Don't talk about college twenty-four/seven to your kid.* Sure, he's thrilled about his future, but he has other important things going on in his life right now like his studies, his job, swim meets, auditions for the musical, a big Model UN conference, or should he ask his latest crush to the winter dance, or not. Pay attention to him as a person doing his thing, not only as a person who has received a nod of approval from a college.

ADMITTED STUDENT'S TO-DO LIST
(FOR BINDING AGREEMENTS)

- ☐ Pay the requested deposit.
- ☐ Withdraw applications from all other colleges ASAP, so they can offer admission to other students who want to go there.
- ☐ Formally thank everyone who helped you arrive at this place. Gifts are nice, but thank-you letters are better.
- ☐ Keep up the grades. You will have to submit your final transcript to the college. Best-case scenario: Your grades stay strong and you're offered a scholarship. Worst-case scenario: Severe premature senioritis and a rescinded offer of admission. The choice is in your power.
- ☐ Return to using your personal email address so important emails from your new college won't become buried in the avalanche of promotions from other colleges.
- ☐ Make a habit of checking email every single day. I get it that email is for old people, but colleges don't. At first, you'll receive emails about orientation and registering for the housing lottery. Later, emails will reveal class registration deadlines and tuition bills, not to be missed.

☐   Though optional, you should visit your new college's social media platforms. In addition to celebrating with future classmates on Twitter, visit the Facebook page, where colleges may post helpful information. Some students even find roommates there.

Deciphering Financial Aid Awards

When a school says they meet 100% of demonstrated need, it does *not* mean that every penny you need will be met with free money. The estimated financial aid package that accompanies an acceptance is not always simple to parse out. Lots of new jargon and information will appear in the offer:

- Total Family Contribution (TFC) shows the actual cash you will have to pay the college. It should more or less mirror the Expected Family Contribution (EFC) you calculated on the college's online calculator.
- Grants are the free money you were hoping for. Depending on the school, grants can come in the form of merit aid (they decide the amount based on your child's academic record), need-based aid (they decide the amount based on the financial aid forms you filled out), or both.
- Loans for which your family qualifies are included in the financial aid package. You'll borrow this money, but you'll need to pay it back plus interest. Loans are the part of paying for college that leads to all that future student debt you've heard about.
- Student employment, a.k.a. work-study, assumes that your child will work during the school year and summers to earn cash to contribute to her own education.
- At or near the time of the ED or EA acceptance to a publicly funded college or university, you'll receive an *actual* (as opposed to estimated) need-based award because the FAFSA you filled out was based on previously filed tax returns. If you've had a dip in your income since, call the college's financial aid office and

alert them. The college will instruct you on next steps, usually submitting updated tax returns and an email explanation.

- If a private college that required the CSS Profile admitted your kid, you'll receive an *estimated* award. In the spring, after you complete your income tax forms and share them with the school, the college's financial aid office will recalculate your estimated offer into a final offer.
- Call if you find anything surprising or unclear. Though your kid will receive all the bills, parents are often the ones calling with the questions.
- Sign up to be copied on emails from the financial aid office. Your kid has matured enough to go to college, but that doesn't mean she'll instantaneously become better about checking email.

Optional Expenses for the Admitted Student

- The college will offer some insurance add-ons (I'm groaning too), such as tuition insurance in case your kid falls ill and must withdraw midyear. Extra medical insurance is usually a good idea if you live out of state. If your kid is staying in state for college, call your insurance company before you refuse this additional coverage, and make sure the present family coverage is sufficient for your kid if she's not living at home.
- At some colleges, housing options come with different price tags (a.k.a. "room").
- Most colleges offer various meal plans with different costs attached (a.k.a. "board").

Deferred or Denied

What were they *thinking* when they rejected my kid?

If your child is not admitted ED, you are in the majority. You may have thought otherwise because news of this type isn't the kind people liberally share. Denial can feel abrupt and harsh, and there's no one-size-fits-all explanation for why this happened. Only one kid is *your* kid, and beyond your social circle, you won't know who else in this vast world appeared within the applicant pool alongside her. One thing I can guarantee you is that a denial does not mean your kid is unworthy — not by a longshot. It just means that this particular path has hit a dead end.

Are you experiencing a lump in your throat whenever you think about this disappointment? Trouble breathing? A tornado of negative thoughts — despair, anger, sorrow, horror, anguish — swirling inside your head? Take a ten-minute timeout, and do this:

1. Go to the most secluded room in your home.
2. Lock the door.
3. Think it.
4. Feel it.
5. Now regroup, unlock the door, and move on to other avenues with more potential.

Keeping your cool is an absolute must. Not to be a Pollyanna about this (because it still feels terrible), but the college has given your child the gift of a clear answer. Not so in the case of a deferral.

Why was my kid deferred?

A flame of hope for acceptance flickers in the distance, and your child has no idea whether she will ever reach the light. There could be a variety of reasons the college deferred your kid, including these:

- She's an excellent candidate, but they decided to wait to see how she stacks up in the RD pool.
- She made it to a committee discussion because she was academically qualified, but she did not receive enough votes by committee members for an acceptance.
- Her academic credentials are "on the bubble" (admissions-speak meaning "on the fence") between students admitted ED and

those who fell short, and they want more information before they commit to her. For example, they may be waiting for semester grades in more rigorous classes or evidence of higher test scores if she reported future testing dates on her application.

- Any of the reasons above, plus your family has some connection to the school and they don't want to alienate you. (If she wasn't qualified, legacy or not, she would have been denied.)

What are my deferred kid's prospects of an acceptance RD?

One client of mine contacted me after his daughter was deferred from a university that's a foundation school for no one. I kept scrolling down his email through the numbers, calculations, and speculations about her chances for being admitted RD, along the lines of *ED admit rate of about 25% equals 1,000 ED acceptances, leaving about 1,000 openings for RD. Assuming a 40% yield for RD acceptance, there would be 2,500 RD acceptances to yield 1,000 students, equating to RD admit rate of 8.1% (2,500/31,000).*

The difference between a 25% and 8.1% admit rate within a pool of highly motivated students would make little difference for his daughter, but this wasn't just any kid applying. This was *his* amazing kid. What a lucky girl to have a dad who believed in her and was so invested in her success that he chose to spend his time making pages of calculations, silently rooting for her, like that. Fully immersing himself in those numbers was his meditation. His daughter had the best fan in town, not only because her dad had faith in her, but also because he shared these numbers in an email only to me from the privacy of his office so he wouldn't burden her with his pain.

I understand why, like my client, you want to know how close your child was and is to acceptance at this school. Your friends will try to comfort you with examples of students deferred ED and then later admitted. There are plenty of examples of that, including Suzy, the swimmer I told you about on p. 215. If your kid has been deferred, I hope he's one of those admitted later. I really do. But I need you to hear me that there are many more examples of students for whom that did not happen. If your child was not selected from the ED pool, it's unlikely he will be chosen out of the much larger RD pool. It's in your child's best interest if he (and you) can move on to other opportunities because there are so very many. Treat that deferral like a gentler rejection, so your kid can write enthusiastic supplements to other colleges and mean it.

The Dos and Don'ts of Coping with Your Kid's Deferral or Outright Rejection

Don't be that parent your child feels like she needs to console, when she's the one who didn't get into a college. I know about that rush of emotions while you sit there, helpless, feeling your child's disappointment deep inside your soul, and perhaps nursing your own disappointment too. However, this is not your disappointment to annex. (Turn to p. 191 for detox instructions or take a ten-minute timeout, see p. 229, and inhale. Now exhale.)

Don't assume your child feels exactly the same way you do. Listen before you console her, and then if she needs it, soothe her in whatever way has worked when she was disappointed in the past. You'll find soothing her can help you soothe yourself.

Don't make excuses. This is not the time to communicate to your kid that she would've gotten in if she'd spent more time on her essays, or studied for her SAT, or hadn't gotten that one C freshman year, or if Tommy from her school hadn't also applied ED, or if she'd applied last year instead of this year. Any reason you can conjure for why she wasn't accepted is a self-esteem killer for your kid. It sends the message that you are disappointed, and possibly that you are disappointed *in her.*

Don't dis the school that denied your kid. No sour grapes. Other kids your kid knows are excited about that college. They might have received an ED acceptance, or they're planning to apply. It's understandable that you might think pejoratively about any colleges that deigned to defer or deny your baby, but you really must keep it to yourself or confide in a partner, therapist, or safe friend far away from your teenager's ears.

Don't pick up the phone and call the college to ask why they did not accept your kid, even if it's just for information. Say you bypass the receptionist and speak to an admissions officer. He will repeat the sound bites on the letter he already sent to your kid—"It was an unusually strong pool of applicants this year, the decision was more difficult than ever, blah, blah, blah"—and you will hang up with no new information, as frustrated as you were before you called. This is a job for the high school guidance counselor, who has a professional rather than an emotional relationship with your kid.

Do honor your kid's moment to grieve if denied. My kids' high school has a tradition. Someone created a Facebook page they call "The Wall of Shame," upon which students post their rejection letters. Students have told me it helped them maintain their sense of humor and support one another during a difficult time.

Do your own version of my client's calculations. Numbers were his coping mechanism. For you, it might be an hour on the treadmill, or calling your best friend, or diving into an intricate recipe for family dinner (though don't expect your family to appreciate it). Do your version of privately comforting yourself through this disappointment. Then lift yourself up, wipe the puddle off the floor, pull out your pom-poms, and start cheering for your kid in the RD round.

Do treat a denial or deferral as another data point that can help determine what to do next. Your child may need to recalibrate which colleges on her list are foundation, target, or reach, or add more options. If she was denied ED, but was accepted somewhere EA and is thrilled, then great! If there's nowhere else she'd rather go, your rollercoaster ride is over.

Do take a cup half full approach toward moving on to plan B. Forward motion is the only option. Progress through those stages of grief, from shock and denial all the way to acceptance and hope, as fast as humanly possible, so you can help your kid set her sights on other colleges that would be eager to have her.

Do reiterate your love for and devotion to your kid. She may roll her eyes, but know that she hears you every single time you say out loud how much you love and are proud of her *no matter what* notification she receives from any college.

Reflections and Advice from Other Parents Who Have Been There

As desperate as you might feel about trying to somehow fix this, now more than ever, *let your child take the lead*. You already know you have my support, but you might've forgotten that you have a whole community of parents propping you up right now. You are far from alone. I want you to hear the voices of some of those in our group who have weathered either ED or RD disappointments, or both, with their own children.

My daughter told me rejections sucked for her (surprisingly more than expected), so the idea of applying to places that are reaches for everyone (MIT, Harvard, etc.) turned out to be a bad idea. After she was deferred from all her EA choices, she was frantically looking for last-minute options she hadn't considered, and one school kept showing up on lists. She literally applied there on January first, using recycled essays from other schools, and now she is a student there, and it's the perfect school for her! So who the #%$ knows?!?!?—Eve

I tried to lower expectations all along, telling my kid that there was a strong possibility she'd get rejected from all her reaches. I think all you can really do is sympathize with what your child's going through and not make it worse by seeming like you're disappointed in her. Needless to say, parental love should not be conditional on success in college applications. I'd recommend being the voice of perspective. "Sure, you'd like to get into your reaches, but denials aren't the end of the world, and they're not some kind of cosmic judgment on you." —Christopher

My daughter was deferred, then applied to seven schools RD and was accepted by four. The acceptances made her feel better about the deferral and rejections. She eliminated the ones in the South because she wasn't crazy about wearing summer clothes all year, and she didn't want her hair to frizz from the humidity. Luckily, she made the right choice for the wrong reasons and had a good experience at a college with what other people might consider bad weather. — Frances

I've seen a lot of people not prepared to go through the RD application process after getting rejected/deferred ED. Kids are in a terrible state of mind after an early deferment, so it's best to have a discussion immediately about all the great possibilities down the road. It's never a good idea to get fixated on one school. There are a lot of great options out there, and generally I agree with the philosophy that you should love the school that loves you. Every school that my son applied to had many pluses that would have made his undergraduate experience a positive one. Reflecting on that during the December process made it a bit more bearable. — Michele

Don't let the disappointment of a deferral/rejection get to you personally. This will be a challenging time, and your child needs you to be there for him in every way — and get ready for him to take all of his hurt and anger out on you, as well. He needs your support, guidance, and unwavering belief in him. And it does work out in the end. — Kate

We've always told our kids that there is no one perfect anything in life — including college. We told them they would grow wherever they planted themselves. Not getting into a particular college is not a reflection of all of the hard work they've put into getting to where they are. Sharing our failures with our kids helped them to see that life is full of disappointments, and it is how you handle them that is a true test of character. Self-worth should not be determined by not getting in on the first try. We reassured our daughter that any school would be lucky to have her! Where I think we went wrong, and what I would like to advise students and families to do, is to have a plan B. We did not. Don't stop preparing those applications — as onerous as they may be. — Lynn (mother of Suzy, the deferred swimmer, p. 215)

STUDENT CHECKLIST FOR A LETTER OF CONTINUED INTEREST (IF DEFERRED OR WAITLISTED)

- Please keep me in the running for admission.
- I'm still excited about this college! Keep an upbeat tone. Don't plead or whine.
- Keep it brief. You can point out what aspect of this specific college makes it well suited to you, and you for them, but this is not an appropriate vehicle for writing a tome professing undying love for the college.
- It is not a good plan to call or email the Office of Admission and ask why you weren't accepted. Discuss that with your guidance counselor. (See How the Guidance Counselor Can Help, below)
- It is, however, an opportunity to provide a succinct update on anything of note that's happened since applying. Good grades or induction into the National Honor Society are of note. Your family trip to Washington, D.C. (even if you're a future political science major) or what you ate for breakfast (even if you're making an effort to eat better) are not.
- Proofread everything you ever send to an admissions office. Ever.

How the High School Guidance Counselor Can Help (There May Be Tears)

- The guidance counselor can provide emotional support. The word *counsel* appears in her title. She has a box of tissues and a prepared pep talk at the ready.

- She can call the college's Office of Admission to gather information. She can even fight for your kid on that call in a way that would sound pushy and annoying coming from a parent or student.
- She can strategize about adjusting your kid's RD list based on how things went down during the early application round.
- She can advise on revisions to the Common Application to make your child's RD candidacy more appealing.

SUBMITTING RD APPLICATIONS

It's the holidays! We bake, buy or make gifts, and gather with friends and family at parties and around cozy fireplaces. Then comes New Year's Day, which looms large this year because it's the most common deadline for RD applications. According to a talk I heard in 2016 at Smith College, almost half of all high school seniors write their college essays the night they're due. I believe it. Teenage theatrics in households of college-bound seniors can register about a 9.5 on the drama Richter scale this time of year. Somehow, it is the parents' fault that it's the last minute and everything is going wrong. My heart especially goes out to parents of perfectionists. This might be the moment your child finally learns that done is better than perfect. Teachers grant extensions, but *if your kid submits her application after midnight of the deadline, it's as if she didn't apply.*

Let's go through the various strategies I've introduced, and a couple of new ones, to avoid the last-minute mayhem:

- Use the shared calendar to save you from headaches. Add "warning" dates that deadlines are coming a few days or a week before those deadlines arrive. (See Keeping Track of Everything [and I Mean Everything], p. 206.)
- Battle college admissions fever within yourself using steps 1–5 of the Six-Step Competition Detox Plan on p. 191. Then employ

step 6 ASAP to help your child shake off any extreme ED/EA disappointments and motivate her to complete her RD applications efficiently.

- I'll admit, I am not above using fear as a weapon against procrastination. If your kid's not on the ball, then well before New Year's Eve, I suggest you share horror stories of kids who got burned by technology or weather when trying to send applications at the last minute. (See "If my kid waits until the last minute, what could possibly go wrong?" on p. 210.)

- If a deadline is closing in and you're starting to feel uncomfortable, discuss with your child exactly what you will and will not do if she waits until the last minute. Prepare her for the moment you might need to go to bed before she's finished her applications so you can work effectively at your own job the next day. Sometimes our children need a reminder that parents are people with lives that extend beyond the scope of theirs.

- Preempt rush fees by letting your kid know that the deadline recorded on the calendar also represents the last day you will brandish your credit card to pay for submitting test scores. (See Sending and Paying for Test-Score Reports, p. 211, and then don't do what I did.)

- If you're a true hard-nose, it's also possible to set your own deadline before the colleges' for the last moment you'll pay for your kid to submit his applications. Money talks.

- As Lynn advised in Reflections and Advice from Other Parents Who Have Been There (p. 233), prepare a plan B in case early front-runners don't work out, so your kid won't put off writing all the RD supplements until the holiday break (at which point, it's no longer a break).

When your child presses "send" on the last college application, you are done (at least, for now). Break out the bubbly! Out with the old, and in with the fresh new year and the billions of topics to think about and talk about besides college.

TO-DO LIST

☐ A gift card for a massage is a good holiday present this year, both to give and to request.

☐ To prepare for ED/EA notifications, some parents order the school's sweatshirt or stuffed mascot to present to their student if admitted (which would explain why my friend who graduated from Wheaton found a plush Swarthmore phoenix in a closet when her parents downsized). You may also want to book a provisional therapist appointment for your child (and for yourself) in case notifications disappoint. Therapists book up fast this time of year.

☐ If your child was admitted ED, wonderful! If she was also accepted elsewhere EA, make sure she tells the other college she's not coming. Someone who was deferred or applied RD will be elated to be offered the spot your kid passed up.

☐ Plunge into the supplement-writing and RD-application-submission scramble, if necessary.

☐ Purchase extra sparkling beverages for the holidays this year, appropriate for everything from celebration to drowning sorrows to lifting stains from carpets (if it's club soda).

PART VI

SECOND SEMESTER SENIOR YEAR AND BEYOND

FIVE NECESSITIES FOR YOUR KICK-TO-THE-FINISH SURVIVAL KIT

1. If you haven't already, subscribe to a magazine like *Us Weekly* or *In Touch* because the latest celebrity train wreck always sounds worse than whatever you're going through.

2. While you're at it, prepare non-college-related dinner table topics. (See p. 183 to get you started.)

3. To fill the unknown void, keep busy, and loop the Serenity Prayer in your head when you feel overwhelmed. (Words for the prayer appear on p. 214, or "Serenity *now!*" works too.)

4. Try to act like everything will be okay (which is true), even if you're not feeling it (which you won't always), because you never know who is watching (which will, at times, be your child, looking to you for encouragement and role modeling).

5. When you stumble (everyone does), make it part of the dance.

Chapter 13

Winter of Senior Year

AND SO WE WAIT

A Sports Mom's Parable

Sportsmanship: *conduct (such as fairness, respect for one's opponent, and graciousness in winning or losing) becoming to one participating in a sport.*

My son is a competitive rock climber. At competitions ("comps"), the climbers sit sequestered from the rest of us in an area known as isolation ("iso"—rock climbing–related terms you can now never un-know). Meanwhile, we parents cluster in the main part of the gym, roped off in the peanut gallery, watching other climbers tackle the climb our children have yet to see. Kids literally climb the walls, then drop forty feet and swing from ropes that parents must trust to catch them. It's like some harrowing rendition of *Peter Pan*.

Though few kids ever suffer injuries at these comps, my fear spikes. The worst moment is when a volunteer ushers my son out of iso and seats him in a plastic chair with its back to the climb. That means my boy is up next. He can't see what I see, the climber behind him scampering up the moonscape of multicolored "slopers," "volumes," and "pockets" screwed onto the wall. Sitting in that chair, my son shakes out his shoulders. I doubt he notices me, or his father, who is holding up a cell phone and videotaping. My son's gray-blue eyes seem focused inward, his expression a mixture of steely determination, desire, and nerves. He has worked *so hard* for this single climb I have come to watch. Waiting for it to happen is the most difficult part.

My son has developed washboard abs that I cannot believe are attached to someone related to me, and he has climbed his way up to national-level competition in this sport. I'm proud of him for so many reasons, but one of my proudest moments happened his sophomore year in high school. He had made it to the final round of divisionals, just one climb away from qualifying for nationals. He stuffed his bare feet into the ridiculously tight climbing shoes they all wear. He tied the rope to the harness buckled around his waist with practiced, intricate knots. He stood up from the chair, turned, faced the wall, and began the traditional "beta dance," pawing at the air with his hands, envisioning each move along the steep climb before him. He dipped a hand into the chalk bag dangling from his harness. At that moment, anything was possible. He could make it to the top of the rock wall without falling ("send" the climb), or his foot could slip on one of the lower holds and he could tank it.

The latter happened. I saw the disappointment register on his face as his shoes sank into the thick blue floor mat. I stood only a few feet away, roped off and helpless, hoping my sixteen-year-old had built up enough physical strength and emotional endurance to withstand the fall on his own. He wasn't injured, but he suffered the next worst possible outcome. He came in dead last.

What he did next is the reason I'm telling you all this. He shook hands with the other climbers, who had climbed better than he had, he laughed (*laughed!*), and then he ducked under the rope that separated us and asked me if we could stick around to watch his teammates in other age groups compete. Of course we could. There would be so many more climbs and falls in his future, and that's when I knew my kid could survive them all.

Meanwhile, at School

With all of her applications in, your child might have something she vaguely remembers from way back in elementary school: free time. What your kid does with it is anybody's guess. My daughter tried a new sport during spring semester, slept more, and enjoyed her classes much more without all the college admissions stress. Her friend, still waiting for regular decision notifications, told me a different story.

Senior spring semester was generally a pretty weird time of year because everyone around me was in that "I'm done" mode with school, and that really sucks you in, even if you don't have everything figured out for the next year. People admitted early were just trying to keep their GPA semi-reasonable, but I was still waiting on my fate, so I couldn't slack off too hard. My parents didn't understand. They told me they didn't think I was the type of student to catch senioritis, which made me feel vaguely guilty when I did slack off on an AP Physics assignment, but I felt "done" too. — Ben

What You and Your Kid Can Do Besides Wait

- Student: Keep striving (or at least chugging along) in school.
- Student: Research scholarships and apply for them.
- Student, if applicable: Interview or audition.
- Student: Update admissions offices if something exciting happens.
- You: Remind your kid to update admissions offices if something exciting happens (because sometimes they need a little nudge to toot their own horn).
- You: Fill out tax returns early to update financial aid forms.
- Both of you: Proofread everything submitted in writing.
- Both of you: Downplay college admissions, and do life. Obsessing about what could happen won't bring your kid any better juju.

FAQS ABOUT WHAT THE *%$! IS GOING ON IN ADMISSIONS OFFICES

Who are the players?

The Admissions Office Administrators Processing Applications

Your child's application will alight in the hands of college admissions office administrators and remain there in processing limbo for a week or longer. During that time, *it is up to your child, not the adults in his life or a Higher Power, to make sure colleges have his completed application.*

I cannot stress this enough. I know a kid who submitted all his applications on time. Then a couple of weeks later, he received a phone call from a kindly administrator at a college admissions office offering him a last chance to submit his transcript. That's when he belatedly checked his applicant portals and discovered that *not one college* had received *anything* he had requested from his high school. Oops. This kid will never know how many colleges denied him admission because parts of his application arrived too late or never arrived at all. He does know that he would not be a college student now if that one kindly office administrator at that one college hadn't gone out of her way to help him. The moral of the story: admissions office administrators, invisible to you, will work hard to ensure your child's application is in working order, but remind your kid not to count on them to play Fairy Godmother.

The Evaluators

In a traditional admissions process known as "holistic evaluation," no single factor will knock a student out of the running or guarantee admission. At many colleges, two, possibly three evaluators thoroughly review each application.

- The first reader is often that regional representative who visited your child's high school in the fall. If your kid attends boarding school, her regional representative is the one in charge of the state where the school is located.
- The second reader might be one of those friendly, extroverted full-time admissions staffers you met at the info sessions you attended, or a hired gun like me (a.k.a. part-time, adjunct, or "outside" reader), trained to help out during crunch time. (I am also friendly and extroverted, in case you were wondering.)
- If the first and second readers disagree about an applicant, the file goes to "adjudication" and a third reader will weigh in.

Every college uses its own methodology. At an information session I attended at Emory University, the presenter said up to six people might read one application before a decision is made. But at every school, no matter what protocol they use, the attitude is similar. Evaluators are hopeful they'll find what they're looking for in your kid. They'll sift through your kid's application looking for reasons to rule her *in*, not to weed her *out*, as many applicants and parents suspect. They want to like her. For admission evaluators, opening each new application is like holding a quarter up in the air, ready to scratch off the silver coating over the lucky number on the lottery ticket.

In case you've forgotten, admission evaluators are human beings. They cry, laugh, think, and find multiple typos distracting. Sometimes I'm one of them, and during reading season, you will find me in my home office, still wearing pajamas at 2:30 p.m., like the romance novelist at the beginning of the movie *Romancing the Stone*. Like her, I'm off on adventures of the mind, crying alone at the keyboard over students' stories, wiping snot off my face with the sleeve of my bathrobe, and sometimes laughing out loud or exclaiming, "Oh no!"

Sometimes my husband, who also works at home, will yell from his office, "Is everything okay?" which is the first time I realize that I've said anything out loud all day. This is what happens when friendly extroverts hole themselves up in a room for months at a time reading hundreds of applications.

So is it true that at some colleges, evaluators spend less than eight minutes on each application?

Sensationalized news headlines have distorted another common evaluation method, "committee-based evaluation" (CBE), in which two admission evaluators partner to read applications as a team. Each will read half of an application simultaneously, discuss it, and then make decisions together. Even if each did spend eight minutes on the application, that would total sixteen minutes, if we're being literal.

Overall, applicants receive an equal amount of airtime as they would in a holistic review, and the news stories neglect to mention the upside of CBE review for the student. When the work is divided, it saves about 200 hours (equivalent to 5 workdays) for a CBE reader evaluating 800 applications. The reader can use that full workweek of saved hours to have a life, so she won't end up burnt out, exhausted, and tempted to skim your child's file when it appears in her queue.

What are they looking for?

Superchildren, Mere Mortals, and Superchildren Disguised as Mere Mortals

Within the context of their high school environments, some kids are positively freaks of nature (in a good way) and widely celebrated for their achievements. You can watch the soccer team captain (also a National Merit semifinalist) score goal after goal under stadium floodlights. You can turn on the TV to witness the brainy Science Olympiad state champ answer the winning trivia question on *As Schools Match Wits*. At the school's orchestra concert, you can marvel at the violinist who has played first chair since middle school and twice at Carnegie Hall.

People hold up these very visible wunderkinds as examples of "kids who will definitely get in everywhere" when they apply to college (not always the case), but high-profile superchildren are not the norm. You may never have heard of the student who quietly creates stunning artwork, earns a black belt in jiu-jitsu and teaches it outside of the school community, or all but raises her little sisters while her parents work double shifts. In your world, she looks like a mere mortal. In my world, when I'm evaluating applications, her superchild powers are revealed.

The important thing to understand as you sit and wait is that colleges' priorities differ. *Your kid might be perceived as a mere mortal at one college but a superchild at another with the exact same rate of selectivity.*

What makes an essay stand out?

Reading essays is my favorite part of the application review process because I get to meet your kid through her teenage voice. I love teenagers. I love the creative way they think with those partially formed frontal cortexes and emote with their raging hormones. Mostly, I love how they dream.

Teenagers still have big, wild, irrational, ambitious dreams, and they should because some of their dreams will come true. I sit there in my home office reading kids' applications, and I think the world will be okay. The ardent environmentalist will devise a way to reverse global warming. The future economics major will someday rescue our country from debt, and the gifted scientific researcher will find the cure for Alzheimer's disease. I just know it. Their earnest voices give me hope that the next generation will solve all of the problems that my own generation has saddled them with.

A good essay will remind me that this application represents a three-dimensional human being who will become someone's college roommate, enhance classrooms, and make an impact beyond the campus gates after he graduates. We readers want to connect with the kid behind his credentials. We want to "get" him. Beyond that, we value a good story and clear, well-written, carefully proofread prose (the reason I keep harping on this).

One friend's kid took six AP classes, but my kid's school only offers two. Does that make my kid look worse?

In case you forgot, the AP program is just another Hydra head of the College Board. Your kid's high school has to buy the rights from this private company to offer an AP class, and many schools can't afford to or choose not to buy in. If your kid attends a high school that offers few or no APs, don't sweat it. She's in good company with kids applying from a cadre of elite private high schools in Washington, D.C., and many high schools offering the notably rigorous International Baccalaureate (IB) program. College admission evaluators are trained to look beyond the AP designation to find rigor on a transcript, in whatever way your kid's high school offers it.

Will the C that the mean PE teacher gave my kid sink her?

A C in physical education may have lowered your kid's GPA, but admission evaluators will focus much more closely on your child's grades in the five "majors" or "solids" (English, math, social studies, science, and foreign language). They'll look favorably upon grades that show an upward trend over the years, but they will also pay attention when a student explains in Additional Information that he spent a month of sophomore year in the hospital after an emergency surgery that affected his grades and everything else. The guidance counselor's letter will probably mention this as well. Evaluators know that even superchildren earn the occasional B or C. If I saw on an application that an uncharacteristic C in PE appeared in the same semester the student suffered emergency surgery, I'd want to lob a dodge ball at that mean PE teacher and see how it makes *her* feel. Then I'd note in my evaluation that the C represents the consequences of a debilitating surgery, not the student's potential to succeed in college.

Will readers be impressed by my kid's crazy-rigorous schedule?

GPAs come in two varieties:

- *Weighted:* Points are added for accelerated or honors classes. For example, on a four-point grading scale, A in AP Bio = 5.0; A in Honors Bio = 4.5; and A in College Prep Bio = 4.0.
- *Unweighted:* Grades in classes of different levels earn the same point value. For example, A in AP Bio = 4.0; A in Woodworking = 4.0.

If your kid's weighted GPA surpasses a 4.0, readers will know that he challenged himself and succeeded. If he's earned that GPA taking six solids (instead of the usual five) plus a college class senior year, it can indicate that he has an insatiable appetite for learning (corroborated by all his recommenders). That's superchild-level impressive.

I am sorry to say that most kids fill up their schedules with rigorous classes for reasons that don't make sense from a personal or admissions standpoint. They sign up for AP classes and IB programs because they think they have to, not because they're ravenous for knowledge. Evaluators can recognize this. A few common tip-offs: a) grades drop; b) activities are discontinued or listed in two-week increments; c) class selection is incongruous with the rest of the application. Students who sign up for superhuman academic programs for the sole purpose of looking good for college admissions make enormous sacrifices in their young lives, only to end up appearing "packaged" and similar to other kids who have done the same thing.

What if my kid's recommendations are bad?

I've only read one terrible recommendation ever, and it was about the most pompous student the teacher had ever met. That same kid wrote his personal essay, without an ounce of irony, about his extreme handsomeness. No joke. Otherwise, the recommendations I've read have ranged from generically positive to gushing. While the handsome student's teacher recommendation confirmed his arrogance, another student's recommendation will confirm his altruistic community service, and another will effuse about how the student juggles serving trays, like he's performing a circus act, at the restaurant where he's a busser. The "It's going to be okay" factor is very high on this one. I say this with genuine affection and all the best intentions: If you're worried about recommendations, you need to let it go.

Do evaluators really stalk applicants' social media or watch those ZeeMee videos?

Most admissions professionals do not have time to troll around the Internet looking for dirt on your kid. Except sometimes, kids do such dunderheaded things on social media that it's impossible for colleges to ignore. As an example, in 2017, at least ten students admitted to Harvard exchanged such egregiously racist and sexist posts on a Facebook group chat that Harvard rescinded their offers of admission.

Warn your kid that his social media's tentacles reach into every component of his life, including this one.

Some colleges accept videos students upload onto ZeeMee (designed for this purpose) as part of their personal profile. It's a new, optional platform and likely weighted similarly to an optional interview—meaning at the bottom of the importance hierarchy.

How do decisions get made?

Every college has its own unique decision-making process, so keep that in mind. I've worked behind the iron curtain in admissions offices, so I can provide a peek at one way this process has happened and will again.

Reader Reports

After reading an application, an evaluator will recommend the student through a written summary and numerical ratings. These "reader reports" will determine if and where an applicant will appear on the committee "docket" (roster of students to be discussed and voted upon in committee meetings). At this point in the process, an evaluator will become a champion for students who have stood out to him. He'll give them high ratings and take time and care to craft a persuasive report documenting why each of those students should be admitted. Next, the evaluator will roll up his sleeves to fight for these kids in committee. He feels invested in them now.

The Infamous Admissions Committee

I hate to shatter the illusion of men wearing tweed blazers and sucking on pipes and humorless women with severe hairdos, but the Admissions Committee is nothing so dramatic. In fact, the committee consists of ordinary-looking people, more or less, ages ranging from recent college graduates to grandparents. Most wear jeans and snow boots in my part of the country and need coffee to keep their engines running.

So there they are, circling a conference room table, grabbing donuts or some equally unhealthy confection from the box in the center. The air feels electric with the anticipation of extroverts who have read quietly for two months straight and are now ready to *talk*. Beside each coffee mug rests a four-inch-thick committee docket filled with the names of all the students who stood out to the people in the room.

Let's get real. Out of 8,000+ applicants to a highly selective liberal arts college, maybe 600 were not academically qualified, since students tend to self-select where they apply. Multiply that by five or so for a larger university. That means the Admissions Committee is in for one heck of a time choosing among the other 7,400 students for 500 spots. (They will use a complicated algorithm to figure out how many students they need to admit to yield those 500 students.) The committee members gathered around the conference table all know full well that any of the students included on the docket would do fine at the college. The question is, which have the capacity to become game changers?

The committee takes its job extremely seriously. Its members maintain an IV drip of coffee to remain alert so they can give every student the full attention she deserves and a fair shot at admission. They will discuss those kids ad nauseum and deliberate for weeks in that room. They will vote. Students on the docket who receive a majority of yeses are admitted, nos are denied, and if the vote is close, the student might be waitlisted. It's no big mystery that this committee decides by committee.

Oh, come on. It's a total crapshoot, isn't it?

At the very end of the evaluation process, as the committee tries to assemble a diverse, dynamic class out of so many superkids, luck does come into play. All else being equal, a kid writing a supplement about how he wants to major in Russian might have a slight edge over a future studio art major (even one with a rocking portfolio) if the college is trying to expand its Russian language program. At another college, the art department strongly supports that same artist for admission;

they've recently built a new art museum with studio space for more students, and that student is voted in unanimously. *Specific, sought-after attributes at one school may not be the same attributes another college seeks, and they may differ from one year to the next.* Therein lies your crapshoot.

I hope this crapshoot business is not all you take away from this section revealing the goings-on in admissions offices. I hope you can remember that a) colleges are working hard to find ways to include your kid, not weed him out; b) invisible forces—from office administrators, to high school recommenders, to college admission evaluators—will fight for your kid; and c) what happens in admissions offices isn't the devil's work.

TO-DO LIST

- ☐ Wait.
- ☐ Sled, ski, snowshoe, shovel the driveway, or hit the beach if you live in a warm climate (lucky you).
- ☐ Attend your kid's hockey game or theater production to show support in ways that have nothing to do with college admissions.
- ☐ Wait some more. As the saying goes, patience is not only how long we can wait; it's how we behave while waiting.

Chapter 14

Spring of Senior Year

THE WAIT IS OVER: RD NOTIFICATIONS ARRIVE

When our daughter was born, my husband (a.k.a. the sugar police) coerced me into banning any processed sugar whatsoever from entering her precious little body. This draconian crusade extended to her first birthday party, for which we recruited our friend Debbie (a talented baker as well as spreadsheet-maker) to bake our daughter a birthday cake sweetened exclusively with banana. A year later, my mother revolted against our sugar ban and snuck our deprived two-year-old out for ice cream. There were no eyewitnesses (at least, none related to us), so we have to take my mother's word for it that with chocolate soft serve smeared across her face, our toddler announced, "This is what I have *always* wanted my *whole life.*"

Your kid's wait for notifications from colleges may have felt like an entire lifetime too. By mid-March, those notifications finally begin to dribble in. One day, toward the end of the month, the Ivies do their big reveal en masse. By April 1, the mystery of college admissions will be solved for your child. Though a spring chill may linger in the air, that day marks the official start of ice cream season, as far as I'm concerned. I'm sure my mother would agree.

The (Ice Cream) Flavors of Notifications

Artificially Sweetened Vegan Vanilla (a.k.a. Denied)

Let's get two things out of the way: 1. Substituting coconut milk and Splenda for cream and sugar defeats the point of ice cream and reduces it to a different (inferior) food. 2. Denials, even the ones your kid expected, can be surprisingly painful for her. They are not boo-boos you can kiss away. See the ED Deferred or Denied section on p. 228 to help you deal with the aftershock.

Triple Chocolate Chunk (a.k.a. Admitted)

Acceptance is always a treat.

Ben & Jerry's Glampfire Trail Mix (a.k.a. New Innovations in College Acceptance)

One variation on the traditional acceptance is "Admitted but not yet." Some colleges accept students to start second semester, or even for the following year. Erika Blauth, one of our consulting college admissions officers, clarified that there are a couple of reasons this notification comes to pass. Some students specify on their applications that they want to start college winter semester if the option is presented. Others fall slightly below the top applicant group slated as admits at highly selective schools, yet evaluators are excited about them. Delayed acceptance provides a way to include those students in the class.

Butter Rum (a.k.a. Waitlisted)

Butter rum is an okay flavor. The rum injects a smidgeon of pizzazz, and it's more appetizing than ice creams that turn gray when you try to make them at home (#blueberry). But it's no mint chocolate chip, and it's not the preferred flavor of anyone I know. (If it's your favorite flavor, you have not yet tasted salted caramel.) A waitlist is exactly what it sounds like—more waiting—the RD version of a deferral, and the butter rum of spring notifications.

Waitlists are much, much longer than when my generation applied to college, sometimes including thousands of kids. They're frustrating as all get-out because there's no official order, making it impossible to know where your kid's situated on them. Many colleges keep huge waitlists' worth of students so they'll have a variety of benched applicants to choose among. One college might keep that kid from Nebraska dangling so they'll have a prospect from every state. Another might add a spare equestrian for the team in case the accepted one doesn't come. In short, waitlists are good for colleges but not for your kid.

(Not) fun fact: By the time a college begins pulling kids off the waitlist, there may be little to no money left to offer financial aid. If this is brand new, unwelcome news to you, siphon out the sweetened rum from the butter and cream, and drink up.

The Meaning of Life on the Waitlist

Inclusion on the waitlist acknowledges that someone out there other than you recognized your child's radiance (because waitlisted is not the same as denied). While some students will receive phone calls in April or early May if selected from the waitlist, I've heard of kids receiving those calls in August. It can happen, but (tough love alert) it probably won't. As an example of the odds, in 2017, Carnegie Mellon University reported waitlisting 3,808 students and admitting 7 of them.

Your child can take all of the proactive steps on the Student Checklist for What to Do Besides Wait When Waitlisted (below), but then she must move on. This shouldn't be as hard as it was after a deferral back in December because by now almost every kid knows other colleges would be thrilled to have her. It's time to start genuinely weighing her options, and that's hard to do if she's still dreaming (along with 3,807 other waitlisted students) that some other school will pluck her from the waitlist.

STUDENT CHECKLIST FOR WHAT TO DO BESIDES WAIT WHEN WAITLISTED

- Write a letter (email) of continued interest to remain on the waitlist. Follow guidelines on the Student Checklist for a Letter of Continued Interest, p. 235, or if a college provides a form to fill out instead, follow their instructions.
- Update the college on new grades when they come in, as school continued past January, when you pressed "send" on your applications.

- Involve the high school guidance counselor, who can ask the probing questions you and your parents want to ask but cannot without sounding neurotic and pushy (which you're not, of course, but colleges don't know that) — like how many kids the college took off the waitlist last year and what's the potential for that to happen for you this year?

- Proofread everything sent to an Office of Admission. I know you're sick of hearing this, but tons of typos in an email leave a worse impression than just about anything else that's within your power right now.

- Assume nothing will come of the waitlist and devote all your energy to deciding which college you will choose. By the way, congratulations on those other schools where you were admitted!

What Disappointing Notifications Can Do to Otherwise Perfectly Rational People

Parents talk smack.

Nobody got in anywhere this year.
My kid didn't get in because he doesn't play a sport.
That one B freshman year knocked him out of the running at all the good schools.

I imagine your local grapevine is as active as mine. I heard repeatedly that a high-profile superstar and co-valedictorian at the local high school in my town "didn't get into *any* of the top colleges" where "everyone thought she was a shoo-in." When I learned that she was choosing between Wesleyan University and Vassar College, I understood the grapevine's definition of the term "top colleges," which was not the same as mine. Even for that highly qualified co-valedictorian, landing one of the 1,890 spots at Princeton University (number one according to *U.S. News* that year) out of the 31,056 applicants would have beaten the 6.1% odds. Those best college rankings mess with otherwise rational people's heads.

Your fellow parents will say what they say for all kinds of reasons. Forgive them. They don't know what you know. Co-valedictorians and junior world chess champions get into "top colleges" every year, but so do "Normal Joes" who have flown under the radar. Every single year, *they all land.* That hot shot, high-profile superchild from your kid's high school might have looked like a shoo-in for prestigious colleges, but on the surface, your neighbors seemed perfectly happy in their marriage right up to the moment they told you they'd filed for divorce. You just don't know, and neither do those parents speculating wildly, spreading rumors, and talking smack.

Students might take disappointments harder than parents realize.

I've invited my daughter's friend who lived through it to share the student's perspective.

> College is where you'll study and live for the next four years, and where you'll make new friends, which is hugely important, but there's an additional social aspect that makes notifications a lot more stressful. It can really feel like not getting into a college means you weren't good enough, and other people in your school will see that failure. It's easy to feel judged in the hyper-competitive environment of senior year in high school. It also feels like the colleges you apply to are a reflection of your opinion of your self-worth. So applying to elite schools and not getting in can seem like you think you're better than you really are, which can feel embarrassing and awkward. It's hard to explain that to your parents. I definitely know that I was terrible to my parents at that time, and although I think they understood, I wish that I could go back and explain better what was going on. — Ben

MAKING THE DECISION

College Visits After Your Kid Is Admitted

Are visits and revisits worth it?

Amber, another of my daughter's friends, had decided that the colleges on her list seemed so similarly wonderful that she'd let them make the decision for her. She'd planned to visit a number of them only if admitted. Then the acceptances rolled in…and in…and in…eight acceptances in all, at colleges about which Amber felt equally enthusiastic. A great problem to have. How was a girl to choose?

Spring break jet-setting (but flying coach and lodging in college dorms). That's how. Amber flew from Massachusetts to Minnesota, Ohio, and all the way to Colorado. She took a few days off from school to drive to open houses and revisit the colleges in New England that had admitted her. She completed homework on airplanes and in the passenger's seat of a car driven by her frazzled father.

When I painted a bathroom in my house, I learned that choosing among slightly varied shades of green was much harder than choosing between green and blue. I think that's what Amber's decision must've felt like when she nibbled cookies in my kitchen on April 30, the day before she had to make her final decision. She'd narrowed it down to four colleges out of the eight she'd visited in the past month. When she left my house that day, it could've gone in any direction.

I do not recommend Amber's extreme April odyssey for every child. However, visits and revisits are a good idea if your kid's having trouble choosing. I'm fairly certain Amber would've been happy at any of those colleges. Visiting them, however, made her feel more confident when she announced to her parents she'd chosen the college that was (wouldn't you know it) the farthest away from home.

Rolling Out the Red Carpet for Admitted Student Visit Days

Admissions offices organize events with balloons, free food, and swag in an attempt to yield as many admitted kids as possible. These events do not represent a typical day at the college, but they can give undecided students the chance to observe classes, stay overnight in a dorm, and learn more about the school (though so can visiting on another day without all the pomp and circumstance). The prospect of going to college starts to feel real to them. It's exhilarating. Plus, it's flattering to feel wanted. Some students love them.

Then there are kids like mine. My daughter, accepted Early Decision, looked forward to attending the Admitted Students Day, where she expected to meet some of her future classmates as excited about the college as she was. Instead, she ended up eating shepherd's pie in a dining hall while listening to other admitted students—who were "meh" about her future college—compare where else they'd been accepted, as if it were a contest. My daughter learned that day that admitted student events are usually not designed with the already committed student in mind. For her, attending the event stoked doubts and anxiety she had to live with all summer. Joining a Facebook group to bond and celebrate with real future classmates would have been a better bet for my child.

The Financial Factor

I am so thrilled for your kid. Really, I am. I don't mean to cut short the celebration, but if you momentarily forgot that colleges are businesses, dealing with financial aid will remind you.

Negotiating (Only Don't Call It That)

Financial aid offers, some better than others, accompany acceptances. You can compare them using my friend Erika's Financial Aid Calculator that she donated to our cause and that I've shared on my website. It will calculate and compare the numbers for you so you don't have to do math! If your child is leaning toward attending Utopia University, but Heavenly College offered her more money, it's time to make a tough phone call. On the plus side, college financial aid offices happily field parent calls, so you won't have to nag your kid to do it. Another plus: If a college accepted your kid, they will now do what they can to yield her.

Your telephone script: *My child is really excited about [name of college], but you only offered [dollar amount] in aid, while [name of another, more generous college] offered [a higher dollar amount] in aid. Can you match it?*

Be prepared to scan or fax that other college's offer as proof. If your kid's first choice has the funds, they might increase the offer. If not, asking is less painful than kicking yourself for not asking while eating instant ramen noodles every night for the next four years.

Even if your kid didn't receive a better financial offer elsewhere, you may have some fodder for negotiation. Return to the Expected Family Contribution (EFC) that appeared on the college's online calculator when you typed in your numbers last fall. If there's a huge discrepancy between the EFC and the amount a college is offering now, you have grounds to ask for more financial assistance. As an example, if the school's tuition is $55,000, your EFC comes to $25,000, but the college only offers you $4,000 in grant money, go ahead and (politely) appeal their lame offer.

If your family's financial circumstances have changed and you need more assistance than anticipated, alert the Office of Financial Aid. For example, if you're an independent contractor, your income fluctuates. (Believe me, I know.) If you reported your numbers from two years ago on your FAFSA, a dry spell since could change your need and a college's aid offer significantly. Or not. You'll never know if you don't ask. You can send them updated tax forms as evidence.

Finally, I have heard that some private colleges that require the CSS Profile might be willing to take your home equity out of the equation. I emphasize *might*. It seems to me you shouldn't have to pay thousands extra in tuition just because you live in your house, but I'm not the one making up the rules. I'm passing along every ounce of information I can to help you make college more affordable.

The Onerous Emotional Task of Helping Your Kid Through This Decision

This right here is the climactic moment of the entire college admissions rite of passage for you. It's not the moment your kid chooses a college, or her graduation from high school, or college drop-off day. Your role in the *act* of choosing represents the crossroads between every ounce of parenting you've accomplished to raise this young adult capable of making an important decision...and letting her go and make it. Put another way, you've taken baby steps leading up to the edge of the crevasse, and now you must leap across it.

Your child has all the facts necessary to make this decision. All you have to do is create the perfect environment for her to feel supported yet not pushed, independent yet not alone, and excited but not anxious as she makes the first big decision of her young adult life. Easy peasy. (Ha!) I hope it brings you comfort to know we understand the precarious perch upon which you're balanced because we are right there with you. We also understand that our reinforcement is not enough. What you need now are strategies (lots and lots of them). Good news! Every chapter in this book has been leading to this decision, so we can recycle strategies you already have stored in your toolbox.

Practical Points You Can Revisit to Help Your Child Choose

- Criteria your child contemplated during college visits (p. 70) can help her compare schools as she deliberates now. Class size, appealing clubs, people she met, etc., could become deal breakers or makers for her. (Try not to bring the adorable or dud tour guide into it.)

- The questions posed on the agendas for both the junior spring and senior fall family meetings (pp. 103 and 196) will help her compare some of the colleges' big-picture features such as big or small, urban or rural, distance from home, and academic programs offered. Ask if her earlier responses to the questions you raised on those agendas still hold true. (If she completely reverses her previously steadfast opinions, avoid muttering phrases like "You have got to be kidding me" or "Holy mother of God.")

- Remind your kid that how her college choice looks to other people is irrelevant. (See p. 191 if the need for a competition detox arises.) All the hype aside, this is your child's life. No matter how highly a college is ranked, or how prestigious its reputation, your kid is the one who has to *live* there. Advise her to base her decision on what *she* wants and feels, not on impressing Aunt Raina or that cute boy in her physics class. (Tell her when she's your age, she won't even remember that boy's name.)

- Outside intervention is still available! The high school guidance counselor can help your child analyze data points, or if this decision sends your kid (or you) into a tailspin, a mental health professional can help restore some clarity.

Strategies for When Your Kid's Emotions Run High

- You've used the positive reinforcement approach a million times throughout your child's life. Apply it now, if she needs reassurance.

- The optimistic approach can come in handy if your kid is so torn up about what to do that she can't see how lucky she is to have this decision to make in the first place.

- If she feels too much pressure to make the one and only right decision, lower the stakes by emphasizing that *there is not only one right college for your child*. Remind her that every college she's considering offers amazing opportunities and she'll make the college she chooses her "perfect fit" once she arrives there.

- Unless it's 11:58 p.m. on May 1, a break from thinking about this might be what your kid needs most. Employ the Magician's Maneuver and use misdirection to distract your kid with a trip to the ice cream shop (under the assumption that ice cream always helps). Sometimes taking a breather will tamp down anxieties and provide a fresh perspective.
- *Tell your child how proud you are of her no matter what decision she makes.* You never know what kind of fear she has roiling inside of her. If she's worried that she might disappoint you, you have the power to remove that obstacle once and for all, so she can think through her decision more clearly.

Strategies for When *Your* Emotions Run High

- Try invoking the Rule of Five (if it won't matter in five years, it's not worth more than five minutes of stressing about it now) when your kid says something out of left field such as "I could *never* go to a college that has Diet Pepsi instead of Diet Coke in the dining hall." Within five minutes, she's bound to come up with other less random criteria.
- Use the Zen (a.k.a. Don't Be a Hater) approach to combatting your assailant if your kid turns on you (p. 112). Remember that teenage hormones still rage within her. If your child works herself up into an agitated state and takes her frustrations out on you while she struggles to decide her path, recall that whatever she's saying has nothing to do with you or your parenting. (You can move beyond Zen to setting limits if her strikes escalate into guerrilla warfare.)
- You can also use the Zen approach when other parents start talking smack. Some parents (who now suddenly know everything there is to know about college admissions) will not be shy about telling you exactly which school is the best and which your child should choose. Some will have the *U.S. News and World Report* rankings of each of your kid's options memorized. Others will tell you it's a miracle your kid got in because *no one*

else did. Don't join them in their smack talk, but try not to judge them too harshly either. This is not their finest moment, but it doesn't mean they're inherently bad people.

- When she asks you where *you* think she should go to college, I recommend a combination of the In Cahoots with Your Kid strategy (which always works) and the Zipped Shut Lips strategy (which works much more effectively with students making college decisions than it does with relentless interrogators). Your kid will take ownership, feel good about her choice, and know you condone it if you zip your lips shut and nod your head in agreement with whatever she says as she weighs options.

- If you feel like you need to say something out loud, the Politician's Defense strategy (a.k.a. saying something without really saying anything)—as in, "I support whatever decision you make"—is the diplomatic solution. The caveat: Your kid might see through it and call you unhelpful or worse. Then you'll need to go back to the Zen approach all over again.

- Careful with the Truth Without Apology strategy. You can use it if that's your jam, though you have to keep in mind that teenagers usually choose the opposite of whatever parents say.

- This one is especially for you type-A parents: Inhale, exhale, and repeat as necessary. You will be tempted to make a pros and cons list or pull out your spreadsheet to review all those carefully recorded details about each college. You can do all that, and maybe it will help propel your child's decision forward, but chances are she'll make her ultimate decision based on a feeling deep within her that you won't see on any list or spreadsheet. It's your job to honor her choice, even if it doesn't make sense on paper. (I know what I'm asking of you. I *empathize*. I'm sure my kids would be happy to describe to you at length my own type-A tendencies. Just keep breathing.)

- Lean in and lean out as needed. Your child did not fundamentally change between the time she submitted her applications and now. If she scrambled at the last minute, then I think you know what's in store for you until midnight on May 1. As previously discussed, you can a) provide last-minute help without helicoptering, or b) go to bed at a reasonable hour and lie there between the sheets reciting the Serenity Prayer in your head while your kid meets the deadline on her own. (See p. 214 if you choose to pray.)

- For help enduring the next strategy on this list, among others, stock up on your beverage of choice, as you did before family meetings. 'Nuff said.

- *Let your child take the lead* has now become the cardinal rule for much more than college visits. Your child will likely make an excellent choice, but she might not, and she'll still be okay in the long run. Trust that you've taught her well how to pick up the pieces if she messes up, and that she knows she can count on you if she needs a little help gluing them back together. (This is championship-level letting go. I'm sending hopes, prayers, and a megadose of courage your way.)

- Always, above all, forgive yourself for anything you say or do wrong during your child's decision-making process and for all eternity. It should go without saying to forgive your kid if she doesn't act her sparkly best either. She'll need to make a number of big decisions in her lifetime, but this is her first, and emotionally (and legally for many) she's still a child.

May 1: National College Decision Day

At midnight on May 1, decisions are due for most colleges. See the Admitted Student's To-Do List (p. 226) for your child's checklist. See the rest of December's Admitted! section (p. 225) for yours. Make sure you've paid the deposit. Then you know that if it were me I'd inject ice cream into the celebration. And maybe a glass of wine. You do your own brand of party.

After the celebration, please make sure everyone who helped make your child's success possible is sufficiently updated and thanked, preferably in your child's handwriting (see Thank-You Note Checklist for Students, p. 124, and tweak it for the occasion). Even though you bore the brunt of the day-to-day drudgery, the financial strain, and the emotional hardship throughout your child's college admissions process, it took a village.

TO-DO LIST

- ☐ Rejoice in the great news!
- ☐ Ignore the denials. Those colleges are now inconsequential for your kid.
- ☐ Follow up on the waitlists, and then ignore those too.
- ☐ Your kid can pay colleges visits if he's having trouble deciding. Register for those admitted student visit days before they fill up, which can happen.
- ☐ Decipher and negotiate (only don't call it that) financial aid offers (for some).
- ☐ Use every strategy in your cache to be your very best, non-controlling self as you help your child make his first big life decision.
- ☐ Remove your credit card from your wallet and remit that deposit.
- ☐ Remind your child to inform any other college that admitted him that he has accepted an offer elsewhere. The sooner they know, the sooner they can offer someone on the waitlist a very pleasant surprise.
- ☐ Revel in the end of not knowing. You made it! I'm sending you and your child congratulatory vibes equivalent to a balloon bouquet, cake, champagne (or sparkling cider), a fruit basket, a heartfelt pat on the back, an armful of fresh-cut spring flowers, *and* ice cream.

Chapter 15

Graduation Through College Drop-Off Day

You dropped your kid off for his first day of kindergarten. You blinked. Now he wears a mortarboard and gown and stands in a row of identically dressed teenagers, some of whom you've known since they were three feet tall, who somehow look old enough to be college students. Your kid climbs the five steps up to the stage in the high school auditorium and glides toward the principal. He shakes the principal's outstretched hand, grasps his diploma in the other hand, shakes a few more hands — the vice principal, his guidance counselor, a teacher or two — climbs down the five steps on the other side of the stage, and takes his place in the line of classmates.

The whole sequence of events that transform your kid from a high school senior into a high school graduate takes a minute, tops, while you fumble in your bag for a tissue. If you can manage to snap a photograph and applaud your child as he walks across that stage, great. If not, it doesn't matter. You have clapped loudly and consistently for this kid his entire life. The sounds of your applause and "Woot! Woot!" amplified through the megaphone of your cupped hands are seared into his mind for the long haul.

The Long, Hot Summer Between High School and College

Communications from Your Kid's New College

You're on the mailing list now. College emails and newsletters include fun things like these:

- Welcome, new parents! Here's what to expect.
- Save-the-date for a special parents' welcome during your kid's orientation. (Light nibbles and beverages served.)
- Directions to the campus
- A list of local hotels and cute bed-and-breakfasts (where you will find no vacancies when you call for reservations)
- A schedule of entertaining drop-off activities for new students
- A list of necessities your kid will need (shopping!)

The communications also include not such fun things like these:

- A schedule of bills to pay
- An invitation to donate even more money to a specific cause (often a construction project)
- An invitation to donate your time to the college version of the PTO (which could skew positive, if you're in the right frame of mind)
- A list of all the things that your kid cannot bring into the dorm rooms, such as candles (fire hazards), electric hot plates (fire hazards), and drugs and alcohol (just plain hazards)

The Big Shop

The school will probably provide a shopping list for dorm necessities, which you can mostly ignore. Here are the real necessities your kid should bring to college:

- She'll need *bedding,* in the form of a comforter, pillow, and a set of extra-long sheets (which made me laugh because my daughter is five-one). My kid also requested a squishy bed topper (everything has to be size extra-long) after she saw the thin dorm room mattress—a worthwhile purchase that will last all four years (or the six years it takes for the average student in the U.S. to earn a B.A.).
- She'll need *toiletries* as well as something to carry them in on her way to the shower. She can bring the basics to get her started.

No need for a lifetime supply of Pantene; there's always a drug-store nearby or the Internet when she runs out, and soap can multitask as shampoo in a pinch.

- Buy some *school supplies*. How many is up for debate. If you're driving and have room in the car, you can hit the big box store before you leave, though every single college I know has a book-store with paper, notebooks, pencils, etc. If you're flying and fill a suitcase with a Costco quantity of Post-it notes, most will end up in the trash at the end of the year when your kid won't want to squander suitcase space to lug them back home.

- As far as electronics go, bring a *power strip surge protector, a long extension cord, and a fan.* There's no such thing as having too many places to plug things in, and on move-in day in a dorm without air conditioning, everyone will be grateful for that fan.

- If a *laptop computer* isn't in the cards for a graduation present, don't worry. Every college has a computer lab, as well as com-puter stations and printers in the library. Eventually, your kid will probably want her own computer for the inevitable all-nighter she'll pull, still a college rite of passage. PSA: Your kid might request a $1,500 Macbook, but a $200 Chromebook serves basically the same purpose.

- Your child does not need most of the *storage stuff* you might think she'll need. Buy a two-decker hanging rod that doubles closet space, a couple of those fabric "drawers" that will fold flat for travel, and hangers (though for many college kids, all the clothes will end up on the floor anyway). Her dorm room will come equipped with a bookshelf, so no need for that. Skip the bed risers, since many dorm beds have adjustable heights, and don't buy the under-bed plastic storage bins that take up all the space in the car until you've seen the room and know what will fit. Suitcases, duffels, or plastic bags work fine for under-the-bed storage.

- Pack *garbage bags.* I know that sounds weird, but hear me out. Garbage bags take up no space. They can be used for storage (under-bed or otherwise), rain ponchos, surprisingly workable sleds, laundry bags, and luggage. They are also useful for collecting trash. Need I go on?

- *Removable adhesive wall hooks* come in handy for bathrobes and jackets, and she'll need *sticky squares or picture-hanging gum* to decorate.
- Buy a *flashlight or headlamp* instead of a reading lamp. Your kid's dorm room might already come equipped with a desk lamp, and if she wants to read in bed while her roommate is sleeping, or the power happens to go out, she will be all set.
- *Appropriate clothing for the weather* is of utmost importance. If you're southern and your kid chooses a college in New England, don't wait until the first snow (which could come within a matter of weeks of her arrival) to buy a parka and boots. If your kid is going to college in a warm climate near an ocean, make sure she packs a swimsuit (because otherwise, skinny dipping).
- Print out a *photo of your family.* This is something she can't buy if she forgets it. Include the dog or cat in the photo, which is usually the family member a college student misses most.

Everything else she can acquire ad hoc, even the items on my list, except for the family photo and extra-long sheets (because by September, stores run out).

Things That You Honest to God Do Not Need to Buy

- Your kid does *not* need a mini-fridge the first day of college. You've paid for three square meals a day in the dining hall, and the only thing needing refrigeration that the college meal plan will not provide is beer.
- There's no sense buying a carpet until you know the room's dimensions, and if it's already carpeted with something not overly disgusting.
- Stereo equipment is obsolete now that everyone has a phone. If your kid needs music in her life beyond earbuds, discount stores

like Marshalls and TJ Maxx sell Bluetooth speakers for a song. (Do you see what I did there?)

- No on the TV. Even if your kid doesn't have her own laptop, she can share her roommate's to watch *Riverdale*.
- I will confirm your instinct that curtains and a string of sparkly lights, though lovely, do not qualify as necessities. The dorm room will have an overhead light and a window shade.
- This is a big one: There is not enough space in the car or in a tiny dorm room for the full body pillow your kid wants to buy at Target.

EMOTIONAL PYROTECHNICS

In every Fourth of July fireworks production, there's a grand finale. A ribbon of glitter streams across the black summer sky with barely a crackle, followed by a whistling rocket that bursts into a fiery pinwheel of light. Then multiple explosions ignite the sky all at once with a thunderous boom. Sparks stream from everywhere. You hardly know where to look until the fireworks dissolve into a cloud of smoke, and the sky quiets and darkens.

Everyone claps. You roll up your blanket and brush off the grass. The woman with the calla lily tattoo packs her folding chair into its nylon sleeve. The half-eaten pie is covered with tinfoil and slipped into the portable cooler. Little children fall asleep on their parents' shoulders, still clutching glow sticks, as they are carried to the parking lot and loaded into car seats. On the drive home, those little guys grow a tiny bit older. By the time their parents pull calico comforters over their shoulders, kiss their pink cheeks, and feel their warm cotton candy breath, these children have grown older still.

When you wake up, it's the fifth of July, the summer before your kid leaves for college. It's hot. Your kid grabs the keys to the family car for a road trip to the river with his friends (whom, he reminds you, he's leaving too). He insists he's an adult now, responsible for his own actions (except buying his own food or filling up the car with gas). He won't commit to what time he'll be home until he sees you assembling lasagna, his favorite, and says he'll be home for dinner. Your child is like that recently celebrated holiday of independence. He's all fire and thunder, exerting his independence and arguing with you one minute, then twinkling peacefully at the dinner table and even thanking you for the delicious lasagna the next. It's confusing for everyone, not just you.

What is happening?

Where to begin? Dr. Appy will help us disentangle the complex concoction of feelings churning inside your kid's brain (and yours), so we can tackle them one by one.

Anger

> *I cannot wait to get out of here!*
> *You are beyond annoying!*
> *I don't know when I'll be home, so stop bugging me about it!*

Okay, I am well aware that it's hard to remember that you love your child more than life itself while he's screaming, "I hate you. You are so [fill in the blank with something horrible]!"

On the inside, however, Dr. Appy says he's subconsciously trying to push you away because it's far easier to leave home angry than to leave while everyone's feeling the love. Most kids who enter this nasty stage will exit it before they exit the house for college. In the meantime, you get a free pass to complain to your heart's content to other adults when your kid acts like Linda Blair in *The Exorcist*. Set your limits (because we all have limits). Then do everything in your power to refrain from engaging in an argument if your kid tries to bait you. Despite his hurtful words, he needs you to provide a solid launching pad so he can blast off safely into the cosmos *in only a month and a half.*

Fear

Will I like my college roommate?
Will I make any friends?
What if I hate all my classes?

Some kids transfer all the fear that simmered throughout junior and senior year—the hours spent worrying, *What if I don't get into college?*—to this new mystery. The nervous child always finds someplace to channel her anxieties, and if you're anything like me, you're also entertaining some fears of your own.

Here's a scripted response from Dr. Appy if you need it: *Of course you're scared, but I'm always here for you. I have all the faith in the world that you'll find your way in college.*

Sadness

I've realized I won't live at home full-time ever again.
I will miss my dog, mom, friends, bed, favorite flowering tree…

If your kid is fixated on how much he'll miss Harry, his pet hamster, it's not all about Harry. Dr. Appy points out that Harry is a stand-in for the more existential loss he's feeling. He's also losing his childhood, innocence, and your daily caretaking. Sure, we feel the depth of this loss too, but we parents are pros at sublimating our own feelings to comfort our kids. By now, it's second nature. Use the script for the fearful child (see above), substituting "sad" for "scared." Once your kid's existential moment has passed…ice cream, anyone?

Excitement

Your kid's excitement can take a sweet, optimistic form, like *I can't wait to go to my first college football game!*

Or his excitement can take a negative turn, as in *I'm finally free of high school, this ridiculous town, and all the people in it!* Of course, one of the people in this ridiculous town is you. Try not to take it too personally.

Ignore the part where your kid's acting like an insensitive pill and focus on what he's really saying: *I am so excited to reinvent myself in college!*

To steer him back toward the pleasant type of excitement, you might respond, "Yes, I'm sure your new college town has way better [pizza, bike lanes, or whatever are your kid's priorities at this moment]. It's going to be awesome!"

Relief

> *I don't have to worry anymore about getting into college!*
> *No more curfew!*
> *I don't have to do another calculus problem ever again!*

While excitement is all about anticipating (with joy) what lies ahead, relief is an emotion that focuses on liberation from the past. Hang tough. It's calculus your kid feels relieved to leave behind, not you (well, maybe your curfew, but not your love). She also wouldn't mind burying the memories of the advent of acne, the bad haircut the day before prom (memorialized in the photograph that you will now remove from the mantel), the sudden abandonment of her childhood BFF when her friend made the cheerleading squad, and every other painful challenge of growing up. You've given it your all as a parent, and you've done an amazing job. Still, no one's childhood is perfect. We all have parts we'd be relieved not to carry with us into our future.

How to Help Your Kid Through His Emotions While You're Having a Few of Your Own

To paraphrase Dr. Appy's advice, you must suck it up. I'm sorry it has to be this way. Although your teenager has entered the realm of adulthood, you are still the elder. It's on you to try to hold yourself together while you handle your adolescent the same way you always have in times of emotional tumult. Do you remember when he gashed his forehead, how it looked like a bloody scene straight out of the movie *Carrie,* and instead of screaming and crying (like you were doing inside), you kept your cool while you called 911? How about that time you blazed with rage at that other sixth-grader who broke your kid's heart while you simultaneously gushed soothing platitudes like "It's her loss," and "You are so much better off without her"? You have done this before and survived. You've got this now.

You do get an exemption from sucking it up if you receive a call from the holding cell at the police station. Strong emotions do not excuse outrageous behavior. Everyone, even your kid, will understand that you cannot manage to hold yourself together every minute. Though you are the elder and a steady force in your child's life, you are not the Dalai Lama.

AND THEN THEY'RE OFF

The College Launch

What to Expect on Drop-Off Day

- You'll arrive on campus and your kid will check in. (FYI, you're supposed to remain scarce.)
- Either the whole football team (which has been training at the college for a week already) will surround your vehicle and help you haul your kid's belongings up the four flights of stairs to her dorm room…
- …or you'll throw out your back because your kid brought more shoes than any person needs and there's no help in sight.
- The posters your kid brought from home that you try to mount on the wall with those adhesive squares will fall down a few times before you can get them to stick. Persevere! The adhesive's not perfect, but it works, and you won't be fined at the end of the year for nail holes in the wall.
- Your kid will meet her roommate, and she'll like the look of her right away, or she won't.
- Your kid's dorm will probably have an activity set up for the new students. Eating lunch in the dining hall together or migrating en masse to Security to have IDs made are popular ones.

- There will be something for you to do, like a meeting for freshman parents in a big auditorium.
- There will be a goodbye.

I don't know how to tell you to do this goodbye, but I can tell you about mine. I am a crier. I see a wedding between two animated pigs on TV, and I'll cry. So it took everything I had during that final hug with my daughter to remain dry-eyed, but I did it. Luckily, we'd parked the car close by, so I could turn my head quickly, duck into the passenger's seat, and take cover before the waterworks began. My sweet husband patted my hand and kept glancing at me (when he should have been watching the road) to make sure I was okay for most of the hour and a half drive home. Our son piped up from the back seat that he was sure she'd be fine, which was such a sweet gesture that it made me cry even harder.

When I exited the car—once full of her belongings, now echoing in its emptiness—I felt forlorn enough to enter the bedroom my daughter had vacated. It had seemed like she'd stuffed everything she owned into the car until I opened that bedroom door. Clothes were strewn everywhere. A bottle of expensive moisturizer sat open on her desk with no sign of the cap. Her crumpled sheets spilled over the edge of the unmade bed. Smack in the middle of the floor she'd left her packing list, a pen uncapped on the white carpet (grrr), and my sewing box gaped open, the tomato-shaped pincushion exposed. Since when did she sew? And the bigger question: Who did she think would clean this up? I resolved to shut the door and make *her* clean it up when she came home for Thanksgiving. The upshot? When sadness mutated into anger, it made that goodbye a lot easier.

Letting Them Go for Real

They will eat bad food, maybe gain the freshman fifteen, work hard, perhaps play hard, meet fascinating people, and become involved in their new lives in ways that will surprise you. They will surprise themselves with their ability to navigate this twilight world between childhood and adulthood, a simulated reality where everyone's the same age and wanting the same thing—a higher education. Never again will they live in such close quarters, sharing such similar life experiences with peers (unless they are incarcerated).

At home, you will set an extra plate at the dinner table for a while. You will pop out of a work trance and wonder what your kid is doing at that very moment. Your fingers will itch to pick up the phone to call her, or at least send a text just to see how she's getting along. Though radio silence is painful, it's what you want. The less you hear from your kid, the better she's adjusting. If your kid calls every day, know that some kids have a tough transition, but by second semester, most are in a much better place (and then they'll neglect you properly). Stay strong and supportive, but don't initiate the calls, and don't hop into a car and rush to campus to rescue your child. You both have to figure this out on your own.

TO-DO LIST

- ☐ Plan some togetherness time with your imminently departing teen. Be flexible; it will probably get canceled.
- ☐ Don't beat yourself up when you wish your kid out of the house already. It's normal.
- ☐ Don't think you've gone insane when in the next breath you want to cling tightly and keep him by your side forever. That's normal too.
- ☐ If your kid is acting like he is ready to leave you and get on with it, it's because he is. (If you dig deeply enough, you might find that you are ready for him to go too.)
- ☐ Remind yourself that parenting is a job with a lifetime contract and no financial remuneration (you actually lose money on it), but it reaps other, more valuable rewards that are hard to define.
- ☐ Savor your child's presence, which you can already feel drifting beyond your reach. He will go, but he will come back. He will go again and again, and each time he will return in a different way.

Epilogue

FIVE LESSONS FROM THE COLLEGE ADMISSIONS PROCESS TO APPLY TO YOUR LIFE

1. Forgive others for their mistakes, and always forgive yourself.
2. Let your child take the lead in his own life, and you do you in yours.
3. Remember the Rule of Five: If it won't matter in five years, it's not worth more than five minutes of stressing about it now.
4. Take time to tell your child, and all your loved ones, how much you love and admire them. Even when you think they can't hear you, they are listening.
5. Inhale. Exhale. Repeat.

THE CHILL PARENTS' REVOLUTION

Let's hold hands and form a closing circle. Sure, it's a little hokey, but we have been through a lot together in this support group of ours. I'll start.

It's been an honor to serve as your facilitator. Thank you for trusting me to guide you on this journey. I knew all along you could get through this with dignity and humor, and now you know it too. We parents are warriors. From the moment our children were born, we've fought for them until we were confident they could fend for themselves. Now they can, and a critical mass of us parents still have quite a bit of fight left in us. Together, we can become a tribe that fights for one another. We've saved our kids and ourselves from college admissions madness, so let's join forces and pay it forward.

It's your turn to be the sane one, the confidante, and the resource during those coffees (or stiff martinis) with the parents of juniors, who are starting to flip out. Do you remember back at the beginning of your kid's junior year, when you were like them? When you look across the table at your friend's face, devoid of lipstick and hope, tell her she is not behind. She is right where she should be. Tell her to forgive herself for any parenting misdemeanors she's committed in the past. Tell her she is more powerful than she realizes, powerful enough to conquer even the College Board's evil empire. Teach her that when she begins to stress out about rankings, prestige, competition, and the interrogators who will incessantly hound her about where her kid's applying, there's another way. Be her guide. Hand her this book.

If she starts to cry or laugh maniacally right in the middle of Starbucks, let her. Tell her you were not (and are not) always the chillest parent in the room either. Then here's what you can do. Remove from around your neck the Medal of Parenting Valor you've earned and ceremoniously drape it around hers. You don't need it anymore (unless you have a younger child—then you can simply show the medal to your friend, tell her she deserves one too, and tuck it back under your blouse for safekeeping).

As for you...you have full permission to experience all the feelings anyone would feel when graduating from one part of the parenting voyage and starting another. Your kid will always be your kid, and you'll evolve into parenting your grown-up child differently. You'll know how to do that, the same way you intuitively knew when she was a newborn that one cry meant she was hungry while another meant she needed a nap. You'll just know; trust me. Most important, trust yourself.

That's all I've got to say, for now, but let's continue holding hands. Who wants to speak next?

TO-DO LIST

☐ College students enduring dining hall food appreciate care packages containing cookies, so you might want to send one. (Storebought is fine. It's the thought and refined sugar that count.)

☐ Turn your kid's vacated room into that craft room you've always wanted, or invite guests to stay in the new extra bedroom in your house.

☐ Spread the word that tests, participating in the cutthroat competition, and even stress are optional parts of the college admissions process, and invite other parents to join our Chill Parents' Revolution. Tell them that actually being a chill parent is not a prerequisite.

☐ Gear up to do college admissions all over again, only wiser and better, if you have another kid.

☐ Treat yourself to wine, a Tahitian vanilla macchiato (with extra whipped cream), or any beverage of your choice. This always has been, and always will be, a judgment-free zone.

Resources

I've shared downloadable PDFs and links to recommended resources on my website, jillshulman.com. What's mine is yours.

TOOLS TO SAVE YOU FROM COLLEGE ADMISSIONS MADNESS

- Organize on paper the Luddite's way:
  - College Shopping Worksheet (p. 98)
  - College Application Checklist (p. 208)
- Organize the fancy, tech-savvy way:
  - Google Calendar
  - Debbie's Dazzling College Planning Spreadsheet (includes checklists and tabs for everything! It's on my website.)
  - Erika's Financial Aid Calculator (will process the numbers for you, so you don't have to do math! It's on my website.)
- Family meeting agendas:
  - Agenda for a Junior Spring Family College-Planning Meeting (p. 103)
  - Agenda for a Senior Fall Family Meeting (p. 196)
- Guidelines for you:
  - A Typical Testing Timeline for Junior and Senior Year (p. 54)
  - How Many Spring Break College Visits Are Too Many? (p. 119)
  - Guidelines for Appropriate Proofreading (p. 156)
  - When and How Students Submit College Applications (p. 192)

CHECKLISTS FOR YOUR KID

- Interview Checklist for Students (p. 123)
- Thank-You Note Checklist for Students (p. 124)
- Student Checklist for Supplemental Essay Prep (p. 178)
- Student Checklist for What to Do Besides Wait When Waitlisted (p. 255)
- Student Checklist for a Letter of Continued Interest (p. 235)
- Student Checklist for Treating Recommenders Right (p. 203)
- Admitted Student's To-Do List (for Binding Agreements) (p. 226)

TESTING

- *Test prep books:* A highly nonscientific survey (of my Facebook and IRL friends) reveals that the old tried and true Stanley Kaplan and Princeton Review books are still most popular.
- *Online test prep:* You can turn directly to the ACT website, or to the College Board, now in cahoots with Khan Academy, to get online test prep help for free. One friend's kid liked the Kranse method for test-taking strategies, endorsed and subsidized by investors from the TV show *Shark Tank* (I remain neutral on whether the Sharks' involvement is a pro or a con).
- *National Organization for Fair and Open Testing (FairTest):* I direct you to this website listing more than 1,000 test-optional and test-flexible colleges for whenever you need a pick-me-up.
- If your kid attends a public high school, the Education Commission of States website will inform you if your kid will automatically take the SAT or ACT as his state-required test. If a test is required, you won't have to pay for it or make any decisions about which test is the better one for your kid (but if you do need to decide, see "Is the SAT or ACT the better test for my child to take?" p. 43).

RESEARCHING COLLEGES

- *College guidebooks: Fiske Guide to Colleges* won the reference book contest among my friends. *Colleges That Change Lives* won as the most helpful under-the-radar book, and *The Insider's Guide to the Colleges*, by the *Yale Daily News,* received a shout-out.
- *Online platforms:*
  - Naviance and College Kickstart are popular online platforms high schools use for college planning. Contact your child's high school guidance office for access (because I'm guessing your kid won't share his password).
  - The National Center for Education Statistics (NCES) website provides basic facts about a host of colleges (not in a very colorful way, but not exaggerated for advertising purposes either).
  - The creators of the College Trips and Tips website have researched the area beyond the campus. They advise where to stay and eat when visiting.

SUMMER AND GAP YEAR

- There are numerous *travel programs* for high school students. A few: The Workaway "community for volunteering, working, and cultural exchange." Putney Travel looks like a fun service trip company, if you can afford it. If you're still interested after you saw the price tag on those Putney trips, Overland offers teen summer expeditions for kids who enjoy hiking or biking.
- *Academic Summer Programs:* Johns Hopkins Center for Talented Youth and Brown University Pre-College Program are popular ones.
- *Indoors:* McDonald's hires high school kids. Locally, your kid can find a university science lab, bicycle repair shop, or froyo store that might hire her too.
- *Outdoors:* The National Parks Service youth programs, Appalachian Mountain Club (AMC), Outward Bound, National Outdoor

Leadership School (NOLS), and other such organizations offer teen wilderness education excursions. Swimming pools and beaches need lifeguards every summer. Little kids need camp counselors and babysitters. Lawns need mowing. You get the idea.

READING (AND VIEWING) TO RAISE YOUR HACKLES

- *Where You Go Is Not Who You'll Be*, by Frank Bruni (an honorary member of the Chill Parents' Revolution)
- *Excellent Sheep*, by William Derceiwics (the author's a little grumpy, but never dull)
- By the end of the documentary *The Test and the Art of Thinking* (Canobie Films), your eyes will be wide open.

FINANCES

- Find a breakdown of expenses you could encounter during the college admissions process, as well as some hidden costs you can avoid, on my website. See p. 55 for the price of testing alone.
- The U.S. Department of Education has a special office entirely devoted to Federal Student Aid for help filling out and understanding the FAFSA.
- You can find information about regional reciprocity, the potential for enjoying in-state tuition rates at out-of-state colleges in your region, on the National Council for State Authorization Reciprocity Agreements (NC-SARA) website.
- Massachusetts Educational Financing Authority (MEFA) is a non-affiliated nonprofit you can trust, if you live in Massachusetts. Hunt for such an organization in your state. Also, the National Association of Student Financial Aid Administrators is a MEFA partner, so I know they'll provide legit input about financial aid.

FINDING SCHOLARSHIPS

- Some big-ticket scholarships include the Siemens Foundation Scholarship and Regeneron Talent Search for science whiz kids; the Gates Millennium Scholars program; and the Coca-Cola Scholars Foundation.
- The Questbridge College Match program finances a college education for high-achieving low-income students. If yours is such a student, also look into the Posse Scholars and Dell Scholars programs.
- Listings for local scholarships are often included on Naviance, or whatever platform your kid's high school uses. Also, high school guidance counselors tend to be on top of things, so use them as a resource for scholarships.

SPORTS, ARTS, AND APPLICATION VIDEOS

- The National Collegiate Athletic Association (NCAA) website explains sports recruiting and includes recruiting calendars for every sport.
- National Unified Auditions for Undergraduate B.F.A. Programs in Theater are offered in three major cities for twenty-six different schools, in case traveling to the college itself is a hardship.
- ZeeMee is a social media platform designed for kids to send images and videos to supplement their college applications.

EMPOWERMENT AND SANITY SAVERS

- Watch Amy Cuddy's TED Talk, or learn from her book, *Presence,* how to strike a power pose right before standardized tests, interviews, a first date, or anything else you or your child might find scary.
- Especially if you have younger children, too, here are recommendations for a few books that will support your beautiful, messy, imperfect, ultimately successful parenting: *How to Be a Happier*

Parent by KJ Dell'Antonia, *The Gift of Failure* by Jessica Lahey, and *Enough As She Is* by Rachel Simmons if you have a girl.

- Dinner table conversation starters can be hand-created, or ready-made TableTOPICS can be purchased, and can save your relationship with your child when he is 100% done with talking about college. (See p. 183 for a few.)

RESOURCES FOR WRITING THE APPLICATION

- Find the essay prompts required for most students at The Common Application and the Coalition for Access, Affordability, and Success websites. (Then ignore those prompts if they stress your kid out, tell him to select "topic of your choice," and carry on. See p. 151.)
- Turn to Application Intel (p. 162) for guidance and insights on writing each part of the application.
- For help with the infamous personal essay, see Time to Write (or Plan to Write, or Think About Writing) the Personal Essay (p. 147), and A Cure for Writer's Block (p. 152).
- Find more essay-writing tips to share with your kid at my website (jillshulman.com).

Acknowledgments

There's no way I could've pulled this book together without the help of my own professional and personal support group, including but not limited to Tracy Behar and the entire team at Little, Brown Spark; Anna Worrall and the Gernert Company team, with a special shout out to Libby McGuire and Alia Habib; and the patience and advice of Dr. Katherine Appy, Psy.D. My cup runneth over with gratitude for the wisdom of so many intrepid parents (including my own), students, and college admissions colleagues too numerous to list here, some named within the pages of this book, and others invisible to you but invaluable to the revolution. My children and husband deserve top billing for providing my greatest inspiration and guidance in art and in life. Thank you, Hannah and Ethan, for graciously letting me steal your stories for the benefit of others, and to Mat, always my first reader and a very handsome (he added that because: first reader) support group unto himself.

Glossary of College Admissions–Related Terms You Can Never Un-Know

Academic merit: This term usually comes into play when financial aid offices award scholarship money to a student for her academic achievement and potential (as opposed to her family's financial circumstances).

Accepted: Your kid got into college. Congratulations!

ACT: An abbreviation (sort of) for a standardized test. ACT once stood for American College Testing, but now it's a brand name for a company.

Adjudication: A third application evaluator steps in to break the tie if two readers disagree on what the outcome should be for an applicant.

Admit: A student who is accepted to a college is an admit. In admissions, it's often used as a noun.

Admitted: The same as accepted to college, or becoming an admit. All good.

AP: Stands for Advanced Placement, usually (and if capitalized like so) referring to rigorous high school classes with a curriculum approved by the College Board's Advanced Placement program.

Arts Supplement: A portfolio of student work in music, film, theater, dance, or creative writing submitted to colleges in the form of a video, slides, or written excerpts as an add-on to the primary application.

Athletic recruiting: Coaches draft high school students to play a sport in college.

Athletic reel: A highlights video taken of an athlete to show how well she will play her sport in college, if the coach will help her get in.

It's like that video footage of your kid's winning goal you proudly posted on Facebook, only more polished.

Binding: A pact your kid makes with a college when she applies Early Decision or Early Decision 2. If she is admitted, she enrolls. No take-backs.

CBE: Committee-based evaluation. Two admission officers sit together in a room and partner to evaluate applications as a team.

Coalition Application: An online form kids can fill out to apply to some colleges—a competitor for the Common Application.

College Board: The purveyor of standardized tests, the AP program, and so much more that will cost you dollars and will cost your kid many hours of her young life that she can never get back.

College Kickstart: An online college planning tool.

College Match: Generally refers to programs, such as Questbridge, that pair outstanding students from traditionally under-represented groups with colleges that will subsidize their education.

Common Application: Your kid fills out this one online application and can fire it off to multiple colleges.

Core curriculum: Specific classes that every student who attends a college must complete to graduate.

CSS Profile: If you can succeed in wiping one college-related term from memory, this is it. CSS stands for College Scholarship Service. The College Board distributes this application for private school financial aid. Let's put it this way—my friend Carin told me she'd rather have another C-section than fill out the CSS Profile again.

Deferred: Instead of either accepting or rejecting your child, a college bumps her from Early Decision or Early Action to the Regular Decision pool of applicants, in which she must wait an extra four to five months for the school to make a bloody decision.

Demonstrated interest: The ways you can show a college you're serious about it, including but not limited to a campus visit or an interview.

Demonstrated need: The amount of money colleges think you need to pay their fees, based on their evaluation of your financial aid forms. (It's never as much as you really need.)

Denied: Your kid didn't get into the college. It can be painful, but it's time to move on.

Distribution requirements: Students must take classes in specified categories (for example: Humanities, STEM, Social Studies) to graduate from the college, though within those categories, students can choose their own specific classes.

Division 1, 2, and 3: Athletic categories designed by the NCAA to determine competition level of athletic contests and resources allocated to athletics for small (D3), medium (D2), and large (D1) colleges and universities.

Docket: The list of students to be discussed and voted upon in Admissions Committee meetings.

Dual enrollment: When your kid takes a college class while still in high school and receives high school credit for it.

EA: An abbreviation for Early Action, meaning your kid can apply to a college in November and find out a month later whether she's in or not, but she doesn't have to make a decision until May 1.

ED: Stands for Early Decision, meaning your child applies to a college around November 1, promises to attend if accepted, and the college notifies her in December. If accepted, the admissions process is done for your child and she can enjoy the rest of her senior year.

ED2: An abbreviation for Early Decision 2. Your child applies around January 1, the same day the RD application is due, only your child signs a binding agreement that she'll attend the school and withdraw all of her other applications if she's accepted.

EFC: Expected Family Contribution is an estimate of how much you'll have to pay the college per year.

Elective: A high school class not considered a "major" or "solid," for example, computer programming, art, or yearbook.

ERW: Evidence-Based Reading and Writing is one of a series of names the College Board has called one of the sections of the SAT test (the one that's not math).

ETS: An abbreviation for Educational Testing Service, which is the company that scores the SAT test.

FAFSA: The Free Application for Federal Student Aid to request money from the government to help pay for college.

FERPA: The Family Educational Rights and Privacy Act (a.k.a. the Buckley Amendment of 1974) gives parents (of students under eighteen years old) and students (eighteen and older) the right to access student records, and requires the student (or parent, if the student is a minor) to give permission before her info is released to a third party.

First generation: If neither parent attended a four-year college, the applicant is among the first generation of her family to attend college.

Fit: The college has the potential to work well for your child once she gets there.

Forced triple: You pay the same amount for your kid to share a room with two roommates as the parent of the kid down the hall pays for him to share the same-sized room with only one roommate.

Gap year: Taking a year off to do something else between high school and college.

GED: Students take a test and earn the equivalent of a high school diploma, called a General Education Diploma (a.k.a. General Education Development, for some reason).

GPA: Abbreviation for grade point average.

Grant: Free scholarship money from the college to help pay for your child to attend.

Handshake: A handshake in college admissions is more like something from a secret society than a friendly greeting. It's usually a coach's hand that's shaken, while the coach says without really saying it that your kid will get into a college if she applies Early Decision (though the admissions office has the final say). I've also heard parents say their kid "verballed" or "committed" to a coach, which amounts to the same thing.

HBCU: Abbreviation for Historically Black College and University. There are 101 of them in the country as of this writing.

Holistic evaluation: No single factor on your kid's application will knock him out of the running or guarantee admission.

IB: International Baccalaureate program, a rigorous high school curriculum.

IDOC: You think you're finally done with the CSS Profile, until the College Board website instructs you to go to IDOC, an acronym for Institutional Documentation Service, where you have to pay five bucks and change to upload your tax returns.

Information session: A.k.a. "info session," in common vernacular. An hourlong presentation at a college during which an admissions office staffer tells you everything the college wants you to know.

Institutional priorities: The college seeks applicants who embody the college's most significant values and needs, which can vary widely among colleges and from year to year.

Khan Academy: A free online study mecca for students.

Late bloomer: Academically, this usually means a student who didn't bother much with schoolwork and his grades showed it, until escalating college talk lit a fire under his butt and he started caring more and performing better halfway through high school.

Legacy: An applicant whose parent or grandparent attended the college to which he's applying.

Letter of continued interest: If your kid applies ED and is deferred, she writes an email to let the college know if she still wants to be considered in the RD pool. She must write a similar letter if she wants to remain on a waitlist.

Liberal arts: Students study a variety of subjects in college, resulting in a well-rounded education.

Loan: Money that you can borrow at a low interest rate to pay for college, but you'll have to pay back with interest. This is the part of your financial aid agreement that places your child in debt.

Majors: Sometimes during the college admissions process you'll hear the five main high school academic subjects — English, mathematics, social studies, science, and foreign language — referred to as academic "majors" or "solids." Once your kid enters college, his "major" will be the main subject he plans to study, and the word "solid" will mean "favor," as in "Do me a solid."

Merit aid: The college decides how much financial aid they will provide based on your child's high school academic record.

National College Decision Day: Enough colleges give students a May 1 deadline to decide whether or not they will accept the college's acceptance that it became a national holiday. (You still have to go to work.)

Naviance: This is a popular online college admissions planning platform used by high schools.

NCAA: National Collegiate Athletic Association is the main governing body of college athletics and creates all the recruiting rules.

Need aware: The college might take into consideration whether or not your kid needs financial aid while they make their admission decision about her.

Need-based aid: The college decides how much financial aid they will provide solely based on the financial aid forms you filled out.

Need blind: The college doesn't take into consideration whether or not you can afford to pay them full tuition when they are making their admission decision about your kid.

On the bubble: The student's credentials place her in between a "maybe" and a "yes" (or a "maybe" and a "no"), and the admission evaluator is on the fence about whether or not to admit her.

Open curriculum: No or few required classes.

Parents: According to many teenagers, this word describes a group of annoying adults whose offspring have miraculously lived through their stewardship (and from whom applying to college may feel like their only escape).

PG: A post-graduate year describes a fifth year of high school as an option instead of a gap year between senior year of high school and college.

Point of contact: Every time your kid visits, interviews, attends a school info session, or sends an email, it's a point of contact (a.k.a.

"touches") with the college admissions office. Some colleges keep track of them, but it's hard to know which.

Pre-read: Someone like a coach asks your child to send an unofficial transcript to a college's admissions office to see if your child's a viable academic candidate. An admissions officer studies it, and if your kid gets a green light, the coach continues the recruitment process.

Princeton Review: A college admission services company best known for its standardized test preparation products.

PSAT/NMSQT: Most people just use the first four letters, which stand for pre-SAT, a test created by the College Board and administered October of junior year (some kids take it as sophomores or even earlier) that activates a deluge of junk mail, a gateway to many more tests, and your first purchase en route to maxing out your credit card during the college admissions process. The second part stands for National Merit Scholarship Qualifying Test because the kids who score highest are eligible for a $2,500 one-time scholarship.

Rankings: An inspired idea some *U.S. News and World Report* employee envisaged in the 1980s to list colleges in order of perceived greatness. College rankings have ballooned into something else altogether, driving parents and students alike to the edge of Anxiety Cliff.

Recruiting calendar: The NCAA calendar that includes times of year when college coaches can recruit athletes and times when they cannot.

Regional reciprocity: If your state university doesn't offer what your kid wants to study, another state university in your region of the country that offers that program will let you pay in-state tuition for your kid to attend.

Regular Decision: The most popular mode of applying to college. Kids submit multiple college applications on or around January 1, and most notifications come out mid-March to April 1.

Restrictive Early Action (REA): Your child can apply early, and learn if she got in early, but it's not a binding decision. However, she cannot apply EA to any other private colleges (public are okay) or anywhere that *is* binding.

Rolling Admission: The college continues to accept applications, and respond to each within a few weeks, until the freshman class is full.

RWL: See ERW, and then I recommend you stop expending your energy trying to figure this out. All you really need to know is that it's the part of the SAT test that's not math.

SAR: The Department of Education sends you a Student Aid Report based on the FAFSA.

SAT: This looks like an abbreviation, but it's not. (The letters SAT don't stand for anything.) It's a brand name for a standardized test created by the College Board.

School profile: This overview reveals basic information about your child's high school (such as number of students enrolled, average GPA, etc.) and provides colleges with a context in which to assess your child's transcript. (Not to be confused with the CSS Profile that asks *you* to reveal much more than basic information.)

Score choice: Your kid can pick and choose which test results she wants colleges to see.

Scores: Most people will just say "scores" instead of "standardized test scores," usually referring to the number of points a student earned on the SAT or ACT.

Single-Choice Early Action: See Restrictive Early Action (REA). I just can't go through the whole thing again.

Solids: See Majors.

Standardized tests: Though there are many standardized tests these days, usually people are referring to the SAT or ACT when they ask, "What are your child's test scores?" (You are under no obligation to answer.)

Stanley Kaplan: A guy named Stanley Kaplan launched this successful test prep system in 1938, and it's still available to your kid today.

STEM: Science, technology, engineering, and math.

Student employment: As part of your financial aid package, your kid is expected to get a campus job and help pay for his own education, a.k.a. work-study.

Superscore: The admissions office only pays attention to the best score your child earned in each section of the SAT or ACT and recalculates a new (better) composite score.

Supplement: Usually students use this word to refer to another essay or set of essays they have to write for a specific college, in addition to the personal essay they will write for the Common Application. However, sometimes it could be short for Arts Supplement (defined on p. 289). Regardless, it means extra work for the student.

Sustained interest: Your kid worked at the soup kitchen every Friday throughout high school, not only once so he could add a community service activity to his college application.

Test-flexible: These schools haven't quite jumped on the no-need-for-testing-at-all bandwagon yet, but they'll give your kid options, like submit any three SAT Subject Test reports instead of an SAT, or submit a graded paper instead of the essay section of a test.

Test-optional: Your kid does not have to send standardized test scores to this college if she doesn't feel they reflect her ability well.

TFC: Total Family Contribution, a financial aid term for the cash you must pay a college.

UCA: Stands for Universal College Application. Introduced in 2007 as a competitor for the Common Application, it's only accepted by a small handful of colleges (so not universal at all).

Unweighted: When calculating GPA, more rigorous classes are allotted the same point value as less rigorous classes.

U.S. News and World Report: This is an online magazine, but now it's most widely known for its college rankings.

Waitlisted: Instead of just saying yes or no in response to your child's application, a college notifies her spring of senior year that she'll have to wait (usually forever) to learn whether or not she can attend that college.

Weighted: When calculating GPA, more rigorous classes are allotted a higher point value than less rigorous classes. Example: An A in AP English = 5.0 points, Honors English = 4.5 points, and College Prep English = 4.0 points. When you see a GPA that's over 4.0 on a four-point scale, it's weighted.

Work-study: See Student Employment.

Writing Supplement: In addition to the Common Application, some colleges require a shorter application called a Writing Supplement that includes brief college-specific questions ("What is your preferred major?" "Is a parent or grandparent an alumnus?"), and often one or more extra essays, as well. (Also see Supplement.)

Yield: When a college offers your child admission, and she says yes, they have "yielded" your baby (along with a huge chunk of your savings account and your heart).

Index

About the Author

JILL MARGARET SHULMAN is the founder of In Other Words, a college essay coaching service. She has spent nearly a decade shepherding high school students and their parents through the college admissions process and reading and evaluating applications at elite colleges. Shulman has also taught writing at the New School and the City University of New York and has written for the *New York Times, Family Circle, Parents, Good Housekeeping,* and *O, The Oprah Magazine,* among other publications. She lives with her husband and two children (whenever they are home from college) in the higher-education mecca of Amherst, Massachusetts.